PENGUIN BOOKS

DIZZY

Hesketh Pearson was born in Worcestershire in 1887 and educated at Bedford Grammar School. After two years working in the City of London, he went on to the stage as a young man to join the company of Beerbohm Tree. Apart from active service during the First World War in Persia and Mesopotamia he continued to act until 1931, when he abandoned his stage career in order to write. His many biographies include *Gilbert and Sullivan* (1935), *A Life of Shakespeare* (1942), *Shaw* (1942), *The Life of Oscar Wilde* (1946), *Dizzy* (1951; Penguin, 2001), *Sir Walter Scott* (1955), *Johnson and Boswell* (1958) and *Charles II* (1960). He also edited Wilde's *De Profundis and Other Writings* for the Penguin Classics and wrote travel books with Hugh Kingsmill. He died in 1964. His autobiography, *Hesketh Pearson by Himself*, was published posthumously in 1965.

Michael Holroyd, who was born in 1935, is half-Swedish and partly Irish. He studied science at Eton College and read literature at the Maidenhead Public Library. As well as an acclaimed biography of Bernard Shaw, he has written biographies of Hugh Kingsmill, Lytton Strachey and Augustus John, and an autobiography, *Basil Street Blues*. He has been Chairman of the Society of Authors, the Royal Society of Literature and the Advisory Council on Public Lending Right, and President of English PEN. He is married to the novelist Margaret Drabble.

DIZZY

Photograph, 1873

DIZZY

The Life and Nature of Benjamin Disraeli, Earl of Beaconsfield

HESKETH PEARSON

With an Introduction by Michael Holroyd

PENGUIN BOOKS

PENGUIN BOOKS

Published by the Penguin Group
Penguin Books Ltd, 80 Strand, London WC2R ORL, England
Penguin Putnam Inc., 375 Hudson Street, New York, New York 10014, USA
Penguin Books Australia Ltd, 250 Camberwell Road, Camberwell, Victoria 3124, Australia
Penguin Books Canada Ltd, 10 Alcorn Avenue, Toronto, Ontario, Canada M4V 3B2
Penguin Books India (P) Ltd, 11 Community Centre, Panchsheel Park, New Delhi – 110 017, India
Penguin Books (NZ) Ltd, Cnr Rosedale and Airborne Roads, Albany, Auckland, New Zealand
Penguin Books (South Africa) (Pty) Ltd, 24 Sturdee Avenue, Rosebank 2196, South Africa

Penguin Books Ltd, Registered Offices: 80 Strand, London WC2R ORL, England

www.penguin.com

First published by Methuen & Co. Ltd 1951
Published with a new Introduction as a Classic Penguin 2001
1

Printed and bound in Great Britain by Cox & Wyman Ltd., Reading, Berks.

To
JOYCE

CONTENTS

ILLUSTRATIONS

The two "Punch" cartoons are reproduced by permission of the Proprietors.

The illustrations not otherwise acknowledged have been photographed at Hughenden Manor by courtesy of the National Trust.

INTRODUCTION

Hesketh Pearson was sixty-two when, in June 1949, he began writing his biography of Benjamin Disraeli. For almost twenty years, since the death of Lytton Strachey in 1932, he had been Britain's most popular and prolific biographer, producing what Richard Ingrams was to call 'a gallery of wits and mischief makers'. His subjects were mainly writers: Oscar Wilde, Conan Doyle, William Hazlitt, Charles Dickens. Though he also published Lives of Tom Paine and Henry Labouchère, he did not usually choose political subjects. But 'something about Benjamin Disraeli had always attracted me', he wrote.

> The mere fact that a Jew should become the chosen leader of a landed aristocracy in a period of snobbish exclusiveness was evocative enough, but added to that his wit delighted me and his mysterious aloofness intrigued me.

'Read no history, nothing but biography, for that is life without theory', Disraeli wrote in his novel *Contarini Fleming*. Pearson appears to have taken this advice to heart. *Dizzy* is not a political biography in the sense that Robert Blake's Life was to be some fifteen years later, and Pearson does not see Disraeli principally as a Tory politician placed, as in a relay team, between Peel and Churchill in the history of outstanding Conservative leaders. Though he acknowledged Disraeli to have been 'the first person to create a party machine,' he was 'not by nature a party man', often found himself in trouble with his own party, and antagonized all parties with his advice to 'rid yourselves of all that political jargon and factious slang'.

Pearson had enjoyed reading André Maurois's *Life of Disraeli*, but his own biography was written as a corrective to Maurois's somewhat romantic and sentimental portrait. His chief source of information, besides Disraeli's letters and novels, was the famous Monypenny and Buckle biography in six volumes. The extraordinary creature who emerges from Pearson's pages resembles the multi-faceted figure pointed to in wonderment by Lytton Strachey in his review of that biography: from one angle, a formidable man of action with the nervous sensibility of an artist; from another, a gorgeous sphinx, poised between flatterers and enemies, and seen against a painted plasterboard of the political landscape; and finally, a romantic comedian performing in his private theatre, determined yet purposeless, who had once dreamed of conquering the world – and then so improbably succeeded in doing so.

Disraeli plays a largely decorative role in Strachey's *Queen Victoria.* He is an understudy to Lord Melbourne, a counterbalance to Gladstone. Strachey and Pearson discussed Disraeli as a biographical subject when they met after the publication of *Queen Victoria* in 1921, Strachey expressing bafflement at the many contradictory qualities in his character, and Pearson suggesting that 'the realist and the showman go hand in hand'.

Pearson's sympathies were immediately engaged by Disraeli's experiences at school. In his autobiography, *Hesketh Pearson by Himself*, he was to write that 'the worst things that have happened to me since leaving it [school] have seemed relatively mild in comparison with those five years of helpless misery'. He quotes with approval Disraeli's very similar conclusion: 'school I detested more than ever I abhorred the world in the darkest moments of my experienced manhood.'

Before turning to biography Pearson had been an actor, and he attributes Disraeli's supreme success in the House of Commons to great acting abilities, the stage business of which (including his devastating use of a handkerchief) he describes with professional delight. He quotes a telling sentence from Disraeli's diary: 'I wish to *act* what I *write*'. This, Pearson suggests, is the reason why Disraeli's parliamentary speeches were so much more effective in influencing public opinion than his novels which, though regarded in part as the first political novels in English, are little more than miraculous fairy tales with preposterous plots and nebulous characters, chiefly interesting for their revelations of the author's dreams and fantasies.

Richard Ingrams has described the 'mass of contradictions' in

Hesketh Pearson who, even when middle-aged, 'retained many of the characteristics of a younger man'. These temperamental anomalies helped to give him a shrewd understanding of Disraeli's dramatically divided nature, the boundless ambition set against a passion for domesticity; a sense of exile and racial isolation which led to an early, 'inscrutable', self-dependence; the highly exotic imagination in opposition to his satirical intelligence.

Pearson recounts with joyful partiality the vivid story of Disraeli's rise from being a figure of ridicule to an object of reverence. He relished the eccentricities of a career that he describes as 'a long fight to cover up his indiscretions ... provoking his declared enemies while appeasing his dubious friends'. His biography provides an impressive list of political achievements and shows an extraordinary triumph over personal disadvantages. It leads to a paradoxical destination. For Disraeli became the leader of an aristocratic party that despised his birth and race, the chief figure in a popular assembly that scorned his fanciful clothes and radical opinions, and Prime Minister of a puritannical country that distrusted his wit, his talent, and his liking for women. But 'was the victory worth the sacrifice?' Pearson asks – and leaves the answer with each reader.

An unusual aspect of this career was the balance Disraeli preserved between the thirst for power and his need for love. The most tender pages of this book are those which describe the last illness and death of his wife, written while Pearson's own wife was dying. 'The person who has once known love is always grateful for life,' Pearson writes, 'because the experience illuminates the whole of existence; and resentment with life is due to the lack of it'. The exercise of power, however potent, had given Disraeli no release from heartache. 'I am certain there is no greater misfortune' he acknowledged, 'than to have a heart that will not grow old'.

Dizzy was published in the autumn of 1951 in Britain and the United States, and sold well in both countries. Most reviewers appear to have agreed with V. S. Pritchett who described the book as 'picturesque, witty, sympathetic, perceptive, and very readable'.

Following its publication, Pearson was sent invitations from the central office of the Conservative Party to address them on the virtues of toryism (he had received similar offers from socialists after the publication of his biography of Bernard Shaw). But he refused them all. 'I think Dizzy an amazing character, the brainiest statesman in English history, and a frustrated poet; intensely interesting on all counts,' he explained; 'but his brand of political partisanship is the least interesting thing about him'.

I

Chapter I

BEGINNINGS

THE romantic story of his ancestry which Benjamin Disraeli composed, and possibly believed, throws a light on his character, but leaves his lineage obscure. He liked to think that they had owned large estates in Spain during the Moorish supremacy, and that with the coming of Torquemada and the Inquisition they had been compelled to seek refuge in the territories of the Venetian Republic, where for more than two centuries they had flourished as merchant princes. Fancy ends and fact begins with the arrival of his grandfather in England shortly after the defeat of the Young Pretender in 1745 had firmly established the Hanoverian succession. This grandfather changed his name Israeli to the more imposing D'Israeli. After some years of struggle as a merchant and stockbroker, he made a successful second marriage and a small fortune. He was a kind-hearted man, who tipped his small grandson Benjamin when his wife was not there to see him do it. She was "a demon" according to her grandson, who remembered with horror his visits to her. He had to walk all the way from Bloomsbury to Kensington, where he received "no kindness, no tea, no tips—nothing." But on one occasion she was so pleasant that Benjamin's mother remarked "Depend upon it she is going to die." And she did.

Benjamin's father, Isaac, was of a dreamy nature, preferring solitude and books to company and business, and when he at length produced a poem his parents were more alarmed than if they had lost an uninsured argosy. Stern measures were called for, and he was consigned "like a bale of goods" to a business connection in Amsterdam, where he continued to read for pleasure, returning home at the age of eighteen with his head full of Rousseau and Voltaire, and a long poem in which commerce was shown to be the cause of man's corruption. To clear his mind of such drolleries, he was sent to France, in the belief that mixing with men of affairs would make him realise the importance of merchandise; but most of his time was spent in libraries, and he arrived back in England with a large assortment of books. After that the family abandoned their attempts to turn a born bookman into an unsatisfactory tradesman and let him go his own way. He married the daughter of an Italian Jew, begat four sons and one daughter, became known to his generation as the author of *Curiosities of Literature*, produced literature's chief curiosity, his son Benjamin, and spent the greater part of his life among the manuscripts in the British Museum, when not similarly engaged in his own library. Byron had a very high opinion of him ("I don't know a living man's books I take up so often . . . as Israeli's") and he had a very high opinion of Byron. But his life was bounded by books; he never went out except to look at them in shops or libraries; he lived with them, carried them about with him, seldom had his nose out of them; took no interest in politics; disliked business; avoided social life; and for relaxation continued his literary pursuits. His disposition was gentle and serene, his character simple and amiable, his conversation ingenuous and pleasing. A life spent in a library usually results in misanthropy or benignity. Isaac D'Israeli was benign. His wife did not share his intellectual interests and apparently exercised no influence on her son Benjamin, who wrote a memoir of his father without mentioning his mother. On reading it his sister Sarah remarked: "I do wish that one felicitous stroke, one tender word had brought our dear Mother into the picture."

Benjamin, the second child of Isaac's marriage, was born on December 21st, 1804, Sarah the eldest having preceded him by two years. The house of his birth overlooked Gray's Inn garden and was in King's Road, later named Theobald's Road.[1] The main feature of his character as a child did not augur well for future eminence in politics, his father declaring that "he never lies." When six years old he went to school at Islington, thence to a school at Blackheath kept by a nonconformist parson, where he showed no inclination for communal exercises but maintained his popularity by telling stories. The games he played were for his own pleasure, such as driving two boys with string reins as

[1] His birthplace at No. 22 still stands (1950) though the bank next-door was destroyed in an air-raid. Just round the corner is Doughty Street, in which Sydney Smith lived in 1804, and Dickens a generation later; so that we may describe this bit of London as Comedian's Corner.

if they were horses, firing at passers-by with a pea-shooter from the top of a coach, and, during the holidays, forming a parliament with his brothers and friends, in which he was permanent Prime Minister and no one else ever came to power. His grandfather died in 1816, and his father, inheriting a fortune, moved to 6 Bloomsbury Square, within a stone's throw of the British Museum, where he could bury himself in books. Here they remained for the twelve most formative years of Benjamin's life.

The old man's death had other effects on the family, all of whom had been brought up in the Jewish faith. But father Isaac was wholly indifferent to it, never attended the Synagogue, and was quite willing to be called a Jew, a Christian, a Deist, or a Buddhist, so long as he was not expected to participate in any religious ceremony. But the Elders were not so pliable and fined him £40 when he declined to act as Warden of the Congregation, an office to which he had been elected. Isaac informed them that he could never take part in their public worship "because, as now conducted, it disturbs, instead of exciting, religious emotions", and that though he had tolerated their ritual, conceding everything possible in matters he held to be indifferent, yet he could not "accept the solemn functions of an Elder" and carry out duties that were repulsive to his feelings. This silenced the Elders for about three years, after which they again became vocal; whereupon Isaac, his father now dead, resigned from their society. Having been bullied by one religion, he did not wish to be browbeaten by another, and so, with his family, was in the soothing condition of avowing no faith, which agreed with his temperament and continued to give him satisfaction for the remainder of his life. But a friend named Sharon Turner considered that Isaac's children would have a better chance in the world if they became Christians; persuaded him with some difficulty to let them be baptised; and Benjamin became a member of the Church of England at the age of twelve. Thus the intransigent attitude of the Jewish authorities made possible his later career in politics.

Having changed his religion, he also changed his school, joining an institution run by an Unitarian minister near Walthamstow, where he settled down to the study of Greek and Latin and for the first time experienced school-life in the raw. Like all boys who are in any way exceptional, he hated the magisterial discipline as much as the juvenile anarchy: "I was a most miserable child; and school I detested more than ever I abhorred the world in the darkest moments of my experienced manhood." The interests of the other boys were not his: "I hated field-sports, indeed every bodily exertion, except riding, which is scarcely one." He felt different from them, did not enjoy what gave them pleasure, and wished he could control them. Recalling his own emotions as a schoolboy many years later, he wrote: "In that young bosom what burning love, what intense ambition, what avarice, what lust of power; envy that fiends might emulate, hate that men might fear!" Recognising that he was at the mercy of any bully who cared to tyrannise over the weak, he spent a part of his holidays in studying the craft of self-defence, practising and taking lessons in boxing. That his efforts were rewarded in term-time need not be doubted; but his biographers have taken too literally the descriptions of the fights which appear in two of his novels, and which probably represent his dreams more nearly than the reality. In *Vivian Grey* the hero, who is also ours, is insulted by a beefy boy named St Leger Smith, and promptly knocks him down:

> Smith instantly recovered, and a ring was instantly formed. To a common observer, the combatants were unequally matched; for Smith was a burly, big-limbed animal, alike superior to Grey in years and strength. But Vivian, though delicate in frame and more youthful, was full his match in spirit, and, thanks to being a Cockney! ten times his match in science. . . .
>
> Oh! how beautifully he fought! how admirably straight he hit! and his stops quick as lightning! and his followings up confounded his adversary with their painful celerity! Smith, alike puzzled and punished, yet proud in his strength, hit round, and wild, and false, and foamed like a furious elephant. For ten successive rounds the result was dubious; but in the eleventh the strength of Smith began to fail him, and the men were more fairly matched. . . .

Smith is saved by the sudden arrival of the headmaster.

Six years after the publication of *Vivian Grey* another fight is described in *Contarini Fleming*, and during that interval the author's wish to defeat his enemies had become more pronounced. He therefore gives his opponent in the second novel a more severe trouncing than St Leger Smith received, and in the process drifted still further from reality, while approximating more closely to his desire. Again the hero starts by felling the bully:

> He was up again in a moment; and indeed I would not have waited for their silly rules of mock combat, but have destroyed him in his prostration. But he was up again in a moment. Again I flew upon him. He fought with subtle energy, but he was like a serpent with a tiger. I fixed upon him: my blows told with the rapid precision of machinery. His bloody visage was not to be distinguished. I believe he was terrified by my frantic air.
>
> I would never wait between the rounds. I cried out in a voice of madness for him to come on. There was breathless silence. They were thunderstruck. They were too generous to cheer their leader. They could not refrain from sympathising with inferior force and unsupported courage. Each time that he came forward I made the same dreadful spring, beat down his guard, and never ceased working upon his head, until at length my fist seemed to enter his very brain; and after ten rounds he fell down quite blind. I never felt his blows; I never lost my breath.
>
> He could not come to time; I rushed forward; I placed my knee upon his chest. "I fight no more", he faintly cried.
>
> "Apologise", I exclaimed; "apologise." He did not speak.
>
> "By heavens, apologise", I said, "or I know not what I shall do."
>
> "Never!" he replied.
>
> I lifted up my arm. Some advanced to interfere. "Off", I shouted; "off, off." I seized the fallen chief, rushed through the gate, and dragged him like Achilles through the mead. At the bottom there was a dunghill. Upon it I flung the half-inanimate body.

But though these fights must not be taken as faithful reports of actual events, we may safely assume that the private thoughts and feelings of Vivian and Contarini, especially the latter, were those of their creator; and the two most noticeable aspects of his nature in youth were independence and ambition. He hated being accountable to anyone for his actions, and could be led but not driven: "A soft word, and I was an Abel; an appearance of force, and I scowled a Cain." His longing for fame was even stronger than his self-will: "The desire of distinction and of astounding action raged in my soul; and when I recollected that, at the soonest, many years must elapse before I could realise my ideas, I gnashed my teeth in silent rage, and cursed my existence." Sometimes a sense of impotence overcame his natural impatience: "To feel the strong necessity of fame, and to be conscious that without intellectual excellence life must be insupportable, to feel all this with no simultaneous faith in your own power, these are moments of despondence for which no immortality can compensate." But as a rule he had faith in himself and his destiny: "I felt within me the power that could influence my kind. I longed to wave my inspiring sword at the head of armies, or dash into the very heat and blaze of eloquent faction . . . I was to be something great, and glorious, and dazzling . . ." Many youths have had these dreams, and then spent their lives sitting on stools entering figures in ledgers. But this youth was to have as much as he needed of eloquent faction, and was to satisfy his longing to wave an inspiring sword at the head of armies by depicting himself as the romantic hero of *Alroy*. Meanwhile his visions of greatness did not cloud his sense of reality. He and the other Church of England boys had to walk two miles to attend morning service on Sundays, returning when the boys who belonged to the faith of their headmaster were half-way through the midday meal, having demolished the choicest dishes. He therefore suggested to his fellow-martyrs that they should all become Unitarians in term-time.

He left school at about the age of fifteen, and for two years continued his studies in Latin and Greek at home, keeping a diary of his reading. He also examined the Lives of what the world called great men, "that is to say, men of great energies and violent volition, who look upon their fellow-creatures as mere tools, with which they can build up a pedestal for their solitary statue, and who sacrifice every feeling which should sway humanity, and every high work which genius should really achieve, to the short-sighted gratification of an irrational and outrageous selfism." But what delighted him more than anything else in these years was the study of politics. "And now everything was solved!" he wrote of himself in *Vivian Grey*; "the inexplicable longings of his soul, which had so often perplexed him, were at length explained. The want, the indefinable want, which he had so constantly experienced, was at last supplied; the grand object on which to bring the powers of his mind to bear and work was at last provided. He paced his chamber in an agitated spirit, and panted for the Senate." His agitation must have been audible, because his father, exercising parental authority for the first and last time in his life, persuaded him to become articled to a firm of solicitors at 6 Frederick's Place, Old Jewry, in the city of London. This happened when, at the age of seventeen, the thought of going to Oxford was rather alluring; but he followed his father's advice, and at a later date comforted himself for the gap in his education: "He was already a cunning reader of human hearts; and felt conscious that his was a tongue which was born to guide human beings. The idea of Oxford to such an individual was an insult!"

Chapter II

SPECULATIVE

FOR some three years he was private secretary to the most active partner in the firm, writing letters from dictation, listening to interviews with bank directors and company managers, and learning a lot about human nature in the process. But outside business his thoughts and interests were elsewhere. He spent hours with the great classical orators, Cicero, Demosthenes, Pericles, read biographies, histories, books of travel, poetry, and passed most of his evenings alone in deep study and meditation. His reading begat restlessness: he longed to be a poet, a statesman, a historian, a soldier; he dreamt of epics in action and epics in composition; he yearned for power: "Power! Oh! what sleepless nights, what days of hot anxiety! what exertions of mind and body! what travel! what hatred! what fierce encounters! what dangers of all possible kinds, would I not endure with a joyous spirit to gain it!" Like many young men of ability, he felt himself to be exceptionally gifted and destined to fame; but his sense of reality was strong enough even in his youth to dispel his more fabulous dreams: "To wake from your bright hopes, and feel that all is vanity, to be roused from your crafty plans and know that all is worthless, is a bitter, but your sure, destiny. Escape is impossible; for despair is the price of conviction." Before he had begun to participate in the social and political world he had reached a conclusion that usually comes with the disillusion of age: "Alas! it is our nature to sicken, from our birth, after some object of unattainable felicity, to struggle through the freshest years of our life in an insane pursuit after some indefinite good, which does not even exist!

In effect his exaltations and agonies resulted in a desire to travel, and his father, after a tentative proposal that Oxford might be more congenial than the city, indulged his whim. In

July, 1824, the father and son, both in poor health, set out on a six weeks' tour of the Continent, accompanied by a friend of Benjamin's named Meredith. Benjamin, by the way, had recently dropped the apostrophe in his surname; and though his father never followed suit, his brothers and sister did. They reached Ostend, which Benjamin thought disgusting and uninteresting, at the end of July, and went on to Bruges, which he called "the city of cities." Ghent, Antwerp, Mechlin and Brussels provided them with sufficient churches, universities, cathedrals and picture galleries, to exercise their feet, excite their eyes, and extend their vocabularies; but in his letters to his sister Benjamin dwelt more lovingly on the meals than on the masterpieces. "Dinner good and Cathedral magnificent, oysters as small as shrimps, but delicately sweet", was his comment on Mechlin, and he declared that "my Mother must really reform her table before our return." He kept a journal of dinners for his own pleasure and a journal of their doings for his father's. One meal made a deep impression: "A *fricandeau*, the finest I ever tasted, perfectly admirable, a small and very delicate roast joint, veal chops dressed with a rich sauce piquant, capital roast pigeons, a large dish of peas most wonderfully fine, cheese, dessert, a salad pre-eminent even among the salads of Flanders which are unique for their delicate crispness and silvery whiteness, bread and beer *ad lib.* served up in the neatest and purest manner imaginable, silver forks, etc; cost only six francs, forming one of the finest specimens of exquisite and economic cookery I ever witnessed." At Ghent he attended High Mass at the Cathedral: "Clouds of incense and one of Mozart's sublimest masses by an orchestra . . . The effect inconceivably grand. The host raised, and I flung myself on the ground." The Rubens pictures at Antwerp inspired a passage of appreciation in his diary, followed immediately by "The dinner was good . . . The *vol au vent* of pigeons was admirable. The peas were singularly fine." Of course they perambulated the field of Waterloo, where their guide harangued them "in a mixture of Dutch, Flemish, French and English—very rich—forming a kind of Belle Alliance lingo, most likely in compliment to the place. We dined at Genappe most admirably . . ."

Passing through "a perfect debauch of gorgeous scenery", they visited Spa and Aix, at both of which they played billiards and "shewed off to great advantage." There was so much to be seen at Cologne that they decided to hire a cab: "To our great surprise a most elegant landaulet with the coachman in military livery stopped at our gate. This, we were informed, was the fiacre, and also nearly the only carriage in Cologne. We were almost stopped in our progress by the stares of the multitude, who imagined we were Archdukes at least. We have always put up at the crack hotels, which we find the most reasonable." They travelled in elegant comfort, lived *en prince*, and drank innumerable bottles of the best Rhenish wines. They visited Bonn, Coblenz, Ems, Mainz, Frankfort, Darmstadt, Heidelberg and Mannheim, and then travelled by boat down the Rhine, of which he declared "that the most glowing descriptions do but imperfect justice to the magnificent scenery." The liberation of spirit effected by this journey helped to change the course of his career. "I determined when descending those magical waters that I would not be a lawyer." This was as well, because he had already felt that he was wasting his time: "The Bar: pooh! law and bad jokes till we are forty; and then, with the most brilliant success, the prospect of gout and a coronet." And he described a true lawyer as one who is "ever illustrating the obvious, explaining the evident, and expatiating on the commonplace." He wanted to be a great man, not a great lawyer; and the same objection held with the other leading professions; though if he had lived three centuries earlier the Church would have appealed to him, for he might have been a Wolsey.

To achieve his end money was indispensable, and when he returned home he tried his luck on the Stock Exchange in partnership with two city friends. "To enter high society", he wrote, "a man must either have blood, a million, or a genius." He was conscious of genius, but his blood was against him, and so he played for a million. A craze for speculation was in the air. Mexico had just thrown off its allegiance to Spain, becoming a republic, and the other Spanish-American colonies were revolting. Companies were being promoted to exploit the resources of these countries, the governments of which were about to be recognised by England. Disraeli and his partners succumbed to the craze, and by faulty speculation lost about £7000 within seven months. Thus at the age of twenty he handicapped himself with a debt which took him nearly thirty years to pay. He also wrote pamphlets for a financier named J. D. Powles, who had made a lot of money out of the boom and wished to make more, their object being to steady the nerves of the investing public, already shaken by the comments of disinterested parties such as Lord Eldon, the Chancellor, who had talked of another South Sea Bubble.

The publisher of these pamphlets was John Murray, who, as a friend of Isaac, had known Benjamin from his childhood and had been sufficiently impressed by his intelligence to ask his advice, before he was eighteen years of age, about the publication of a play. Shortly after that young Disraeli wrote a satire on society and sent it to Murray, who was not enthusiastic; so the author told him to put it in the fire. But the success of the pamphlets on the American Mining Companies, or the fact that he had been persuaded to speculate in their shares, induced Murray to send a Life of Paul Jones to Disraeli with the request that he should prepare it for the press. Altering a word here and there, deleting a passage now and then, and writing a preface that showed every sign of complete indifference, Disraeli finished his one piece of pure hack-work; after which he plunged into another scheme that promised wealth. John Murray had made a big success of *The Quarterly Review*, and wanted to start a monthly or even a weekly periodical. Having a high opinion of young Disraeli's judgment, he consulted him on the subject. But Disraeli at that time was thinking in thousands, and proposed a Conservative daily paper that should compete with the non-party *Times*. His enthusiasm affected Murray, and in August, 1825, the publisher signed an agreement with Disraeli and J. D. Powles, whereby half the property in the forthcoming morning paper would be owned by Murray and the remaining half in equal shares by the other two, the capital being provided in similar proportions. As Disraeli's capital consisted wholly of expectations, it is probable that Powles made himself responsible for their share of the cash. But though the young man's pockets were empty, his mind was full, his energy overflowing, and whenever he was not tackling the details of present organisation he was teeming with ideas for future expression.

Murray was anxious that Sir Walter Scott's son-in-law, J. G. Lockhart, should be the editor, and towards the end of September Disraeli was sent to Scotland, with letters of introduction, in the hope that he would be able to persuade Lockhart to accept the post. The journey by coach took four days, and he slept at Stamford, York and Newcastle, reading Froissart on the way, enjoying the scene of social gaiety in York, and spending an hour in the Minster, which, he wrote, "baffles all conception. Westminster Abbey is a toy to it. I think it is impossible to conceive of what Gothic architecture is susceptible until you see York. I speak with the cathedrals of the Netherlands and the Rhine fresh in my memory." He found Edinburgh exactly as he had fancied it, "the most beautiful town in the world", and he reported favourably on the various delights of a Scotch breakfast, adding "cold grouse and marmalade find me, however, constant." He was invited to Chiefswood, Lockhart's country cottage near Abbotsford, where his youthful appearance caused a frigid reception: "Lockhart had conceived that it was my father who was coming . . . In addition, therefore, to his natural reserve, there was, of course, an evident disappointment at seeing me. Everything looked as black as possible . . ." But Disraeli's intelligence and eloquent fervour soon captivated Lockhart, who entirely approved the establishment and aims of the periodical, but said that if he undertook the editorship of a daily paper he would lose caste in society; for in those days a *perfect gentleman*, as Disraeli described Lockhart, could not be a journalist. Scott, who was soon brought into consultation, said that Lockhart could not accept an official situation of any kind, as it would compromise his independence, but that he ought to have a seat in parliament. Disraeli stayed some three weeks at Chiefswood, dined frequently at Abbotsford, and talked much with Scott, whom he thought kind, extremely hospitable, but rather stately. Seeing that the word 'editor' was unpalatable to them, he suggested that Lockhart should be the Director-General of their paper, and he enlarged on the vast influences behind them, both commercial and political. But neither Scott nor his son-in-law could face the dreadful prospect of lowering themselves socially by journalistic contamination, and nothing had been settled when Lockhart and Disraeli arrived in London about the middle of October. There, however, Lockhart's gentility waning at the prospect of a fat salary, he signed two agreements: (1) to edit *The Quarterly Review* at an annual salary of £1000, this being more reputable than the editorship of a daily newspaper, and (2) to assist in the production of the latter, to write articles for it, and "by all other means consistent with his rank in life" to promote its sale and character, for £1500 a year.

Disraeli now proved himself a man of affairs, taking offices, arranging for the printing, interviewing the prospective staff, appointing home and foreign correspondents, raising contributions, and superintending a hundred matters. Meanwhile John Wilson Croker, Secretary to the Admiralty, with other contributors to the *Quarterly*, objected to Lockhart's appointment as editor, and Murray became so alarmed that he asked Disraeli to re-visit Scotland and request Lockhart to use what influence he had to propitiate his opponents. Scott wrote to several friends and also sent a firm note to Murray, who in his agitation replied that Disraeli should have gone direct to Scott, not to Lockhart. On his return home Disraeli had several exhausting scenes with Murray, who at length calmed down, took a determined line with the Croker cabal, and wrote to Lockhart that "after this Heaven and Earth may pass away, but it cannot shake my opinion." It did not, however, require a cosmic black-out to shake Murray's opinion. A panic in the city was sufficient for the purpose. In December '25 the bubble of speculation burst; Powles and Disraeli were unable to raise their share of the capital; and Disraeli, after 'naming the new paper *The Representative*, quitted the organisation before the first number appeared and ceased to be Murray's right-hand man. Bad management and bad editing completed what the city smash began, and the newspaper lasted only six months, leaving Murray poorer by £26,000.

The experience was good for Disraeli. It taught him to put no further trust in speculation, and to beware of speculators. It made him more self-reliant than he had been; and by forcing him to realise that he must depend on himself if he wished to make money, turned his mind to a form of industry that could not be injured by the actions of others. He had also learnt much about business men in the course of his negotiations, and he made use of the knowledge in his future writings. Among others, two famous publishers had come under his observation. At Abbotsford he was introduced to Archibald Constable, publisher of Scott's works and *The Edinburgh Review*, and "It struck me that I had never met before such an ostentatious man, or one whose conversation was so braggart. One would think that he had written the Waverley Novels himself, and certainly that Abbotsford belonged to him." They returned to London in the same coach: "He informed me that he intended to build a new wing to Abbotsford next year . . . Something had gone wrong on the journey; the guard or coachman had displeased. He went into an ecstasy of pompous passion. 'Do you know who I am, man? I am Archibald Constable', etc." A week later came the crash which ruined both Scott and Constable. While in the north Disraeli must have run across several Scottish dialecticians, because he introduces a typical North British bore in an early novel, one who "cut up the Creation, and got a name", and whose "attack upon mountains was most violent, and proved, by its personality, that he had come from the Lowlands . . . he avowed that already there were various pieces of machinery of far more importance than man; and he had no doubt, in time, that a superior race would arise, got by a steam-engine on a spinning-jenny."

But the man he liked and knew best was John Murray, whom he considered noble and generous-minded but inconsistent and vacillating. There was a coolness between them when Disraeli left *The Representative*, due largely no doubt to Murray's feeling that he had been let in for a too ambitious project and then let down by the failure of half the capital to materialise. When, a little later, he thought that he detected a caricature of himself in Disraeli's first novel, he refused to have anything more to do with Benjamin or his family, and spoke freely of Disraeli's "outrageous breach of all confidence and of every tie that binds man to man in social life." Less than a year before he had written to Lockhart about Disraeli in these terms: "I can pledge my honour, therefore, with the assurance that he is worthy of any degree of confidence that you may be induced to repose in him—discretion being another of his qualifications." It is difficult to reconcile these conflicting certificates of character; but a sudden loss of money is liable to warp judgment.

ISAAC AND SARAH D'ISRAELI, 1828

By Daniel Maclise, R.A.

THE AUTHOR OF " VIVIAN GREY "

By Daniel Maclise, R.A.

BENJAMIN DISRAELI, 1834

By Count D'Orsay

Chapter III

BEN-VIVIAN

WITHOUT stopping to count his losses in the city Disraeli started to write a novel, which he completed in four months at Hyde House, near Amersham, which his family had rented for the autumn of '25. It was an early start in literature, for the book was finished by his twenty-first birthday, though he probably revised it in the early part of '26, a great deal of the previous autumn having been devoted to *The Representative*. A solicitor named Benjamin Austen, an acquaintance of the Disraeli family, had arranged for their rental of Hyde House, and his wife arranged for the publication of *Vivian Grey* by Colburn, whom she knew. Mrs Austen was a pretty woman of many accomplishments, a musician, a painter, a literary critic, who loved flattery as much as she longed for social eminence. Disraeli was able to supply the first because he soon perceived the necessity of making himself popular with the other sex. "Perhaps he affected gallantry, because he was deeply impressed with the influence of women both upon public and upon private opinion", he writes of a character modelled on himself; and he was in no need of the advice he puts into the mouth of someone else: "Talk to women, talk to women as much as you can. This is the best school. This is the way to gain fluency, because you need not care what you say, and had better not be sensible." It came quite easily to him, as he was greatly attracted to women and found their company very refreshing. There is a revealing passage in *Vivian Grey* in which he speaks of the moment when the ladies retire from the dinner-table leaving the men to their port: "How singular it is, that when this move takes place every one appears to be relieved, and yet every one of any experience must be quite aware that the dead bore work is only about to commence."

Mrs Austen thought highly of *Vivian Grey* and advised Colburn to bring it out, though she would not disclose the author's name.

The mystery appealed to the publisher, who was able to start gossip about the forthcoming work in several leading papers, the readers of which were informed that the book was full of satirical portraits of living people, that the hero was "a sort of Don Juan in prose", and that he knew everybody worth knowing in the social and literary world. As a result it was reviewed at considerable length in many of the periodicals; the game of spotting the originals of the various characters became a seasonal amusement, only equalled in popularity by the sport of detecting the author; and the book was a success; though the author had to content himself with the sum of £200, the successful speculator in this instance being the publisher.

It gave Disraeli pleasure to hear people talking of his novel, especially when they did so to him. "You must look at it", someone advised. "It is the oddest book that was ever written. Immensely clever, I assure you. I cannot exactly make it out." To which he gravely replied: "This is certainly much in its favour. The obscure, as you know, is a principal ingredient of the sublime." Gradually it leaked out that he had written it, and the papers which had remained silent during the excitement it had caused promptly gave tongue. The advance puffery was described as "shameful and shameless", the novel was dismissed as "a paltry catchpenny" by "an obscure person for whom nobody cares a straw"; and though Disraeli had been entirely innocent of the methods whereby Colburn had aroused the public interest, he was accused of a "total disregard of all honourable feeling", of a "ludicrous affectation of good breeding," and of having, in effect, obtained money by false pretences. He was stunned by these attacks; but as he was to endure fifty years of vituperation, in the course of which he trained himself to sustain it without noticeable discomposure, it is interesting to read his account of the reception of *Vivian* written some five years later, before he had ceased to smart from the memory. The passages are in *Contarini Fleming*, where *Vivian Grey* is called *Manstein*, and the great Edinburgh journal which he mentions was *Blackwood's*, the critic being 'Christopher North':

I can give no idea of the outcry. Everybody was in a passion, or affected to be painfully sensitive of their neighbours' wrongs . . . Those who were ridiculed insisted that the ridicule called in question the very first principles of society. They talked of confidence violated, which never had been shared; and faith broken which never had been pledged. Never was so much nonsense talked about nothing since the days of the schoolmen. But nonsense, when earnest, is impressive, and sometimes takes you in. If you are in a hurry, you occasionally mistake it for sense. All the people who had read *Manstein*, and been very much amused with it, began to think they were quite wrong, and that it was a very improper and wicked book, because this was daily reiterated in their ears by half-a-dozen bores, who had gained an immortality which they did not deserve. Such conduct, it was universally agreed, must not be encouraged. Where would it end? Everybody was alarmed. Men passed me in the street without notice; I received anonymous letters, and even many of my intimates grew cold. As I abhor explanations, I said nothing . . . I found even a savage delight in being an object, for a moment, of public astonishment, and fear, and indignation.

About two months after the publication of *Manstein* appeared a new number of the great critical journal of the north of Europe. One of the works reviewed was my notorious production. I tore open the leaves with a blended feeling of desire and fear, which I can yet remember. I felt prepared for the worst. I felt that such grave censors, however impossible it was to deny the decided genius of the work, and however eager they might be to hail the advent of an original mind, I felt that it was but reasonable and just, that they should disapprove the temper of the less elevated portions, and somewhat dispute the moral tendency of the more exalted.

With what horror, with what blank despair, with what supreme, appalling astonishment, did I find myself, for the first time in my life, a subject of the most reckless, the most malignant, and the most adroit ridicule. I was sacrificed, I was scalped. They scarcely condescended to notice my dreadful satire; except to remark, in passing, that, by-the-bye, I appeared to be as ill-tempered as I was imbecile. But all my eloquence, and all my fancy, and all the strong expression of my secret feelings! these ushers of the court of Apollo fairly laughed me off Parnassus, and held me up to public scorn, as exhibiting a lamentable instance of mingled pretension and weakness, and the most ludicrous specimen of literary delusion that it had ever been their unhappy office to castigate, and, as they hoped, to cure.

The criticism fell from my hand. A film floated over my vision; my knees trembled. I felt that sickness of heart, that we experience in our first serious scrape. I was ridiculous. It was time to die.

But instead of dying he wrote another volume of *Vivian Grey* during a tour of northern Italy in the autumn of '26. This second part of the story is so feeble that he must have written it solely for the £500 which he received for it. The sparkle of the early chapters disappears completely from the sequel; the writing becomes pretentious and wearisome; and the incidents are either ridiculous or incredible; as when an Archduchess, condemned to marry an unattractive Prince, succumbs to a passion for Vivian, and a beautiful woman, madly in love with him, falls dead in the tempest of her emotions. Not seeing a clear way out of this morass of nonsense and verbiage, he brings the novel to a close with an earthquake, a cataract, a tornado, death, desolation, and elemental chaos, which, if theatrical seems apposite.

In the first part of the book, however, he gives a portrait of himself as Vivian and a pleasantly satirical picture of the world as it appeared to one in his nonage, the affectation of cynical disillusionment always making a strong appeal to clever young men. "I wish to *act* what I *write*", he noted in a diary seven years after the appearance of this first novel: "My works are the embodification of my feelings. In *Vivian Grey* I have portrayed my active and real ambition." This confession makes it possible for the biographer to see at once how Disraeli saw himself, and to make the necessary deductions therefrom, because one or more aspects of the author is dramatised in each of his novels. Vivian is an invaluable index to the mind of his creator, a full-length portrait of whom, on the brink of manhood, could be painted from his protagonist's character. All that we need notice here is his thirst for power, his quick intelligence, his sense of being an alien in a strange land, his conviction of his own superiority, his adroitness in handling people far more experienced than himself, his overmastering ambition, his awareness of the value of a rich and mellifluous voice—"I can perform right skilfully upon the most splendid of musical instruments, the human voice"—and his recognition of the necessity to "mix with the herd", to sympathise with their sorrows, to partake of their merriment, "to inspire them with feelings which they could not share, and humour and manage the petty weaknesses which he himself could not experience."

The first thing he had learnt about human nature was its susceptibility to flattery, and for a young man his early exercises in that art were curiously subtle; for he put his own ideas into the mouths of others, making self-important people feel that they were thinking and saying what really came from him. The misunderstanding with Murray, when he re-visited Scotland to see Lockhart, may have arisen from his over-confidence in this technique. Incidentally he was able to send Murray £150 out of the sum he received for *Vivian Grey* to pay for the printing of the mining pamphlets, the cost of which should have been discharged by others; but Disraeli regarded it as a debt of honour for which he was responsible. His action, however, did not mollify Murray, who probably regarded it as blood-money and who may have been biased against him by Lockhart. Why the latter should have become hostile we do not know. Perhaps he had decided that Disraeli was not a perfect gentleman. Or, like so many others, he may have seen himself in *Vivian Grey*. Or, more likely, his pretentiousness had called forth a Disraelian epigram which would not have amused him as much as it pleased the friend who had repeated it. For already the young novelist, along with some queer tricks of style like his description of a lark as "shrill chanticleer's feathered rival", could turn a phrase neatly, e.g.:

"The Marchioness is the most amiable of women: at least I suppose her lap-dog thinks so."

"How those rooks bore! I hate staying with ancient families; you are always cawed to death."

"If you wish to win a man's heart, allow him to confute you."

"When a man is either going to talk sense, fight a duel, or make his will, nothing should be seen at dinner save cutlets and the lightest Bordeaux."

"No one likes his dependants to be treated with respect, for such treatment affords an unpleasant contrast to his own conduct."

"There is no act of treachery or meanness of which a political party is not capable; for in politics there is no honour."

"Rest assured that in politics, however tremendous the effects, the causes are often as trifling."

"He who anticipates his century is generally persecuted when living, and is always pilfered when dead."

"Observe how much more men's conduct is influenced by circumstances than principles."

"A good offer should never be refused, unless we have a better one at the same time."

"No one is petted so much as a political apostate, except, perhaps, a religious one."

"It is not in human nature to endure extremities, and sorrows soon destroy either us or themselves."

By a freakish coincidence a character in the novel is named Lord Beaconsfield, who is dismissed by another character as "a dolt"; and in view of the author's future career it is amusing to come across this passage: "Nothing is more undignified than to make a speech. It is from the first an acknowledgment that you are under the necessity of explaining, or conciliating, or convincing, or confuting; in short that you are not omnipotent, but opposed."

His visit to Switzerland and Italy from August to October '26 was in the company of the Austens, who found him a most accommodating, kind and amusing fellow-traveller; though Mrs Austen thought he was unnecessarily troublesome over his buttons, which had to be put on his shirt almost daily, an operation that provoked extreme irritation. "They cannot have been good at first", she complained. "I'll tell my Mother you have abused my linen", he threatened. They crossed the Channel from Dover to Boulogne and stayed a few days in Paris doing the usual 'sights'. Thence they went to Geneva, and from various letters to his father we discover that the descriptions of travel in his novels resemble those in his correspondence. For example: "At the termination of the Jura ridge . . . did I on Friday morning witness the most magnificent sight in the world—the whole range of the high Alps with Mont Blanc in the centre *without a cloud*; the effect was so miraculous that for a long time I did not perceive the lovely scene under me, the plain and city and lake of Geneva, the latter of ultra-marine blue." In *Contarini Fleming*, written five years after, we read this: "Standing upon the height of Mount Jura, I beheld the whole range of the High Alps, with Mont Blanc in the centre, without a cloud . . . I was for some time so entranced that I did not observe the spreading and shining scene which opened far beneath me." He rowed on the lake every night with Maurice, Lord Byron's boatman, who told him much about the poet, and, anxious to experience a storm like that described in *Childe Harold*, he was lucky enough to enjoy the effects without the danger: "It was sublime—lightning almost continuous, and sometimes in four places, but as the evening advanced the lake became quite calm, and we never had a drop of rain." The people and country of Switzerland gave him a feeling of repose. "I wish that the world consisted of a cluster of small States", he mused. "There would be much more genius, and, what is of more importance, much more felicity." He had not been well before leaving home, but now he knew the comfort of returning health:

> I was content to exist. I began from this moment to suspect, what I have since learnt firmly to believe, that the sense of existence is the greatest happiness; and that, deprived of every worldly advantage which is supposed so necessary to our felicity, life, provided a man be not immured in a dungeon, must nevertheless be inexpressibly delightful. If, in striking the balance of sensation, misery were found to predominate, no human being would endure the curse of existence; but, however vast may be the wretchedness occasioned to us by the accidents of life, the certain sum of happiness, which is always supplied by our admirably contrived being, ever supports us under the burden.

The passage of the Alps produced in him all the symptoms of the poetic temperament except the poetry; while his reception at the Great St Bernard hospice was of a severely practical nature, the Brotherhood expressing a keen desire to hear whether the new tunnel under the Thames had been successful. He had to confess that he had never seen it. On reaching the Italian lakes he declared that "in speaking of Italy, romance has failed for once to exaggerate"; though realism, he considered, was sometimes carried too far, as in the Villa d'Este, where the ornaments were without exception "so universally indelicate that it was painful to view them in the presence of a lady." They saw all the famous places in northern Italy: Milan, Verona, Padua, Bologna, Pisa, Florence, Turin, Genoa, and of course Venice. They admired innumerable pictures and palaces, met many agreeable people, and enjoyed themselves thoroughly.

At that time Disraeli had not conceived, or convinced himself of, his Venetian ancestry, and his letters about Venice lack the emotion he describes in *Contarini Fleming*, where the hero makes the city the Mecca of his pilgrimage. Contarini sees the same things and sometimes depicts them in the same words, but when Disraeli wrote that novel he gave the hero sensations which his creator had not shared when he first beheld Venice: "I felt like a man who has achieved a great object. I was full of calm exultation . . . The marble palaces of my ancestors rose on each side, like a series of vast and solemn temples . . . I viewed them with a devotion which I cannot believe to have been surpassed in the most patriotic period of the Republic . . . I stood upon Rialto . . . Within these walls my fathers revelled! I bowed my head, and covered my face with my hands." Pleasing dreams, but they were dreamt at a later date. Indeed that early tour of Italy closed with a reflection that Contarini-Disraeli, his head full of Venetian forefathers, would scarcely have approved: "I trust I have not travelled in vain. Nature and Art have been tolerably well revealed to me . . . Five capitals and twelve great cities, innumerable remains of antiquity and the choicest specimens of modern art, have told me what man has done and is doing. I feel now that it is not prejudice when I declare that England, with all her imperfections, is worth all the world together . . ."

Chapter IV

PARTLY SARTORIAL

"LIKE all great travellers, I have seen more than I remember and remember more than I have seen", wrote Disraeli, and we may say of his early novels that he wrote more than he knew and knew more than he wrote. In time he became very critical of his early work, recognised that it affected a knowledge of the world that he had not gained while ignoring the self-knowledge that he had reached, and described it as full of conceit; but he added in extenuation that "every man has a right to be conceited until he is successful." His second long novel was in some respects even more fantastical than his first, but this was partly because it was written with the object of repeating the same sort of success that had attended the first and also to the fact that he was weakened by a long illness.

In the spring of '27 he was entered at Lincoln's Inn with the apparent intention of being called to the Bar, but beyond eating his dinners he seems to have taken no further interest in the matter. For about three years he was prostrated by an illness described by his doctor as "chronic inflammation of the membranes of the brain", and throughout that period he lived almost as a recluse, though during one brief interval of fairly good health he produced a short satire called *Popanilla*, which was issued by Colburn in '28 and received with no enthusiasm by press and public. It ridiculed the industrial civilisation of England, its politics, economics, religion, trade, agriculture, colonial expansion, literature, science and pretty well everything else; and a good deal of the satire is as timely today as it was a century ago. The present age has known many politicians like Popanilla: "Bigotry, and intolerance, and persecution, were the objects of his decided disapprobation; resembling, in this particular, all the great and good men who have ever existed, who have invariably maintained this opinion so long as they have been in the minority."

We have seen the result of Popanilla's advice to a backward people: if only they would develop all their resources, he "had no hesitation in saying that a short time could not elapse ere, instead of passing their lives in a state of unprofitable ease and useless enjoyment, they might reasonably expect to be the terror and astonishment of the universe, and to be able to annoy every nation of any consequence." And several modern dictators have done their best to illustrate the truth of this: "Free constitutions are apt to be misunderstood until half of the nation are bayoneted and the rest imprisoned." Not even the announcement that *Popanilla* was "by the author of *Vivian Grey*" attracted the reading public, who wanted something more like *Vivian Grey* from its author, and as his statement that English women had more manners and tact than the women of other races was followed by the remark "This is a clap-trap, and I have no doubt will sell the book", he was clearly of opinion that nothing could sell the book, an opinion that was fully justified.

In spite of his illness his few public appearances were rendered noteworthy by his striking attire. At the age of nineteen he had been seen in a black velvet suit with ruffles, and black stockings with red clocks, which, with his black curly hair and rather affected manner, had jarred on some of his acquaintances; and two years after the publication of *Popanilla* we hear of him walking up Regent Street in a blue surtout, a pair of military light blue trousers, black stockings with red stripes, and shoes. "The people", he reported, "quite made way for me as I passed. It was like the opening of the Red Sea, which I now perfectly believe from experience. Even well-dressed people stopped to look at me." That same season he dined with Lytton Bulwer, when he wore green velvet trousers, a canary-coloured waistcoat, low shoes, silver buckles, lace at his wrists, and his hair in ringlets. Obviously he intended to make an impression even at a time when he felt himself doomed to inaction and possibly insanity.

In 1829 the Disraelis left Bloomsbury for Buckinghamshire, Isaac having taken a manor house built in the time of Henry VIII at Bradenham, a few miles from High Wycombe, which he hoped would prove beneficial to his family. Here Benjamin lived quietly for twelve months, trying to get back his health and managing to evade his creditors. Neither illness nor debts made him despair of ultimate success, and he wrote to a friend "I advise you to take care of my letters, for if I become half as famous as I intend to be you may sell them for ten guineas apiece. . . ." He complained to another friend that his hair was growing badly and getting grey, "which I can unfeignedly declare occasions me more anguish than even the prospect of death." In the intervals of his prostration he worked on a novel which he prophesied would be successful. "It will complete the corruption of the public taste", he announced. He showed the manuscript to his new acquaintance Lytton Bulwer, who praised it highly but suggested the excision of many flippancies. This discouraged Disraeli, who would have suppressed the novel if he had not needed the money. But he wanted to visit the East, and as his father would not finance the trip he was forced to try his luck with the publishers. Anxious to restore harmonious relations with John Murray, he wrote to suggest an interview. Murray refused to see him, but said that if he cared to submit his novel it would be judged on its merits. Disraeli then sold the book to Colburn for £500, and wrote to Murray that when he returned home from the East he would try "for the third time" to persuade that publisher to bring out one of his works. Such perseverance after a rebuff was typical of the novelist who had just described someone as "always offended and always offending. Such a man could never succeed as a politician, a character who, of all others, must learn to endure, to forget, and to forgive."

The Young Duke appeared in the spring of '31, and sold well. Disraeli was in Egypt at the time, in a frame of mind wholly out of tune with the social atmosphere of the book, which can be suggested by a few phrases:

"Let me die eating ortolans to the sound of soft music."

"The proof of the general dullness of polite circles is the great sensation that is always produced by a new face."

"Unless we despise a woman when we cease to love her, we are still a slave, without the consolement of intoxication."

"A want of tact is worse than a want of virtue."

"It destroys one's nerves to be amiable every day to the same human being."

"When you have been bored for an hour or two on earth, it sometimes is a change to be bored for an hour or two on water."

"Something unpleasant is coming when men are anxious to tell the truth."

"The consciousness of a noble action is itself ennobling. His spirit expanded with the exciting effects which his conduct had produced. . . ."

"Mankind are not more heartless because they are clothed in ermine; it is that their costume attracts us to their characters, and we stare because we find the prince or the peeress neither a conqueror nor a heroine."

"Poor creature! that is to say, wicked woman! for we are not of those who set themselves against the verdict of society, or ever omit to expedite, by a gentle kick, a falling friend."

The novel shows the effect of the romantic movement on one whose temperament is romantic but whose intelligence is sceptical and satirical. Disraeli pictures himself as a young aristocrat who goes through all the experiences considered necessary to his station in life, from flirting to dissipation, from gaming to duelling. A fair sample of the writing is this description of two slightly inebriated dukes accosting two pretty women in the public ball-room at Doncaster:

> "We are attracted by observing two nymphs wandering in this desert", said his Grace of Burlington. This was the Burgundy.
>
> "And we wish to know whether there be any dragon to destroy, any ogre to devour, any magician to massacre, or how, when, and where we can testify our devotion to the ladies of our love", added his Grace of St James. This was the champagne.

The young Duke ruins himself, but love rescues him from the pit of debauchery, and his career is crowned by marriage with the loved one. It is a tale told by a wit, full of society and fatuity, signifying little; yet perhaps it is no more absurd to us than the clever novels of today will appear to our descendants a century hence.

With a loan from Austen, and the sum he had managed to raise on the book, Disraeli set forth with his friend Meredith to visit the land where his "holy ancestry" had lived. Already he had started a novel on the twelfth century Jewish hero, David Alroy, and he longed to see the places that he wished to describe. They left London by steamer on May 28th, 1830, and spent two months in Spain, using Gibraltar as their headquarters, and travelling on horseback through brigand-infested country to Ronda, Cadiz, Seville, Cordova and Granada: "The air of the mountains, the rising sun, the rising appetite, the variety of picturesque persons and things we met, and the impending danger, made a delightful life", which he would have enjoyed fully if the symptoms of his malady had not continued to manifest themselves in palpitation of the heart and a feeling of heaviness in the head. Even these abated after a while, an improvement he ascribed to the perpetual sunshine. They were most hospitably received wherever they went, and Disraeli's dandyism made him the subject of much comment: "I have also the fame of being the first who has passed the Straits with two canes, a morning and an evening cane. I change my cane as the gun fires, and hope to carry them both on to Cairo. It is wonderful the effect these magical wands produce. I owe to them even more attention than to being the supposed author of—what is it?—I forget!" Everyone in Spain, male and female, carried a fan. "I also have my fan", he wrote home, "which makes my cane extremely jealous." He suffered a grave set-back when the news of the death of George IV reached Gibraltar, for he had to abandon his gaudy dress waistcoats. "I truly grieve", he lamented. But there was plenty to distract his mind: bull-fights, bandits, and boleros.

Andalusia fascinated him: "I was never less than ten hours out of the twenty-four on my steed, and more than once saw the sun set and rise without quitting my saddle, which few men can say, and which I never wish to say again." Everywhere he was reminded of Cervantes, and the constant menace of robbers gave excitement to their journeys. Once their guide heard the distant trampling of horses at night-time. "Ave Maria! A cold perspiration came over me. Decidedly they approached, but rather an uproarious crew. We drew up out of pure fear, and I had my purse ready. The band turned out to be a company of actors travelling to Cordova." At Granada they were shown over the Alhambra by an old lady who felt positive that Disraeli was a Moor, because he behaved as if it belonged to him, saying "This is my palace." His general health had never been better: "All the English I have met are ill, and live upon a diet. I eat everything, and my appetite each day increases." Some months later he mentioned what had chiefly delighted him in Spain: "The Alhambra, and other Saracenic remains, the innumerable Murillos, and, above all, their *olla podridas*." Nevertheless he continually missed his family and his home. Begging his sister Sarah to write regularly, he said: "Do not let the chain of my domestic knowledge be broken for an instant. Write to me about Bradenham, about dogs and horses, orchards, gardens, who calls, where you go, who my father sees in London, what is said . . . A thousand, thousand loves to all. Adieu, my beloved. We shall meet soon. There is no place like Bradenham, and each moment I feel better I want to come back."

They had a rough and unpleasant journey from Gibraltar to Malta. Disraeli was a good sailor, and liked the life on a ship, but "it destroys the toilette, and one never feels, or is indeed, clean." Not even his morning and evening canes pleased the officers of the Malta garrison, his foppery proving intolerable, and after a while they ceased to invite "that damned bumptious Jew boy" to their mess, where he dined in an Andalusian costume. He was also to be seen dressed as a Greek pirate: a blood-red shirt with silver studs the size of shillings, a many-coloured sash, a jacket and trousers of broad blue stripes, red cap and slippers, and a belt stuffed with pistols and daggers. In this astonishing rig-out he paraded the streets of Valeta, followed by a gaping crowd; called on the Governor, a grave person whom he reduced to helpless laughter; and made himself the talk of the place. "To govern men, you must either excel them in their accomplishments, or despise them", he wrote to his father. The young officers played rackets, billiards and cards; and so, aware that he could not excel them, he despised them. "Affectation tells here even better than wit. Yesterday, at the racket court, sitting in the gallery among strangers, the ball entered, and lightly struck me, and fell at my feet. I picked it up, and observing a young rifleman excessively stiff, I humbly requested him to forward its passage into the court, as I really had never thrown a ball in my life. This incident has been the general subject of conversation at all the messes today!" In addition to his social achievements he soothed his solitude "with a Turkish pipe six feet long, with an amber mouthpiece and a porcelain bowl . . I not only have become a smoker, but the greatest smoker in Malta. The fact is I find it relieves my head."

An acquaintance named James Clay hired a yacht and took Meredith and Disraeli on their further travels as paying passengers.

First they went to Corfu, where they heard that Turkey had just put down an Albanian insurrection and was busy "pacifying" the country. Disraeli wished to congratulate the Grand Vizier, and proceeded to Yanina accompanied by Clay, Meredith, their servants, and a guard of Albanians. Half-way to the capital they spent a night in a large khan where their host was a young Bey, who produced an excellent supper with wine that was not so excellent but which they were compelled out of politeness to drink "in rivers." This, capped with their own brandy, removed the barriers between East and West: "The room turned round; the wild attendants who sat at our feet seemed dancing in strange and fantastic whirls; the Bey shook hands with me; he shouted English—I Greek. 'Very good' he had caught up from us. 'Kalo, kalo' was my rejoinder. He roared; I smacked him on the back. I remember no more." At Yanina they spent a week in a scene that recalled the *Arabian Nights*. "When I was presented to the Grand Vizier I made up such a costume from my heterogeneous wardrobe that the Turks, who are mad on the subject of dress, were utterly astounded." On this occasion his blood-red shirt and silver studs were set off by green pantaloons with a velvet stripe down the sides, a silk Albanian shawl with a long fringe of many hues round his waist, red Turkish slippers, and his Spanish jacket almost hidden with embroidery and ribbons. He had been informed by the Austrian consul that the Grand Vizier had destroyed in the course of the last three months, not in war, some "four thousand of my acquaintance"; but Disraeli took his seat on the divan with the self-possession of a morning call. Compliments were paid, and "we congratulated him on the pacification of Albania. He rejoined, that the peace of the world was his only object, and the happiness of mankind his only wish: this went on for the usual time." Disraeli found it delightful to be made much of "by a man who was daily decapitating half the province."

Leaving the Grand Vizier to the arduous duties entailed by his utopian dreams, they sailed through the Ionian islands, dodging pirates, touching at various places, and staying at Athens, of which he wrote "I never witnessed anything so truly beautiful, and I have seen a great deal." They made an uncomfortable excursion to Marathon, and then sailed for Constantinople, where he and Clay idled for over a month, Meredith, more active, going on to Smyrna. Disraeli was enthralled by the coloured costumes of the Turks, Greeks, Armenians and Jews, and the atmosphere of luxury and laziness appealed strongly to him: "The life of this people greatly accords with my taste, which is naturally somewhat indolent and melancholy . . . To repose on voluptuous ottomans and smoke superb pipes, daily to indulge in the luxuries of a bath which requires half a dozen attendants for its perfection; to court the air in a carved caïque, by shores which are a perpetual scene; and to find no exertion greater than a canter on a barb; this is, I think, a far more sensible life than all the bustle of clubs, all the boring of drawing-rooms, and all the coarse vulgarity of our political controversies." All the same after a month of it, he looked forward to his return home: "A mingled picture of domestic enjoyment and fresh butter, from both of which I have been so long estranged, daily flits across my fancy."

But Palestine and Egypt had yet to be visited, and they sailed for Jaffa, calling at Cyprus on the way. From Jaffa they set out for Jerusalem, "a party of six, well mounted and well armed." They put in a week at Jerusalem, and Disraeli was suitably impressed: "Except Athens I never saw anything more essentially striking . . . Athens and Jerusalem in their glory must have been the finest representations of the beautiful and the sublime . . . I could write half a dozen sheets on this week, the most delightful of all our travels." One incident was attended with danger. Entering the Mosque of Omar he was detected, instantly surrounded by a bevy of turbaned fanatics, and got away with difficulty. At a later period he recalled the spiritual peace that had come to him during that sojourn in Syria; and if, like all romantics, he overstated its effect, the impression at the time was considerable and never entirely left him:

> There is a charm in oriental life, and it is Repose. Upon me, who had been bred in the artificial circles of corrupt civilisation, and who had so freely indulged the course of his impetuous passions, this character made a forcible impression. Wandering over those plains and deserts, and sojourning in those silent and beautiful cities, I experienced all the serenity of mind which I can conceive to be the enviable portion of the old age of a virtuous life. The memory of the wearing cares, and corroding anxieties, and vaunted excitement of European life, filled me with pain. Keenly I felt the vanity and little-

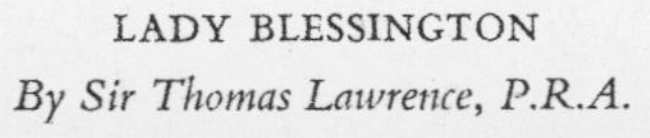

LADY BLESSINGTON

By Sir Thomas Lawrence, P.R.A.

COUNT D'ORSAY, 1841

By James Wood, R.A.

BENJAMIN AND MARY ANNE DISRAELI, 1840

By A. E. Chalon, R.A.

ness of all human plans and aspirations. Truly may I say that on the plains of Syria I parted for ever with my ambition. The calm enjoyment of existence appeared to me, as it now does, the highest attainable felicity; nor can I conceive that anything could tempt me from my solitude, and induce me once more to mingle with mankind, with whom I have little in common, but the strong conviction that the fortunes of my race depended on my effort, or that I could materially advance that great amelioration of their condition, in the practicability of which I devoutly believe.

This of course was a dramatised version of his emotion; and though he may, in his imagination, have parted for ever with his ambition, the newspapers which he received at Cairo announcing the introduction of the Reform Bill in the British parliament quickly made it apparent that his worldly aspirations, dead in the desert of the Holy Land, would be resurrected on the floor of the House of Commons.

The travellers reached Alexandria in March '31, and Disraeli remained in Egypt for four months, climbing the great Pyramid, voyaging up the Nile for seven hundred miles, and spending a week at Thebes, the sight of the ancient remains in Upper Egypt overpowering him: "My eyes and mind yet ache with a grandeur so little in unison with our own littleness." Clay fell ill in Cairo at the end of May and Disraeli had to face the prospect of looking after himself: "You know that though I like to be at my ease I want energy in those little affairs of which life greatly consists; here I found Clay always ready." Clay's view of his own readiness was expressed in the statement that Disraeli was the sort of person who "ought never to travel without a nurse." The next disquieting event was that Disraeli's favourite servant, a Greek from Cyprus, had to leave him. This was particularly annoying because "he wore a Mameluke dress of crimson and gold, with a white turban thirty yards long, and a sabre glittering like a rainbow. I must now content myself with an Arab attendant in a blue shirt and slipperless."

While in the capital Disraeli met Mehemet Ali, who, after a career of bribery, treachery, extortion and wholesale assassination, had made himself Pasha of Cairo and master of Egypt, and would later have become master of the Middle East if the European powers had not kept him out of Constantinople. Mehemet was toying with the idea of establishing parliamentary government, and asked Disraeli what he thought of it. Disraeli seemed to think there were difficulties in the way of an Egyptian democracy and mentioned a few of them. Mehemet was silent and thoughtful; but at his next levée he gave Disraeli the benefit of his meditations: "God is great!" he began. "You are a wise man. Allah! Kerim, but you spit pearls. Nevertheless I will have a parliament, and I will have as many parliaments as the King of England himself. See here!" he flourished two lists of names: "here are my parliaments; but I have made up my mind, to prevent inconvenience, to elect them myself."

Meredith and Disraeli were about to leave Egypt for England when the former caught smallpox and died on July 19th. This was a terrible blow, not only on account of their friendship, but because Meredith was engaged to be married to Disraeli's sister Sarah, to whom Benjamin was devoted; and he had to break the news by letter, which he did in the overwrought manner peculiar to him. First to his father: "Oh! my father, why do we live? The anguish of my soul is great. Our innocent lamb, our angel is stricken. Save her, save her . . . I wish to live only for my sister. I think of her all day and all night." Then to his sister: "Oh! my sister, in this hour of overwhelming affliction my thoughts are only for you. Alas! my beloved, if you are lost to me where, where am I to fly for refuge? I have no wife, I have no betrothed; nor since I have been better acquainted with my own mind and temper have I sought them. Live then, my heart's treasure, for one who has ever loved you with a surpassing love, and who would cheerfully have yielded his own existence to have saved you the bitterness of this letter. Yes, my beloved, be my genius, my solace, my companion, my joy."

He arrived home at the end of October, 1831, in excellent health but in sombre attire.

Chapter V

LARGELY PERSONAL

RETURNING to England just after the House of Lords had thrown out the second Reform Bill, Disraeli found himself in an atmosphere of semi-revolution, riots all over the country, physical combats between political disputants, communal uproar, domestic strife. He decided to stand as a parliamentary candidate for Wycombe at the next election, but in the meantime he completed one of two novels on which he had been working during his travels, and then, after removing his name from the books of Lincoln's Inn, plunged into social life. He took lodgings in Duke Street, St James's; and, sponsored by Bulwer, at whose parties in Hertford Street peers hobnobbed with penmen, he made the acquaintance of eminent scribes and prominent lords, and was soon calling at every house of distinction in Mayfair. He once admitted that, before the spring of '32, he "had lived a very secluded life, and mixed not at all with the world." At one of Bulwer's parties, on April 27th, 1832, he was introduced, at her request, to Mrs Wyndham Lewis, wife of the M.P. for Maidstone, whom he described as "a pretty little woman, a flirt, and a rattle; indeed, gifted with a volubility I should think unequalled, and of which I can convey no idea. She told me that she liked 'silent, melancholy men'. I answered 'that I had no doubt of it'." He little realised that his melancholy was to find its ideal complement in her volubility. After the party had broken up he remained with Bulwer to enjoy a pipe. Another guest, Colonel Webster, who had a reputation as a *roué*, said to him: "Take care, my good fellow; I lost the most beautiful woman in the world by smoking", and he added that the custom had prevented more *liaisons* than the dread of a duel or a divorce. "You have proved that it is a very moral habit", replied Disraeli between puffs.

His ability to make swift rejoinders while maintaining an air of indifference aroused the admiration of women and the resentment of men. "Be ever ready with the rapier of repartee", he wrote in an early novel, " and be ever armed with the breastplate of good temper. You will infallibly gather laurels if you add to these the spear of sarcasm and the shield of nonchalance." Men thought him affected, a coxcomb, his complete self-possession placing them at a disadvantage; and while secretly laughing at his origin, his manners and his clothes, were inwardly irritated by his success with women and the fact that they could not get the better of him in conversation. Even the haughty Sir Robert Peel was careful to be polite to him, which at least proves that he had become a notable figure in society within three months of his initiation. Furthermore his assumption of superiority was not entirely a pose. He had witnessed debates in the House of Commons and had decided that the level of intelligence was not of a high order: "I have seen the House convulsed with raillery which, in other society, would infallibly settle the rallier to be a bore beyond all tolerance. Even an idiot can raise a smile. They are so good-natured, or find it so dull." And long before there was any likelihood of his appearing in the Commons, or any conceivable chance of his being seen in the Lords, he had made up his mind to succeed in each: "One thing is clear, that a man may speak very well in the House of Commons, and fail very completely in the House of Lords. There are two distinct styles requisite: I intend in the course of my career, if I have time, to give a specimen of both. In the Lower House Don Juan may perhaps be our model; in the Upper House, Paradise Lost." After hearing such speakers as Macaulay, Peel, Bulwer and the rest, he was as confident as ever, writing to his sister: "Macaulay admirable; but, between ourselves, I could floor them all. This *entre nous*; I was never more confident of anything than that I could carry everything before me in that House. The time will come . . ."

At the height of the season which saw his entry into the Mayfair drawing-rooms his novel *Contarini Fleming* was published by Murray, and the notabilities he met were able to smile over a piece of advice in it: "Always know eminent men, and always be master of the subject of the day." Less successful aspirants to social fame could comfort themselves with his confession "Impertinent and flippant, I was universally hailed an original and a wit", but quickly perceived that they could not emulate him: "There are times when I am influenced by a species of what I may term happy audacity, for it is a mixture of recklessness and self-confidence which has a very felicitous effect upon the animal spirits. At these moments I never calculate consequences, yet everything seems to go right. I feel in good fortune; the ludicrous side of everything occurs to me; I think of nothing but grotesque images; I astonish people by bursting into laughter, apparently without a cause. Whatever is submitted to me I turn into ridicule. I shrug my shoulders and speak epigrams." A few of these epigrams must find a place here:

"She was one of those women who have the highest respect for furniture."

"Never argue. In society nothing must be discussed; give only results."

"Amusement to an observing mind is study."

"Read no history, nothing but biography, for that is life without theory."

"I think that, ere long, science will again become imaginative, and that, as we become more profound, we may become also more credulous."

"Never apologise for showing feeling, my friend. Remember that when you do so you apologise for truth."

"Among all men there are some points of similarity and sympathy. There are few alike; there are some totally unlike the mass."

"When a man really believes he is dying, he does not like to lose the interest which such a situation produces."

Disraeli always had a high opinion of *Contarini Fleming*, in which he traced "a development of my poetic character" and expressed his inmost thoughts and feelings. He thought it "the perfection of English prose and a *chef d'œuvre*." It describes how a misunderstood boy, full of poetry, romance, and high thoughts for the betterment of his species, runs away from school because he hates control, leaves his university for the same reason, and becomes the chief of a band of robbers, erstwhile fellow-students, whose headquarters are in a forest-girt castle. After their dispersal by the forces of law and order, he joins his father, a leading politician, is made an Under-Secretary of State, writes a satirical book (*Vivian Grey* of course) which creates a sensation because of its portraits of eminent people, throws up his job, and travels. First he goes to Venice, where he falls in love, and flies to Candia with his wife, who, after a brief interlude of ecstatic happiness, dies in childbirth. Then he travels through Greece, Turkey, Asia Minor, Palestine, Spain and Egypt; and drawing on the author's memory and correspondence, he becomes a Baedeker of information concerning the people, scenery, costumes and architecture of every country he visits. His father dies; he inherits great wealth, builds a palace near Naples, gives himself up to composition, but thinks he will yet be called upon to ameliorate his species.

The novel was acclaimed by Heinrich Heine, and William Beckford was so entranced that he asked his publisher to call on the author of "that transcendent work" and send a description of his appearance and conversation. The publisher duly called and reported that Disraeli was the most conceited person he had ever met in his life. But he was no more conceited than his hero Contarini, who is pictured in one place as walking up and down in a frenzy of ambition, thirsting for action: "There seemed to me no achievement of which I was not capable, and of which I was not ambitious. In imagination I shook thrones and founded empires. I felt myself a being born to breathe in an atmosphere of revolution." Which may explain why the poetic character he tries to develop in the course of the story is not very convincing. In spite of Heine, Beckford, Thomas Campbell, Madame D'Arblay and other encomiasts, the book did not pay its expenses; and Disraeli turned to another tale that he had worked on while in the East.

Strolling up and down the Yew Terrace at Bradenham, he meditated in poetic prose, and soon completed the narration of "a gorgeous incident in the annals of that sacred and romantic people from whom I derive my blood and name." Byron and the romantic movement were responsible for much, but for nothing quite so astonishing as *Alroy*, which is among the prime aberrations of an exotic talent. This is how Alroy avenges an attempt on the virtue of his sister: "Pallid and mad, he swift upsprang, and he tore up a tree by its lusty roots, and down the declivity, dashing with rapid leaps, panting and wild, he struck the ravisher on the temple with the mighty pine. Alschiroch fell lifeless on the sod, and Miriam fainting into her brother's arms."

In his pilgrimage Alroy is fed by the birds, and natural forces give way to magic when he wishes to cross a precipice. Wild beasts quail before him; he wakes up and looks into the flaming eyes of a hungry and indignant lion: "For a moment, their flashing orbs vied in regal rivalry; but at length the spirit of the mere animal yielded to the genius of the man. The lion, cowed, slunk away, stalked with haughty timidity through the rocks, and then sprang into the forest." The hero's arrival as a conqueror at Bagdad is celebrated with several passages of this order: "Yes! yes! upon the bounding plain fleet Asriel glances like a star, and stout Scherirah shakes his spear by stern Jabaster's scimetar . . ." And the love-scene between Alroy and the caliph's daughter, the princess Schirene, is heralded thus: "It is the tender twilight hour, when maidens in their lonely bower, sigh softer than the eve! The languid rose her head upraises, and listens to the nightingale, while his wild and thrilling praises, from his trembling bosom gush: the languid rose her head upraises, and listens with a blush." It is quite possible that the enthusiastic and ambitious author thought this as good as anything in *Romeo and Juliet*, because over forty years later he said that he had aimed in places at the highest bursts of poetry; and that if politics had not intervened and he had pursued his plan of writing "poetry without numbers", he might have brought about "a literary revolution." No doubt.

The Bible as well as Byron, Scott as well as Shakespeare, are forced to contribute to a style which Flaubert, Flecker and Maeterlinck may have studied to their disadvantage but which fortunately has had little effect on English literature, though it turned the attention of Oscar Wilde to that form of artificiality known as poetic prose. Yet Wilde never explored the possibilities of human imbecility so thoroughly as Disraeli. Few people would be willing to assert that *The Picture of Dorian Grey* is a lifelike representment of human beings or a vivid narrative of probable occurrences; but compared with *Alroy* it is a masterpiece of photographic reality and scientific exactitude. All Disraeli's books contain dream-pictures of himself and what he would like to achieve; and *Alroy* is a fantasy in which its author is depicted as the descendant of David, the conqueror chosen by God to lead the Jews to victory and revive their ancient glory. Several famous warriors and statesmen have begun life by writing fantasies in which they appear as supermen; and more than any of his other novels *Alroy* might have suggested to a clever political contemporary that Disraeli would become Prime Minister, for nothing less would satisfy his ambition, and no one but a born man of action could have written that particular sort of rubbish.

Fortunately for John Murray's peace of mind, he returned it to the author unread, and Colburn brought it out in '33. Naturally Beckford went into raptures over it; but it did not attract the reading public, even though baited with a short story called *The Rise of Iskander*, a tale of love, war, and patriotism, in which a hero is portrayed as a god, and the Cross beats the Crescent by double-crossing it.

Disraeli's interest in the East never subsided, and was to bear fruit in an English occupation of Egypt, an English Empress of India, and an English settlement of eastern affairs at the Berlin Congress. His interest in his own personality was also to be more permanent than he believed. Confessing that *Vivian Grey*, *Contarini Fleming* and *Alroy* contained the secret history of his feelings, he declared that he would write nothing further about himself. But he was to appear, thinly disguised, in every novel that came from his pen; though he followed *Alroy* with two short pieces for Bulwer's magazine *The New Monthly* in which he attained a measure of light-hearted objectivity. They were called *Ixion in Heaven* and *The Infernal Marriage*, and they did for the gods what Bernard Shaw was later to do for the Romans: brought them up to date. The second contains some characteristic epigrams:

"Next to knowing when to seize an opportunity, the most important thing in life is to know when to forego an advantage."

"Those who want to lead must never hesitate about sacrificing their friends."

"I have often observed that nothing ever perplexes an adversary so much as an appeal to his honour."

"There are exceptions to all rules, but it seldom answers to follow the advice of an opponent."

In *Ixion* appears Disraeli's famous phrase "Adventures are to the adventurous", which he liked so much that he repeated it eleven years afterwards in *Coningsby*, and which was certainly true of himself, as he was about to demonstrate in the field of politics.

Chapter VI

SOCIAL, POLITICAL AND AMOROUS

DISRAELI was not by nature a party man. He had affinities and antipathies, like everyone else, but he was too individualistic to subscribe to any political programme. For this reason he was distrusted by all the sheep-like members of parliament, both whigs and tories; and though he soon realised that he would achieve nothing without a label, the question of his sincerity remained an open one to the end of his days, the large majority of people being so made that they invariably suspect the integrity of those who have minds of their own. In many respects he was the most consistent and sincere politician of his age, though naturally his views expanded and were partly dictated by the changes and circumstances of the time. But this must be said at the outset: he was, like every politician who comes to the front, a careerist. No one fights political battles for the sake of peace and quiet; no downright incorruptible idealist could endure the wire-pulling, charlatanry, humbug, chicanery, place-seeking, time-serving, and power-snatching, which are the necessary ingredients of politics; and the spectacle of a successful and mainly disinterested statesman, whether right, left or centre, is one that the world awaits in vain.

> Get thee glass eyes,
> And, like a scurvy politician, seem
> To see the things thou dost not,

is Shakespeare's comment on that profession, and on the whole a true one. Only a saint could be quite honest in politics, and saints do not enter politics; but Disraeli was as honest as a man can be who is chiefly devoted to his own interests. He was less impressionable and less emotional than his great antagonist of later years, Gladstone, and consequently a better ruler of men, but he was just as sincere and quite as honest. Both of them played the power-game for all it was worth, and neither was therefore primarily concerned with the welfare of mankind; but each believed that his own policy was for the good of the country, Gladstone passionately, Disraeli calmly.

Their personalities were as different as their achievements. Disraeli was perhaps the only figure in English political history who started public life as an object of ridicule and ended it as an object of reverence: it was as if Oscar Wilde, the aesthete of Gilbert's *Patience*, had closed his career in the atmosphere of sanctity that surrounded the last years of Tennyson. But behind the negligent figure and coloured costume and long hair ringlets of "this miserable, circumcised, soi-disant Christian", as the actor Macready called him, were the determination, fortitude, prevision and persistence of Richelieu, with a patience that Richelieu might have envied, and a sense of humour that he lacked. Rebuff followed rebuff from the moment he entered the political scene.

Before the Reform Act came into operation, he stood for High Wycombe as a radical, declaring that he was neither a whig nor a tory and that his politics could be described in one word: England. He also made it clear that he was sprung from the people, that neither he nor his family had ever received a shilling of the public money, and that not a drop of Plantagenet blood flowed in his veins. After his opponent had paraded the town with a band and a hired mob, he "jumped up on the portico of the Red Lion and gave it to them for an hour and a half." He made a surprising appearance, with his profuse black hair, his rings and chains, his lace and cambric, his white face and elaborate waistcoat; and the people were amazed when this foppish figure let loose a stream of eloquence, with dramatic gestures to enforce his arguments, in a voice that could be heard far down the street. "When the poll is declared, I shall be there", he concluded, pointing at the head of the lion above the portico, "and my opponent will be there", indicating the lion's tail. "I made them all mad", he reported. "A great many absolutely *cried* ... All the women are on my side and wear my colours, pink and white." But however popular he was with the mob, the Corporation and burgesses who controlled the election placed him at the lion's tail, his opponent at the head; upon which he publicly asserted that "the whigs have opposed me, not I them, and they shall repent it", and that the nearest thing to a tory in disguise was a whig in office.

This was in June '32, and at the close of the same year he stood, again at High Wycombe, for the first reformed parliament. But again he antagonised the chief parties by saying in his election address: "Rid yourselves of all that political jargon and factious slang of whig and tory—two names with one meaning, used only to delude you—and unite in forming a great national party . . .", and he defined himself as a conservative to preserve what was good in the constitution, a radical to remove what was bad. The tories were more friendly than the whigs, who did their best to defeat him because, he said, he was not nobly born, and once more he was at the bottom of the poll. Without pausing, he put himself forward for the county of Buckinghamshire; but discovering that a second tory candidate had just been nominated, he withdrew his own name and supported the other. The following year there was a chance of standing for Marylebone and he issued an address; but the vacancy did not occur, so he consoled himself by writing a pamphlet explaining his political faith and advising the tories to merge with the radicals. He disliked the whigs, who had substituted a selfish oligarchy for a kingdom, and he thought the tories, who had lost their traditions, could be purged of retrogression and reinstated in their historical position as leaders of the people and supporters of the monarchy. To bring this about was to be his own work for nearly half a century; but no one in the eighteen-thirties could have guessed that it was feasible, still less that the flashy young Jew would be the motive-force. Lord Melbourne, then Home Secretary, who met him at a dinner-party in '34, was attracted by his conversation and asked "Well now, tell me, what do you want to be?" "I want to be Prime Minister", replied Disraeli with quiet gravity. Melbourne gave a weary sigh and then explained the utter impossibility of such an achievement, ending with "You must put all these foolish notions out of your head; they won't do at all." But Melbourne lived to feel less confident, and when towards the close of '48, just before his death, he heard that Disraeli was to become tory leader in the Commons, he exclaimed "By God! the fellow will do it yet."

It certainly did not seem as if he would live to do it after his second defeat at High Wycombe, and for some years his activities were almost wholly social. We hear of him at Bath with Bulwer, smoking latakia over their conversation and being mobbed at a public ball. Wherever he went his clothes aroused comment; at one dinner he appeared in a black velvet coat lined with satin, purple trousers with a gold band running down the outside seam, scarlet waistcoat, long lace ruffles reaching the tips of his fingers, white gloves with jewelled rings outside them, his well-oiled black ringlets touching his shoulders. His conversation, which ranged from the sarcastic to the eloquent, according to his mood, made him popular with hostesses who were not solely satisfied with the movement of their guests' jaws in mastication, and his table was covered with invitations, many from people he did not know. He could be extremely cutting when the occasion called for it. One of his hosts, after praising a certain wine, urged him to drink it. He agreed that it was very good. "Well", said the host, "I have got wine twenty times as good in my cellar." "No doubt, no doubt", said Disraeli, glancing round the table, "but, my dear fellow, this is quite good enough for such *canaille* as you have here today." He talked much about poetry and about the East, and he told one girl that the great thing in life was repose, that nothing repaid exertion; but she noticed that his temperament was such that not even a glorious old age could compensate him for obscurity in youth. Naturally he thought a good deal about marriage, and in a letter to his sister asked "Would you like Lady Z— for a sister-in-law, very clever, £25,000, and domestic? As for 'love', all my friends who married for love and beauty either beat their wives or live apart from them. This is literally the case. I may commit many follies in life, but I never intend to marry for 'love', which I am sure is a guarantee of infelicity." All the same he was quick to notice physical blemishes in those women who engrossed his attention. "Handsome, brilliant, and young", he thought Lady Lincoln, "but with one great fault, a rabbit mouth."

In the autumn of '33 he began a diary, which however only engaged him intermittently while resting at Bradenham after the whirl of the social season. A few phrases in this document are revealing: "I have passed the whole of this year in uninterrupted lounging and pleasure . . . My life has not been a happy one. Nature has given me an awful ambition and fiery passions . . . My disposition is now indolent. I wish to be idle and enjoy myself . . . Alas! I struggle from Pride. Yes! It is Pride that now prompts me, not Ambition. They shall not say I have failed . . . All men of high imagination are indolent . . . I have an unerring instinct—I can read characters at a glance . . . I am only truly great in action. If ever I am placed in a truly eminent position I shall prove this. I could rule the House of Commons, although there would be a great prejudice against me at first . . . Imagination governs mankind." On another occasion he wrote "I am never well save in action, and then I feel immortal . . . Dyspepsia always makes me wish for a civil war."

Except for his father and Bulwer, he now derived little pleasure from conversing with men: "As I never get anything in return, I do not think the exertion necessary." But he entered into their sports to prove that he was as tough as they: "I hunted the other day with Sir Henry Smythe's hounds, and although not in scarlet was the best mounted man in the field, riding Lady Sykes's Arabian mare, which I nearly killed; a run of thirty miles, and I stopped at nothing. I gained great kudos. The only Londoner I met was Henry Manners Sutton . . . He asked me to return with him; but as Lady Manners was not there, I saw no fun and refused." His fellow-sportsmen would have been surprised to learn that he was then engaged on a long narrative poem. He had "an unconquerable desire of producing something great and lasting", and when wandering over the plains of Troy had conceived the idea of a revolutionary epic which would do for the Napoleonic saga what Homer had done for the ancient Greeks. He envisaged a work of some thirty thousand lines, and his intention was to read a canto to the Austens, if alone, when he dined with them in January '34. But Mrs Austen no doubt felt that a treat of this sort should not be confined to the family, and asked a number of people to dinner. The poet was undeterred, and the curious figure, dressed in a fantastic style that did not harmonise with Miltonic blank verse, stood with his back to the fire and declaimed pages of stuff that had nothing in common with the *Odyssey* except length. After he had left the room, a humorous member of the party recited an impromptu parody, guying the manner and matter of the epicist, and sent everyone into fits of laughter. But ridicule, even had he heard of it, was not enough to dishearten a poet who longed to be the Homer, Virgil, Dante or Milton of his age; and the first three parts were soon submitted to the indulgence of readers, with a preface implying that there was a good deal more to come, but that as "I am not one who finds consolation for the neglect of my contemporaries in the imaginary plaudits of a more sympathetic posterity" the decision of the public would be final, and, if unfriendly, his lyre would be hurled into limbo without a pang. Readers were as apathetic as posterity has been, and he stopped the manufacture of verse for three years, when he corrected what he had written and might have completed the work if, happily, politics had not intervened. He wished to dedicate the first volume to the Duke of Wellington, but the man who had faced Napoleon's bombardment without blenching quailed at the prospect of reading Disraeli's pentameters, and politely refused his permission.

While the second and third books of the heroic poem were going through the press he made the acquaintance of Lady Blessington and was soon a constant visitor at her house in Seamore Place, where all the male celebrities of the day were to be met. It was commonly supposed that she and Count D'Orsay were lovers, though he had married her step-daughter in order to benefit from her late husband's estate, and she was therefore outlawed by the other famous hostesses of the day, and married men called on her without their wives. Michael Sadleir has suggested that D'Orsay was probably impotent; on the other hand, Samuel Rogers told Henry Crabb Robinson that D'Orsay kept one of the dancers at the opera but dared not look at her in Lady Blessington's presence. Anyhow there was quite enough uncertainty about the whole affair, as well as her own past, to make Lady Blessington a theme for scandal; and the fact that she was beautiful and witty made her imaginary transgressions all the more unendurable, jealousy being the strongest incitement to moral indignation. A good example of her stingless wit was her remark to Walter Savage Landor, who was violently attacking the Psalms to the discomfort of a Roman Catholic fellow-guest: "*Do* write something better, Mr Landor." This silenced him without leaving him resentful.

D'Orsay was the great dandy of the time and led the fashion in men's clothes; but as he was able to give the whole of his leisure to the subject he dressed with exceptional distinction and never appeared over-dressed or ostentatious, like Bulwer, Ainsworth, Dickens, above all Disraeli. In addition D'Orsay was a tall handsome man, with an athletic figure and a personality of great charm; and both he and Lady Blessington evoked the admiration and affection in equal degree of many remarkable people, in particular Dickens, Disraeli and Bulwer, the second of whom gives a pleasant portrait of D'Orsay as 'Count Mirabel' in the first novel he wrote after entering the Blessington circle, *Henrietta Temple*, wherein the Count is described as "the best-dressed man in London, fresh and gay as a bird, with not a care on his sparkling visage, and his eye bright with bonhomie . . . Care he knew nothing about; Time he defied; Indisposition he could not comprehend. He had never been ill in his life, even for five minutes . . . There was something in Count Mirabel's very presence which put everybody in good spirits. His lightheartedness was caught by all. Melancholy was a farce in the presence of his smile; and there was no possible combination of scrapes that could withstand his kind and brilliant raillery." D'Orsay takes the hero of the novel for a drive, and we may feel sure that this is a personal reminiscence: "The Count Mirabel enjoyed the drive to Richmond as if he had never been to Richmond in his life. The warm sun, the western breeze, every object he passed and that passed him called for his praise or observation. He inoculated Ferdinand with his gaiety, as Ferdinand listened to his light, lively tales, and his flying remarks, so full of merriment and poignant truth and daring fancy." They arrive at their destination, and we learn that "Count Mirabel, who had the finest tact in the world, but whose secret spell, after all, was perhaps only that he was always natural, adapted himself in a moment to the characters, the scene, and the occasion." Several of D'Orsay's remarks are recorded:

"If a man be convinced that existence is the greatest pleasure, his happiness may be increased by good fortune, but it will be essentially independent of it."

"Feel slightly, think little, never plan, never brood. Everything depends upon the circulation; take care of it. Take the world as you find it; enjoy everything. Vive la bagatelle!"

"Men were made to listen as well as talk", says Lady Bellair. "Without doubt", replies the Count, "for Nature has given us two ears, but only one mouth."

From the accounts of certain fellow-guests, it seems that Disraeli used his ears more than his mouth at the Blessington dinner-parties, where he was habitually silent and observant, though when his interest was aroused he would hold the table with a burst of eloquence, enlivened with satire and sarcasm, displaying such a grasp of his subject and command of language that people thought him the most wonderful talker they had ever heard. He was asked everywhere and got to know everyone of importance, being as popular with Lord Durham, a leading whig, as with Lord Lyndhurst, a leading tory. "I have had great success in society this year in every respect", he informed his sister. "I make my way easily in the highest set, where there is no envy, malice, etc, and where they like to admire and be amused", and he asserted that he was as popular with first-rate men as he was hated by the second-rate. Water-parties up the Thames to Richmond, singing all the way, water-parties down the Thames to Greenwich, fêtes, picnics, supper-parties, receptions, balls: he enjoyed them all, and basked in an atmosphere of admiration.

Also he had found a mistress, whose christian name was Henrietta and who was a member of the set he moved in. Their intimacy in 1833 made that year the happiest of his life; and in the autumn of '34 he wrote in his diary: "What a happy or rather amusing society Henrietta and myself commanded this year. What delicious little suppers after the Opera!" Her husband had a title, which no doubt added to her attraction, but Disraeli loved her with ardour and separation from her made him feel ill and sad. On reaching Bradenham in August '34 he confided to Lady Blessington that he was "very ill indeed from the pangs of parting. Indeed, I feel as desolate as a ghost, and I do not think that I ever shall be able to settle to anything again. It is a great shame, when people are happy together, that they should be ever separated; but it seems the great object of all human legislation that people never should be happy together." Ten days later he declared himself "quite at a loss how to manage affairs in future as I find separation more irksome than even my bitterest imagination predicted." And he told Bulwer that all the barriers of his life seemed to be failing simultaneously. He found relief in writing, and began a love-story. But he only finished one volume, his attention over the next two years being fully engaged by the social round, by politics, and especially by Henrietta herself, whose extravagance seems to have increased his debts until, his ardour waning and his ambition waxing, he determined to break the *liaison*, noting in his diary for the autumn of '36 that he had parted from her for ever. Then, with his love-affair behind him and his load of debts before him, he completed the story; and *Henrietta Temple*, dedicated to D'Orsay, repeated the success of *Vivian Grey*.

One does not expect a picture of real life from a born politician, and *Henrietta Temple*, because it deals mainly with the emotion of love, is further from reality than any of Disraeli's stories except *Alroy*. Having already depicted himself as a great conqueror, thinker, writer, leader, he now sees himself as a great lover, out-Romeoing Romeo, his intensity of feeling ending in delirium, prostration, and almost annihilation. The woman he loves is of course the most glorious creature in the universe, whose beauty outvies art; while he is the most sensitive and imaginative of creatures, who loves at first sight, overwhelmingly and for ever. Sentimentality and rhetoric result from the suppression of what a writer really feels in favour of what he would like to feel, and the emotionalism in *Henrietta Temple* is heightened to absurdity. This is how Disraeli liked to imagine himself as a lover: "An immortal flame burns in the breast of that man who adores and is adored . . . The cares of the world do not touch him; its most stirring events are to him but the dusty incidents of bygone annals. All the fortune of the world without his mistress is misery; and with her all its mischances a transient dream. Revolutions, earthquakes, the change of governments, the fall of empires, are to him but childish games, distasteful to a manly spirit . . . Nothing can subdue him. He laughs alike at loss of fortune, loss of friends, loss of character . . ." Such elevation of feeling must have a worthy setting; and though we are informed that love can irradiate a hovel and lighten the fetter of a slave, nevertheless "fortunate the passion that is breathed in palaces, amid the ennobling creations of surrounding art, and greets the object of its fond solicitude amid perfumed gardens, and in the shade of green and silent woods!" Disraeli's isolation in aristocratic society is suggested by the hero being a Roman Catholic, unemancipated at the period of the story, and his romantic view of that society is rather more than suggested by such comments as: "The young marquis was an excellent specimen of a class inferior in talents, intelligence, and accomplishments, in public spirit and in private virtues, to none in the world, the English nobility."

But even in such an over-fervid and unnatural romance the author's worldly sense occasionally breaks through, and we are reminded that he was suffering from duns when we come across the sentence: "As men advance in life, all passions resolve themselves into money. Love, ambition, even poetry, end in this."

Chapter VII

TURMOIL

"ONE event makes another", wrote Disraeli in *Henrietta Temple*: "what we anticipate seldom occurs; what we least expected generally happens; and time can only prove which is most for our advantage." This was particularly true of his political career, the ups and downs of which were scarcely ever predictable. Once more he put himself forward as a radical candidate for High Wycombe at the General Election of '35, and now he was backed by the chief tory of the realm, the Duke of Wellington. In his address to the electors he hinted at possible adaptations in his own programme: "The conduct and the opinions of public men at different periods of their career must not be too curiously contrasted in a free and aspiring country. The people have their passions, and it is even the duty of public men occasionally to adopt sentiments with which they do not sympathise, because the people must have leaders . . . I laugh, therefore, at the objection against a man, that at a former period of his career he advocated a policy different to his present one. All I seek to ascertain is whether his present policy be just, necessary, expedient; whether at the present moment he is prepared to serve the country according to its present necessities." The objection to this opportunistic philosophy, apart from the turning of leaders into followers, is that it can be used to excuse knavery as well as to explain statecraft; but the candour of it must have been refreshing from a youthful politician; and another passage from his address has a far greater significance today than when he wrote it: "I cannot force from my mind the conviction that a House of Commons, concentrating in itself the whole power of the State, might—I should rather say would—establish in this country a despotism of the most formidable and dangerous character." In spite of his popularity as a speaker, the whig forces were too much for him, and for the third time he was at the bottom of the poll. He now realised that, if he wanted to enter parliament, he must join one of the two chief parties; and when Sir Robert Peel, the new tory Prime Minister, issued an address to his electors which advocated many of the reforms favoured by Disraeli, he applied for membership of the Carlton Club, declared himself henceforth a tory, and within a week or two was dining with some of the party leaders. A fellow-guest was "young Gladstone", and the dinner was "rather dull, but we had a swan very white and tender, and stuffed with truffles."

In April '35 the party wanted a good man for an election at Taunton and sent Disraeli to contest the seat, which he did "in a rage of enthusiasm." The fatigue was awful, he reported: "Two long speeches today, and nine hours' canvass on foot in a blaze of repartee." His personal appearance made the usual dramatic effect: the lividly pale face, black eyes, luxuriant glossy hair, half-smiling half-sneering mouth; the bottle-green frock-coat, startling waistcoat, ornamental trousers, chains and rings galore. All his eloquence and finery were wasted on the electors, and he sustained his fourth defeat; but at a great banquet after the fight he made a speech in which he said that his was the democratic party because it stood for the King against a usurping aristocracy, for the freedom of the people against a tyrannical executive. He commenced the speech in a lazy affected manner, using gestures that displayed his rings; but quickly warmed to his theme and spoke with fervour and rapidity, his voice becoming rich and resonant, the dandiacal manner changing to that of a skilled orator.

The Tory Administration had just been turned out by a Whig and Irish alliance; and as these two had previously been abusing each other in what is miscalled unparliamentary language, Disraeli remarked on the fact. The Irish leader was Daniel O'Connell, the first of those fiery figures who maddened English politicians and made melodramatic scenes in the House of Commons between the passing of the Act of Union in 1801 and the establishment of the Irish Free State in 1922. His personal idealism and unpleasant tactics were summed up by Sydney Smith: "The only way to deal with such a man as O'Connell is to hang him up and erect a statue to him under the gallows." In one of his Taunton speeches Disraeli described the whigs as "that weak and aristocratic party in the state who could only obtain power by leaguing themselves with one whom they had denounced as a traitor." The London papers made the most of this, and in their version Disraeli was reported to have called O'Connell an incendiary and a traitor. O'Connell was nettled, and at a meeting in Dublin he indulged in one of those flights of invective which gave colour to political oratory in the nineteenth century but which have now gone out of fashion, not because politicians love one another more than they did but because they are more nervous: the hatreds are still there; but so is the law of libel; and people have become more touchy. Several passages in O'Connell's speech, if the antagonists had been living today, would have made Disraeli financially solvent:

"At Taunton this miscreant had the audacity to call me an incendiary! . . . Then he calls me a traitor. My answer to that is, he is a liar. He is a liar in action and in words. His life is a living lie. He is a disgrace to his species. What state of society must that be that could tolerate such a creature . . . He is the most degraded of his species and kind; and England is degraded in tolerating or having upon the face of her society a miscreant of his abominable, foul and atrocious nature. The language is harsh, I must confess; but it is no more than deserved, and if I should apologise for using it, it is because I can find no harsher epithets in the English language by which to convey the utter abhorrence which I entertain for such a reptile. His name shows that he is of Jewish origin. I do not use it as a term of reproach; there are many most respectable Jews. But there are, as in every other people, some of the lowest and most disgusting grade of moral turpitude; and of those I look upon Mr Disraeli as the worst. He possesses just the qualities of the impenitent thief on the Cross, whose name, I verily believe, must have been Disraeli. For aught I know, the present Disraeli is descended from him, and, with the impression that he is, I now forgive the heir-at-law of the blasphemous thief who died upon the Cross."

A decade later Disraeli would have thoroughly enjoyed this, and shown how O'Connell had missed many telling points; but he was not yet hardened to abuse, and moreover he still had his way to make in politics. As it happened O'Connell, having killed a man in a duel, had sworn never to fight again, and his son had defended his name against a recent opponent. Disraeli therefore sent a challenge to the son, who replied that he was not responsible for what his father said, only for what was said against his father. Disraeli promptly said it in an open letter to O'Connell published by the press, from which we extract two passages:

"If it had been possible for you to act like a gentleman, you would have hesitated before you made your foul and insolent comments upon a hasty and garbled report of a speech which scarcely contains a sentence or an expression as they emanated from my mouth; but the truth is you were glad to seize the first opportunity of pouring forth your venom against a man whom it serves the interest of your party to represent as a political apostate. . . .

"I expect to be a representative of the people before the repeal of the Union. We shall meet at Philippi; and rest assured that, confident in a good cause, and in some energies which have not been altogether unproved, I will seize the first opportunity of inflicting upon you a castigation which will make you at the same time remember and repent the insults that you have lavished upon

BENJAMIN DISRAELI."

The moment this letter appeared in print Disraeli again wrote to O'Connell's son, saying that he had done his best to insult Daniel and to express "the utter scorn in which I hold his character, and the disgust with which his conduct inspired me. If I failed in conveying this expression of my feelings to him, let me more successfully express them now to you. I shall take every opportunity of holding your father's name up to public contempt. And I fervently pray that you, or some one of his blood, may attempt to avenge the unextinguishable hatred with which I shall pursue his existence." But instead of the duel for which he had hoped, a friend of the O'Connells warned the police, and Disraeli was arrested, taken before a magistrate, and bound over to keep the peace in sureties of £500. "All men agree I have shown pluck", he was able to tell his sister, and he received countless letters of congratulation from all over the kingdom. He soon proved his ability to play the Irishman's game, and in the course of a series of letters to *The Times* on the statesmen of the day, signed 'Runnymede', he referred to O'Connell as "a systematic liar and a beggarly cheat, a swindler and a poltroon . . . His public and his private life are equally profligate; he has committed every crime that does not require courage." In December '36 he attacked O'Connell in a speech at Aylesbury, and the Duke of Wellington said "It was the most manly thing done yet; when will he come into parliament?"

Some ten years afterwards O'Connell sent a message to Disraeli admitting that he had been misinformed and deeply regretting the misunderstanding between them. "I sent him a very courteous reply", noted Disraeli, "but avoided any personal communication. He always made me a very reverential bow afterwards." But by that time Disraeli had learnt how to treat the attacks of his opponents, and was practising what he preached: "Never complain and never explain."

Following the defeat of his fourth attempt to get into parliament, Disraeli went to work with his pen and in December '35 published a "Vindication of the English Constitution", a tract of two hundred pages containing his political creed, written to instruct "this perplexed, ill-informed, jaded, shallow generation", a description that covers every generation since the Flood. It contains an attack on the utilitarians, an argument to prove that the House of Lords was a more representative body than the Commons, a long dissertation on the party system, and a statement of more urgency today than when he made it: "The peers and the Commons of England are the trustees of the nation, not its masters." Early in '36 the 'Runnymede' letters appeared: they trounced such notable whigs as Palmerston, Melbourne and Lord John Russell in terms that moved the editor of *The Times* to tell the writer "You have a most surprising disdain for the law of libel", and eulogised such eminent tories as Peel and Stanley in terms that should have moved the editor of *The Times* to moderate the writer's transports. The result of all this journalistic energy was soon apparent: Disraeli was elected to the Carlton Club; dined on fish with the tory leaders at Greenwich, the only guest who was not a member of parliament; and when he proposed the toast of the House of Lords at a banquet, his was the only speech to be reported verbatim in *The Times*.

But these glories were attended by discomforts. His financial affairs had become more and more complicated, and he was now at the mercy of money-lenders. A legal friend named William Pyne was constantly helping him to raise the interest for his various loans, to settle his "blasted bills", and in other ways to keep the usurers at bay; but the sheriff's officers were constantly hunting him and their presence at High Wycombe made him stay indoors for weeks on end between sunrise and sundown, his freedom during the daylight being practically restricted to Sundays. In the autumn of '36 he commenced another novel, from which he hoped to make three or four thousand pounds; but his creditors were closing in on him, he dared not tell his father how much he owed, and he feared he might be "nabbed" if he went to dinner with Sir Robert Peel or attended a tory banquet. Sometimes he applied to his intimate friends for small loans to pay his necessary expenses, and there is a note from D'Orsay beginning "I swear before God that I have not six-pence at my banker now, having lost the night before last £325", but offering his name as security for a loan. The fact that Disraeli had just become a Justice of the Peace for his county did not minimise the risk of arrest, and he dreaded "a family exposé." In January '37 he stayed with D'Orsay, who lived in "an elegant residence" which adjoined Lady Blessington's "magnificent mansion", Gore House, Kensington, to which she had recently moved. Here he continued to write his novel, had many talks with Lady Blessington, and dined with D'Orsay's friends whenever the Count was not dining out, which happened every other day. In February he returned to Bradenham to help in a bye-election. After canvassing one day, he drove through the night to Aylesbury, where, chatting with friends before the George inn, he fell down in an epileptic fit. He was bled, taken to Bradenham, and partly disclosed his financial position to his father. But he was soon back with D'Orsay, writing hard, and wondering what his father would say if he wholly disclosed his financial position. He did not do so because his momentary distress was alleviated by his kindly parent's assistance.

The novel, written so to speak in the shade of the sponging-house, came out in May '37, under the title of *Venetia*, and was dedicated to Lord Lyndhurst. It is a much toned-down love-story, the author having receded from the frenzies of *Henrietta Temple*, with a heroine as beautiful as ever, though far less emotional, and a less ecstatic hero. It is the only novel Disraeli wrote in which he was not a leading character, the two chief figures being Byron (Cadurcis) and Shelley (Herbert), but as Byron had been his youthful hero there is more than a little of himself in the portrait. The period is the eighteenth century. Byron blazes into fame, is eclipsed, and Macaulay's famous passage on English hypocrisy is quoted in full to account for his sudden disgrace. Shelley appears as the heroine's father and hero; also as a general who fights for America against England in the War of Independence. An atmosphere of revolutionary ardour envelops the book, due perhaps to a reaction against the author's recent affiliation with Toryism; but the longueurs are excessive, the scenic descriptions would have been more appropriate in a guide-book, and the characterisation has less life in it than usual. Byron and Shelley are drowned together in the gulf of Spezzia; the heroine loses lover and father; her mother, an idealised and quite impossible person, loses her husband; and the story ends happily because an unhappy ending would have displeased both public and publisher; though one may say of the average hero in a Disraelian novel that his death would be a happy release for the reader. Naturally a poet has to produce poetry, but when Disraeli writes Shelley's sonnets for him something of Shelley vanishes, and we may search the Golden Treasury in vain for such charmingly innocuous lines as:

> And one soft accent from those gentle lips
> Might all the plaudits of a world eclipse.

Disraeli finally dismisses the real Henrietta from his mind with words that he puts into the mouth of Shelley-Herbert: "The gratification of the senses soon becomes a very small part of that profound and complicated sentiment, which we call love. Love, on the contrary, is an universal thirst for a communion, not merely of the senses, but of our whole nature, intellectual, imaginative, and sensitive. He who finds his antitype, enjoys a love perfect and enduring; time cannot change it, distance cannot remove it; the sympathy is complete." There is also more of Disraeli than of Shelley in the remark: "Some find a home in their country, I find a country in my home." Byron, on the other hand, is accurately portrayed in sentences like: "Men have always been fools and slaves, and fools and slaves they always will be." His illusion that he himself was among the poets prompted Disraeli to say, through Shelley: "Poets are the unacknowledged legislators of the world." But his sense of his own position was expressed in the phrase: "Want of love, or want of money, lies at the bottom of all our griefs." He was right in telling his lawyer-friend Pyne that the book bore marks of his recent anxieties.

"It is a vile trade", he wrote to Lady Blessington in January '37, referring to the business of publishing, "but what is better? Not politics. I look forward to the coming campaign with unmitigated disgust; and should certainly sell out, only one's enemies would say one had failed, to say nothing of one's friends." Pending the resumption of political hostilities, he went to innumerable dinners, entertainments, balls, and what-not, rubbing shoulders with half the peerage but not receiving much satisfaction from the contact: "The more I feel, the more I am convinced that man is not a social animal", he declared. King William IV died in June '37 and Disraeli accompanied Lord Lyndhurst to Kensington Palace, where the young Queen received the homage of her illustrious subjects. Parliament was dissolved, and Disraeli was asked to stand as a candidate for Ashburton, Derby, Chichester, Dartmouth, Marylebone, Taunton and Barnstaple, which shows that he was already a popular figure in the political world. But he chose Maidstone, which had decided to put up two tory candidates, the other being Wyndham Lewis, who had represented the borough in the recent parliament.

Disraeli opened his campaign with a speech attacking the new Poor Law, which had been passed by the whigs, because "it went on the principle that relief to the poor is a *charity*. I maintain that it is a *right*! . . . I consider that this Act has disgraced the country more than any other upon record. Both a moral crime and a political blunder, it announces to the world that in England poverty is a crime." Since he was expecting to be arrested for debt, he was glad to find that the local Sheriff's officer was his staunch supporter. But he was subjected to much whig animosity, and for nearly an hour at one meeting he was interrupted with cries of "Shylock!" and "Old clothes!" from the recently ensuffraged townsmen. This time however he was successful, being elected to parliament at the end of July, and Mrs Wyndham Lewis wrote to her brother "Mark what I say—mark what I prophesy: Mr Disraeli will in a very few years be one of the greatest men of his day." He returned home to find that High Wycombe had celebrated his success the previous day, the church bells ringing, the band parading the streets, the town illuminated. He also found that "it makes a sensible difference in the opinion of one's friends; I can scarcely keep my countenance." For himself, he was a believer in Fate and was not unduly elated: "We are the children of the gods, and are never more the slaves of circumstance than when we deem ourselves their masters. What may next happen in the dazzling farce of life the Fates only know." Wyndham Lewis and his wife went to stay at Bradenham, and Fate had a hand in that too. Mrs Wyndham Lewis was already calling him Dizzy; and as the Houses of Parliament were shortly to follow suit, and the rest of the world were about to do the same, we may take a similar liberty. No other leading politician up to his time had been celebrated throughout the country with a nickname that has persisted, which is a seal of comradeship and a higher distinction than monarchs can bestow. It is inconceivable that Gladstone could ever have been called 'Gladdy' or Pitt 'Billy' or Peel 'Bobby' by his most intimate friends; but Disraeli has been 'Dizzy' to millions he could not know.

Before the opening of parliament he went a round of house-parties, ending up at Woolbeding, near Midhurst, where his hostess was Lady Caroline Maxse and there was a gathering of "shooting dandies", Whyte Melville among them. But pheasant-slaughtering was not for him a pleasant pastime, and he visited Cowdray, Petersfield, and other places in "a region of picturesque and sylvan beauty I have never seen equalled." Back at Bradenham for ten quiet days, he wrote the last passage in his diary just before he left home to take his seat in the House of Commons: "I am now as one leaving a secure haven for an unknown sea. What will the next twelve months produce?"

Queen Victoria's first parliament assembled on November 15th, 1837, and the man who was to become her favourite Prime Minister sat with the Tory Opposition just behind his leader Sir Robert Peel. No one could have guessed that the bejewelled fop would one day drive the great Peel from office, reanimate the whole Tory party, and lead it to victory. There were several future Prime Ministers in the new house. The then whig leader, Melbourne, was in the Lords; but Lord John Russell, whig Home Secretary, Lord Palmerston, whig Foreign Secretary, and W. E. Gladstone, at present a tory, were to fill the chief office under the Crown for one Party, while Peel, Lord Stanley and Disraeli were to fill it for the other. The reading of the Queen's Speech in the Upper House, the debate that followed in the Commons, the division that followed the debate, and all the other exciting events, were described by Disraeli in a long letter to his sister, which concluded with the words: "I dined, or rather supped, at the Carlton with a large party off oysters, Guinness, and broiled bones, and got to bed at half-past twelve o'clock. Thus ended the most remarkable day hitherto of my life."

On December 7th he rose to make his maiden speech, following Daniel O'Connell, whose party gave the whigs their majority. He had decided to impress the House with a well-phrased and well-delivered oration criticising the Government's Irish policy; but the Irish members and some of the radicals had also decided that he should be punished for his attacks on O'Connell, and they were further irritated by his curious appearance and stylish manner. They began by laughing boisterously at his over-elaborated sentences, and he broke off to say that if they did not wish to hear him he would sit down without a murmur. For a short space there was silence, but another well-conned phrase produced an outburst of ironical laughter, accompanied by hoots, cat-calls, and a great variety of farmyard noises. He appealed once more for a hearing, without effect, and the remainder of his speech was punctuated by sounds that might have emanated from a jungle. But he steadily persisted, and even commenced his carefully prepared peroration, which was lost in howls of laughter. Having remained on his feet for the exact period he had intended, the lungs of his opponents began to show signs of fatigue, and his final remarks were partly audible: "I am not at all surprised at the reception I have experienced. I have begun several things many times, and I have often succeeded at the last—though many had predicted that I must fail, as they had done before me." More hubbub. Up to this point he had appeared unruffled and good-humoured. But now, in a voice that could be heard well above the prevailing din, a voice that was described as almost terrific, he shot out the words: "I sit down now, but the time will come when you *will* hear me."

He would not have been human if he had not felt deeply depressed by this humiliating experience; but he was fortified by the advice of Richard Lalor Sheil, O'Connell's right-hand man, who, after annoying a number of radicals by saying "If ever the spirit of oratory was in a man, it is in that man; nothing can prevent him from being one of the first speakers in the House of Commons", met Disraeli at a dinner-party given by Bulwer and assured him that what he thought a failure was really a success. "Now get rid of your genius for a session", said Sheil. "Speak often, for you must not show yourself cowed, but speak shortly. Be very quiet, try to be dull, only argue and reason imperfectly, for if you reason with precision they will think you are trying to be witty. Astonish them by speaking on subjects of detail. Quote figures, dates, calculations. And in a short time the House will sigh for the wit and eloquence which they all know are in you; they will encourage you to pour them forth, and then you will have the ear of the House and be a favourite." Disraeli took this advice, and addressed the House for the second time ten days after his maiden speech; but that the effort called for some nerve may be inferred from a humorous passage in *Coningsby*:

> Music, artillery, the roar of cannon, and the blare of trumpets, may urge a man on to a forlorn hope; ambition, one's constituents, the hell of previous failure, may prevail on us to do a more desperate thing; speak in the House of Commons; but there are some situations in life, such, for instance, as entering the room of a dentist, in which the prostration of the nervous system is absolute.

However his second speech earned him "a general cheer", and he began to think that "Next to undoubted success the best thing is to make a great noise, and the many articles that are daily written to announce my failure only prove that I have not failed." Already he was feeling the temper of the House and criticising the speeches of the other members; and when Sir John Pakington, who sat beside him, made a "confident, fluent and commonplace" maiden speech, Disraeli supported him zealously, while noting that Sir John probably went to bed thinking he was an orator and doubtless wrote to his wife to that effect. After his second speech he prophesied that his third effort would be received with loud cheers, and it was; so much so that he wrote to his sister: "I think I have become very popular in the House; I ascribe it to the smoking-room", where, presumably, his conversational ability quickly made him an acceptable person. Yet he did not really feel comfortable away from Bradenham, and he told Mrs Wyndham Lewis "I never leave home without feeling as I did when I went to school." In April '38 he supported Talfourd's Copyright Bill in the House. In those days an author's property in his work only lasted for 28 years or his own lifetime, whichever was the longer, and Sergeant Talfourd wished to prolong this period for sixty years after the author's decease. Disraeli spoke eloquently for justice to authors, but it was not until 1911 that their families were allowed to profit from their work for fifty years after royalties had ceased to interest them. Disraeli's triumph on this occasion was not witnessed by Wyndham Lewis, his fellow-member for Maidstone, who had died the previous month, leaving his widow grief-stricken but wealthy. "You are too young to feel that life has not yet a fresh spring of felicity in store", wrote Disraeli, to cheer her up. He told her that she must not *indulge* her sorrow and not brood over the past, and that his advice, assistance and society were hers to command, "for, as you well know, I am one of those persons who feel much more deeply than I ever express."

The Coronation of Queen Victoria took place at the end of June, and though Disraeli loved imposing shows he decided not to attend the ceremony in Westminster Abbey because he had not a court dress; so he consoled himself with the reflection that "to get up very early (eight o'clock), to sit dressed like a flunkey in the Abbey for seven or eight hours, and to listen to a sermon by the Bishop of London, can be no great enjoyment." But at the last moment he could not resist the temptation and obtained a dress at 2.30 on the morning of the event. "It turned out that I had a very fine leg, which I never knew before!" He was fascinated by the pageant, though he observed that there was a "want of rehearsal." The gold medal which he received as M.P. on the occasion he presented to Mrs Wyndham Lewis, from whose house opposite Grosvenor Gate in Park Lane he witnessed the review in Hyde Park a fortnight later. Lord and Lady Londonderry received 150 guests at Holdernesse House (now Londonderry House) after the review, and Disraeli, who became a close friend and constant correspondent of Lady Londonderry, was invited. "It was the finest thing of the season . . . the very flower of fashion being assembled." The band of Londonderry's regiment played on the staircase, which was crowded with "the most splendid orange-trees and Cape jessamines"; the jewels of the women and the uniforms of the men made a dazzling scene; and the banquet was "so magnificent that everybody lost their presence of mind."

At the end of July he went down to Maidstone to address several gatherings, stopping at Rochester en route to drink a glass of brandy and water and to scribble a note to Mrs Wyndham Lewis telling her that she had not been absent from his thoughts for a moment throughout the day. Arrived at Maidstone he wrote to her again: "Let me avail myself of this moment, which I seize in a room full of bustle and chatter, to tell you how much I love you." During one of his speeches he "never began a sentence with the slightest idea of its termination; really in a funk, but never made a more successful one." His pluck and perseverance were demonstrated at the close of the parliamentary session, when, as on the occasion of his maiden speech, he followed O'Connell and again attacked the Government's Irish policy; but within eight months his prophecy had been fulfilled: the time had come when they wished to hear him.

Chapter VIII

LOVE AND MONEY

EXCEPT when he is carried away by passion, nothing is more difficult than to disentangle a man's motives in choosing a wife. In the case of Disraeli it is especially difficult because the evidence is as conflicting as the two main strands in his nature: a passion for domesticity and a boundless ambition. In one of his early novels, *Contarini Fleming*, he writes: "Talk of fame and romance, all the glory and adventure of the world are not worth one single hour of domestic bliss", which quite truthfully expresses what he felt. But in his last novel, *Endymion*, we read this: "Partly from my temperament, still more perhaps from the vicissitudes of my life, I have considerable waiting powers. I think if one is patient and watches, all will come of which one is capable; but no one can be patient who is not independent. My wants are moderate, but their fulfilment must be certain . . . I am sometimes conceited enough to believe that I shall succeed, and to back myself against the field." When that passage was written, he had achieved his ambition, Endymion being himself in retrospect; and it shows that his main concern in early life was to be free of financial embarrassment in order to pursue his way in politics. From a letter quoted in a previous chapter it is clear, too, that he had no intention of marrying for love; and he was certainly not thinking solely of a certain nobleman in *Tancred* when making the comment: "I suppose he intends to marry for love, as he is always in that way; but the heiresses never leave him alone, and in the long run you cannot withstand it; it is like a bribe; a man is indignant at the bare thought, refuses the first offer, and pockets the second." Finally we have his personal confession in a letter to his future wife: "When I first made my advances to you, I was influenced by no romantic feelings"; and also his wife's evidence many years after their marriage: "Dizzy married me for my money, but if he had the chance again he would marry me for love." That seems conclusive; but in the strange see-saw and complexity of human motives and emotions, nothing is conclusive.

After the death of Wyndham Lewis, the relations between his widow and Disraeli quickly became more than cordial, and he was writing to her that the company of other people was insipid to him, that he was apathetic in her absence, and that there was "no hell on earth like separated love." He began to compose a poetic drama, into which he poured his feelings of love, doubt and misery. He had heard the painful story of Count Alarcos while in Spain and had planned his drama then; but now he set to work on it in the belief that he could be the Shakespeare of his age as he had previously tried to be its Milton. The play, which is packed with Websterian horrors, was absurdly over-praised by his friends; but he was one of those who could not bear to be an "also ran", declaring in a short story called *Walstein* that "Mediocrity disgusts me. In literature a second-rate reputation is no recompense for the evils that authors are heir to"; and again in *Coningsby* that he was not content to excel in his own circle if he thought there was one superior to it, absolute not relative distinction being his aim. "I see no use in writing tragedies unless they be as fine as Shakespeare's", he said. Feeling like that, and perceiving that *Alarcos* fell short of *Othello* and *King Lear*, he abandoned blank verse. But the occupation of writing it had helped him over several weeks of despair, due to his belief that Mrs Wyndham Lewis did not reciprocate his feelings. And in this he was right. To begin with, she was forty-five years old, while he was thirty-three, and at her age "the hey-day in the blood is tame . . . and waits upon the judgment." Then she owned a fine house in Park Lane, with an income of about £4000 a year, while he was heavily in debt. Also she would not consider marriage until a year had passed since the death of her husband. Further she was by nature a flirt, a chatterbox, "cold in love" she called herself, superficial, vain, undependable, socially silly, and bored by politics.

Although, as we have seen, Disraeli was at first attracted by her money, he realised at a later date that she was not so rich as he had supposed, and we need not doubt his word that, from a worldly point of view, he could have made a far more advantageous match; but by that time he had become deeply attached to her, had discovered that she fulfilled a permanent need of his nature, and that separation from her was painful: "I wish to be with you, to live with you, never to be away from you—I care not where, in heaven or on earth, or in the waters under the earth." That is the language of love, if not of passion, for it expresses the one and all-sufficient desire of the human being who can forget himself in the existence of another. He told her that he did not care for politics as much as usual because love swallowed up everything else: "In Fame as well as Love my motto is 'All or Nothing', because I prefer happy obscurity to mediocre reputation." In December '38 he was distraught because she had not written to him, and he declared that his health had been affected by the agitation and excitement of the previous months, that all the goodness and kindness of friends meant nothing when there was a cloud between lovers; and the relief he felt when she wrote again to say she would see him was certainly heartfelt: "I am mad with love. My passion is frenzy. The prospect of our immediate meeting overwhelms and entrances me. I pass my nights and days in scenes of strange and fascinating rapture . . ."

In life as in letters his feelings, when touched, were too lavishly expressed; and though he could have said with Macbeth

> The expedition of my violent love
> Outran the pauser reason,

his effusive prose does not help us to forget the "pauser reason". Nor, apparently, did his outpourings entirely convince Mrs Wyndham Lewis, though she may have been playing with his affection when, one day early in February '39, she more than hinted that her money was the real bait. It seems that this provoked a violent rebuttal on his part, and he was asked to leave her house. He went away and wrote her a long letter, honestly stating that her fortune had been the first incentive, but that from the moment he had declared his love he had devoted to her all the passion of his being. "My nature demands that my life should be perpetual love", he said. Having assured her, in the usual manner on such occasions, that he would not upbraid her, he went on to say that she had broken his spirit and poisoned his life, outraged his heart, wounded his pride and tainted his honour. In conclusion he could not affect to wish her happiness, as it was beyond her capacity to obtain it; she would frivol away her life until the moment when she would "sigh for any heart that could be fond . . . Then will be the penal hour of retribution: then you will think of me with remorse, admiration and despair; then you will recall to your memory the passionate heart that you have forfeited, and the genius you have betrayed." Whether she had been trifling with him or serious, this letter made her realise that he was in deadly earnest, and she sent a distracted note, begging him to come to her, telling him that he had misunderstood her, and assuring him of her devotion.

When, in later life, she used to say that he had married her for her money, she was probably thinking of the one passage in his letter that would have remained in her memory: that he had no romantic feelings for her at first. But she confided to an intimate friend, Mrs Duncan Stewart, that she was aware of his affection long before their marriage. "After the death of my first husband I was still a good-looking woman and had a good fortune", she said. "I had many admirers who wanted to marry me, but I knew they were all thinking of my money and not of myself. There was one exception to this, namely Dizzy. I knew that he was in love with me and not with my money because he showed his affection and love to me while my first husband was alive." Speaking of their engagement, before the misunderstanding to which allusion has been made, she continued: "He used to come to my house nearly every day and spend some time in talking to me. He was evidently attached to me, and wished to propose, but was embarrassed by the difference in our fortunes. One day he spent some time with me but did not come to the point. I brought the matter to a head by laying my hand on his and saying 'Why should not we two put our two fortunes together?', and thus it came about that we were engaged."[1]

Following the misunderstanding and reconciliation already noted, Disraeli's interest in politics was renewed, and he was in excellent form for the rest of the parliamentary session. One evening he dined with Sir Robert Peel, arrived late and "found some 25 gentlemen grubbing in solemn silence. I threw a shot over the table and set them going, and in time they became even noisy. Peel, I think, was quite pleased that I broke the awful stillness . . ." People in those days fed on a generous scale, which may have accounted for the long pauses in the conversation, and

[1] Ref. *T.P.'s Weekly*, Dec. 13, 1912.

when we learn that the second course that evening consisted of "dried salmon, olives, caviare, woodcock pie, foie gras, and every combination of cured herring, etc", we are inclined to wonder what the diners were expected to face when the remaining courses were laid before them. Disraeli was fond of his food and occasionally drank "a great deal too much wine", but speechless guzzling did not appeal to him and many people besides Peel must have found him an invaluable guest. Dining with his leader did not however make him vote for his leader, and he was often with the radicals against the tories, still hoping for a fusion between the two. The various political crises fascinated him. "One cannot walk down Parliament Street under such circumstances without some degree of exultation", he wrote to his sister just before the Bedchamber crisis, when Peel refused to take office unless the Queen changed her female personnel, substituting the wives and sisters of incoming tories for those of outgoing whigs. The Queen was adamant, and the whigs owed their continuance in office to a point of etiquette.

Disraeli was already a popular speaker in the House of Commons: "I rose with several men at the same time; but the House called for me, and I spoke with great effect, amid loud cheering and laughter." A little later he made "by universal consent the best speech on our side on the most important party question." The subject was national education, which he favoured, but he did not like the idea of state education, foreseeing its inevitable result: "It had been discovered that the best way to ensure implicit obedience was to commence tyranny in the nursery . . . It was always the state, and never society—it was always machinery, never sympathy. By their system of state education all would be thrown into the same mint, and all would come out with the same impress and superscription . . . The time would come, if they persisted in their present course, when they would find that they had revolutionised the English character; and when that was effected, then they could no longer expect English achievements." At the end of the session he was able to report that "The complete command of the House I now have is remarkable, and nothing can describe to you the mute silence which immediately ensued as I rose, broken only by members hurrying to their places to listen."

The day after the rising of parliament, on August 28, 1839, his marriage with Mrs Wyndham Lewis took place at St George's, Hanover Square, and henceforth she must be known to us, as she was to her husband and their friends, as Mary Anne. They went at once to the Kentish Hotel, Tunbridge Wells. It rained throughout their stay and they scarcely left their rooms, except to drive through squalls to see Lord Camden at Bayham, through showers to see the Sidneys at Penshurst, and, during a transient lull, to walk one day on the Pantiles. The moment the weather cleared up they drove to Dover and left for the Continent: "A rough but very rapid passage carried us to Calais, only two hours and twenty minutes, but Mary Anne suffered dreadfully, as indeed all the passengers except myself." They made for Baden-Baden, which Mary Anne thought little better than Cheltenham, and after a week there drove through the Black Forest to Stuttgart, thence to Munich, where they stayed several weeks, seeing everything and deciding that "Since Pericles no one has done so much for the arts as the King of Bavaria." Ratisbon, Nuremberg and Frankfort were visited, and their holiday ended in Paris, where they stayed at the Hôtel de l'Europe in the Rue de Rivoli and had a very gay time: "Mary Anne is particularly well, and in her new costumes looks like Madame de Pompadour." At the end of November they arrived at his wife's house in Park Lane, which was to be his London home for over thirty years, and a fortnight later they dined *en famille* with a party of Rothschilds, Montefiores, Alberts and Disraelis—"not a Christian name", said Dizzy, "but Mary Anne bears it like a philosopher."

She was to bear everything like a philosopher; for though the more obvious features of her character were those of a feather-headed and irresponsible gadabout, her marriage to Disraeli brought out her sterling qualities: a sound judgment in worldly matters, founded on swift intuitions and practical ability; steadfastness of purpose, fortitude, good humour, honesty; and a belief in her husband's greatness that was only equalled by a devotion to his interests; the compulsion of these qualities arising out of her love for him. "There was no care which she could not mitigate, and no difficulty which she could not face. She was the most cheerful and the most courageous woman I ever knew", said Disraeli after her death. Their life together was serenely happy, wholly unmarred by the egotistical quarrels of most married people, his unvarying affection, patience and gentleness, her high spirits, shrewdness and impulsiveness, contributing to a harmony as rare as their natures were remarkable.

His nature indeed was unique, its curious composition being due to an acute intelligence disjoined from an exotic temperament, which resulted from the division and juxtaposition of his race and nation. For various historical and ethnological reasons, the Jews who have not intermarried with gentiles have never become assimilated with the nations of their adoption; they have remained foreign in outlook and oriental in spirit, a condition that has sometimes produced men whose intelligences are supernational and whose emotions are intensely racial, largely because they are outside the culture of the countries to which they belong. This accounts for Disraeli's oriental imagination and satirical intellect. He saw and felt things differently from the average Englishman; wrote in a style which, though spawned by the Romantic Movement, had a voluptuous and more profusely rhetorical quality than the outpourings of purely occidental romantics; yet, when his mind was solely engaged, produced apothegms that revealed a cynically realistic view of life. But his isolation engendered another element in his nature. It has often been observed that alien minorities tend to admire the traditions and structure of the society in which they live but of which they are not a part. With the Jews this is especially so; and along with his sceptical outlook and exotic constitution, Disraeli had a profound respect for English custom and an exaggerated veneration for English caste. With him this did not degenerate into mere snobbery, for he had no illusions about individuals and did not confuse the peer with the peerage. It was simply his romantic idealisation of something from which he felt himself cut off. Thus in politics he was an intellectual radical, an emotional tory, and what has just been said will explain what is to come.

Ambition was the child of his imagination. Most human beings have a mysterious urge to excel in something, but Disraeli wished to excel both as a man of action and as an artist, and even tried to convince himself that the two spheres were alike. "Action is the exercise of our faculties", he wrote. "Do not mistake restlessness for action . . . A great student is a great actor, and as great as a marshal or a statesman." But therein he deceived himself. When a born man of action takes to letters, his main concern is propaganda, his chief object to impress his personality upon the world. For that reason no man of action can be a great writer, the temperament which produces great literature being opposed to the temperament which produces practical results, the first being reflective and objective, the second active and subjective. Disraeli's novels are solely interesting as revelations of his personality and as political documents, his desire to excel as a writer of fiction being due to an ambition which was stronger in him than in other men because of his racial isolation, a wish to astonish and beat the gentiles in artistry as well as statecraft. "The moment that I mingled again with men, I wished to influence them", says Contarini Fleming, and this longing to make himself felt in a hostile world was Disraeli's. Yet his intelligence told him that ambition was a demon: "When all is gained, how little then is won! And yet to gain that little, how much is lost!" he wrote as a young man; and in middle-age, though he had achieved notoriety, he had not changed his mind: "Fame and power are the objects of all men. Even their partial fruition is gained by very few; and that too at the expense of social pleasure, health, conscience, life."

The only alternative to fame was an obscure but happy domestic life; and his nature was strongly inclined to this because, as a Jew, his real country was his home. Like others of his race, he had a far keener susceptibility to family life than the average Englishman, whose home is his country. Because of his ever-present sense of being an exile, a stranger, Disraeli became self-dependent at a very early age, detaching his mind from the prejudices and opinions of the outside world. "The breath of man has never influenced me much", says Contarini, "for I depend more upon myself than upon others. I want no false fame. It would be no delight to me to be considered a prophet, were I conscious of being an impostor." But he was determined to succeed in society, a necessary step to success in politics, and for this purpose he built up an enigmatic personality, of whom the only thing that could be predicted was the unpredictable. Like most of his fictional heroes, he was gifted with a rich melodious voice, the effect of which was much enhanced by careful modulation and a sphinx-like immobility of countenance. Quite early in life he observed: "No error so common or so grievous as to suppose that a smile is a necessary ingredient of the pleasing. There are few faces that can afford to smile. A smile is sometimes bewitching, in general vapid, often a contortion." Therefore he seldom smiled, and always looked inscrutable. This studied personality was also a form of self-defence; it helped him to bear, and even to exploit, his origin; and since his nature demanded that his relationship with people should be either intimate or distant, the mask he wore suited his peculiar organisation, for he could take it off in private and put it on in public. Had he really disliked society, he could not have borne, even for the sake of political success, the endless performance of himself in the part of Disraeli; but he had an oriental love of glitter, colour and rank, and he found people entertaining in small doses: "Anybody amuses me for once. A new acquaintance is like a new book. I prefer it, even if bad, to a classic."

Chapter IX

REBELLION AND BREAD

THE Kingdom of Heaven had not come on earth, though confidently expected, with the passing of the Reform Bill. All that had actually happened was the substitution of the middle-classes for the aristocracy as rulers of the realm; and the great body of toilers, still unenfranchised, began to suspect that their condition was not likely to improve. Disraeli believed that the whigs, who had forced the measure through parliament by working on the passions of the labouring class, by incitements to revolution, and by threatening to turn the House of Lords into a puppet-assembly, were themselves the cause of all the trouble. Having placed William III on the throne of England, they had transferred power from the crown to a parliament "the members of which were appointed by a limited and exclusive class, who owned no responsibility to the country, who debated and voted in secret, and who were regularly paid by a small knot of great families that by this machinery had secured the permanent possession of the king's treasury." For more than a century, Disraeli asserted, "a people without power or education had been induced to believe themselves the freest and most enlightened nation in the world, and had submitted to lavish their blood and treasure, to see their industry crippled and their labour mortgaged, in order to maintain an oligarchy, that had neither ancient memories to soften nor present services to justify their unprecedented usurpation." All of which had been accomplished by the artful orators and toilsome patricians among the whigs, who "had convinced their unprivileged fellow-subjects that government was a science, and administration an art, which demanded the devotion of a peculiar class in the state for their fulfilment and pursuit." Disraeli therefore made it his business, whenever addressing parliament or his constituents, to trace effects back to their causes, to teach them the history they had forgotten or never learnt or wrongly learnt, for of written history he said that "Generally speaking, all the great events have been distorted, most of the important causes concealed, some of the principal characters never appear, and all who figure are so misunderstood and misrepresented, that the result is a complete mystification." These historical lessons did not make him popular even with his own colleagues, the tories having supported many whiggish measures and lapsed into laissez-faire; and though Sir Robert Peel appeared to value his services, the party as a whole felt rather nervous when he was entertaining the House.

With the advent of the chartists in 1839 his attitude became less tolerable than ever. Chartism sprang up as a result of working-class discontent over the failure of the Reform Bill to improve their lot. The Factory Act of '33 and the Poor Law of '34 had done little to appease the workers, who had been antagonised by the reluctant concessions of the first and the harsh administration of the second. The wealthy manufacturers of the north were the mainstay of the whigs; and as their sole object was to make money, their main concern was to get labour cheap and keep it cheap. In short the factory conditions amounted to serfdom, the workers in the big manufacturing towns were ill-treated, half-starved, scandalously housed and utterly miserable, while the bad harvests which commenced in 1837 made the plight of the agricultural labourers equally deplorable. Disraeli, as we have seen, attacked the new Poor Law during the Maidstone election, and when he was returned to Parliament it was gently hinted to him that for the sake of his political future he had better keep his mouth shut on the subject. He promptly reacted to this hint by voting for a repeal of the Act, finding himself in a minority of thirteen against the combined whig and tory powers. Having thus imperilled his political future, he then proceeded to undermine it.

The leaders among the chartists consisted of those who favoured violence and those who favoured amelioration by petition. They drew up 'The People's Charter', their hope that the world could be a better place being founded on annual parliaments, universal male suffrage, vote by ballot, abolition of the property qualification for a seat in the Commons, and payment of members. First of all they tried peaceful methods, and a petition signed by a million and a half people, so formidable that a special machine had to be constructed for its transport, was taken to Westminster in June '39, trundled into the Commons, and left on the floor of the House until the close of the debate which took place a month after its arrival. Disraeli was under no illusion that the granting of political rights would ensure social felicity, and would have agreed with Dr Johnson:

> How small, of all that human hearts endure,
> That part which laws or kings can cause or cure.

But in his speech he said that, while rejecting the remedy proposed by the chartists, parliament should try to cure the disease. This he attributed to the Reform Act, which had given the new ruling class power without responsibility, for they had eagerly transferred to a centralised government the social duties they should have accepted along with their new political privileges. He regretted that his own party had supported the new Poor Law, which was a prime example of making government responsible for what ought to be the obligation of the rich, and he told the tories that they had acted contrary to what should be their principle: of opposing everything like centralised government and favouring the distribution of power. He accused the Home Secretary, Lord John Russell, of treating the Charter with derision because it was incompatible with the retention of political power by the class which he had helped to create. In conclusion, Disraeli regretted the fact that the whole subject was distasteful to both parties in the House, but affirmed that, however much he disapproved of the proposed remedies of the chartists, he fully sympathised with them, for their grievances were great, and it would be a serious error if the House treated the movement as a temporary ebullition instead of a social insurrection.

The House committed the error and rejected the petition without going further into the matter. But the direct-action chartists, tired of waiting for the debate, engineered a riot in Birmingham; and Lord John Russell asked the House to authorise an advance to the Birmingham Corporation for the establishment of a police force. Disraeli voted against it in a minority of three, and accused Russell of levying five thousand troops against his former allies, the very people who had shouted loudest for the Reform Bill. The Chancellor of the Exchequer, Spring Rice, sharply reproved Disraeli for this tactless remark, and an Under-Secretary described him as "an advocate of riot and confusion." Disraeli replied: "How he became Chancellor of the Exchequer and how the Government to which he belongs became a Government, it would be difficult to tell. Like flies in amber 'One wonders how the devil they got there'." Russell asserted that the outbreak was due to a well-known tory chartist. Disraeli rejoined that he could trace the pedigree of sedition to a higher source; to the whig leaders themselves, who had threatened parliament with the arrival of two hundred thousand men from Birmingham to frighten the House of Lords into passing the Reform Bill. Having made their arrangements for the maintenance of law and order, the House rose; and while M.P.s were resting from their labours, the country was agitated by riots, rick-burnings, machine-smashings, and other signs of political disapproval. In fact England remained in a state of social insurrection for some years, until good harvests and increasing trade did what the Reform Bill had failed to do; and throughout that period Disraeli sympathised with the chartists, writing a novel (*Sybil*) to show that their grievances were justified, voting always in a small minority against the severity of the punishments inflicted on their leaders, asking in the House how it was that "the same thing obtained impunity in Ireland under the name of agitation, which in England was punished under the name of sedition", and stating his opinion "that in a country so aristocratic as England even treason, to be successful, must be patrician . . . Where Wat Tyler failed, Henry Bolingbroke changed a dynasty, and although Jack Straw was hanged, a Lord John Straw (Russell) may become a Secretary of State."

He was clearly becoming as hazardous an ally as he was a dangerous adversary; and when Peel called together a conference of sixteen leading tories in 1840, Disraeli was the only one present who had not held office. To prove that such attempts to make him a dependable party man were useless, he voted against his leader in the House on the same day that he was invited to attend the conference. Meanwhile he and his wife were giving large dinner-parties to radicals and tories, and being entertained at all sorts of literary, social and political gatherings. Once they went to a breakfast-party at Bulwer's place on the Thames, and Prince Louis Napoleon rowed them out in a boat, getting stuck on a mudbank in mid-stream. Disraeli was much amused by his wife, who rated the future Emperor for his handling of the oars: "You should not undertake things which you cannot accomplish. You are always too adventurous, sir", and so on. The Prince took it in good humour, and eventually they were retrieved by a boatman. "I could not have borne the scolding better myself", related Dizzy, who was reminded of the episode a year later when the Prince had a more serious aquatic adventure at Boulogne in an attempt to seize power in France, which resulted in his imprisonment.

On the whole Disraeli was liked in society, but certain people were prejudiced against him, partly because of his notoriety, partly on account of his manner and appearance. The poet-banker, Samuel Rogers, was one of these. As far back as 1834 Disraeli noted "Rogers hates me. I can hardly believe, as he gives out, that *Vivian Grey* is the cause. Considering his age I endeavoured to conciliate him, but it is impossible. I think I will give him cause to hate me." Six years went by and Disraeli found himself next to Rogers at dinner: "He made one or two efforts at conversation which I did not encourage; but after the second course (Rogers having eaten an immense dinner), both of us in despair of our neighbours, we could no longer refrain from falling into talk, and it ended by a close alliance . . ." Sometimes he and Mary Anne went away for a quiet holiday. "We have found this place pleasant enough, the weather being very fine", he wrote from the York Hotel, Brighton, in April '40. "I have eaten a great many shrimps, which are the only things that have reminded me I am on the margin of the ocean; for it has been a dead calm the whole week, and I have not seen a wave or heard the break of the tide."

But the dead calm did not extend to the political world, which was in the early stages of the commotion for the repeal of the Corn Laws. During four successive years the harvests had failed; trade was bad; wages were dropping; food prices were rising; and the state of the poor was insufferable. For some two centuries England had managed to feed herself and to export corn, but by the period of the French Revolution the home supply had dwindled, and in 1791, to encourage the English farmer, a duty was placed on foreign corn when the home price was beneath a certain figure. In the stress of the Napoleonic wars the home price soon surpassed that figure; but by that time there were no foreign supplies, and in 1812 the price of corn had doubled. For the poorer classes there were several years of famine, and they attributed to the Corn Laws what was largely due to depreciated currency. To increase home production new taxes were levied on foreign imports in 1815; but the distress in the agricultural community was not relieved, and in 1828 a sliding scale of duties was imposed, which in effect benefited everyone except the consumer. In the early eighteen-thirties the situation was saved by good harvests, but when the bad harvests commenced in '37 the position again became acute, and the following year an Anti-Corn-Law Association was founded in Manchester, three of its leading members being Charles Villiers, John Bright and Richard Cobden. Out of this Association grew the Anti-Corn-Law League, of which Cobden, a successful calico merchant, became the mouthpiece and prophet, or, as Carlyle called him, the "inspired bagman with his calico millennium."

The middle-classes responded enthusiastically to the annunciation of the new faith, because they were vaguely conscious that it would mean the end of the old landowning aristocracy which benefited by the Corn Laws, as indeed it did; while the labouring classes, rendered frantic by the indescribable filth of their slums and hovels and the appalling mortality of their children from starvation, would have swallowed any theory that seemed to promise more and cheaper bread. Even the chartists, who opposed the plan on the ground that it would favour the middle-classes by reducing the wages of the workers, were forgotten in the excitement aroused by something that promised money to the industrialists and food to the industrious. Nothing could have halted the movement of which Disraeli makes Lord Roehampton (really Palmerston) say in *Endymion*: "What cry can be better than that of 'Cheap bread'? It gives one an appetite at once." And no one in parliament except Disraeli could foresee its result: the rise to political power of the middle-classes, the industrialisation of the country at the expense of its agriculture, the denationalising of England by Liberalism, and the ultimate decline of the British Empire along with the specifically British character. Cobden devoted his life to his creed, becoming known as "the saviour of the poor"; and when his work for the cause had led to the failure of his own business, a grateful nation presented him with £120,000 for services rendered. But all that was in the future. At the period we have now reached, 1840, he was stumping the country and proclaiming his gospel, while Disraeli was telling the House of Commons that the repeal of the Corn Laws would merely benefit the manufacturing capitalist. Eight years before he had said: "Reduce the burdens that so heavily press upon the farmer, and then reduce his protection in the same ratio. That is the way to have cheap bread."

The Whig Government was defeated early in '41, and Disraeli, who had been having trouble with his supporters at Maidstone, decided to stand for Shrewsbury at the General Election, making it clear in his speeches that he would resist the sacrifice of any class in the community to the fancied advantage of the others. "We had a sharp contest, but never for a moment doubtful", he told his sister. "They did against me, and said against me, and wrote against me all they could find or invent; but I licked them." The crest he had adopted, the Castle of Castile, appeared on a tory banner, with his motto *Forti nihil difficile* (Nothing is difficult to the brave), which was translated by a whig newspaper "The impudence of some men sticks at nothing." His opponents certainly stuck at nothing, accusing him of trying to get into parliament in order to keep out of prison and publishing a list of his unpaid debts. Although he asserted that these particular debts had all been settled, he was still in financial straits and apparently had not confessed his real position to his wife, because he wrote to his solicitor: "A writ delivered in my absence to my lady and other circumstances have produced a terrible domestic crisis." He was again attending to his own affairs, with disastrous consequences, because his only method of paying what he owed was to borrow more money from the usurers at phenomenal rates of interest, and then, when that had to be repaid, to borrow more. He certainly owed more than £20,000 at this date, and the ramifications of his affairs were so complicated that his explanations to his wife baffled her as much as they confused himself.

However, his financial position did not worry the electors of Shrewsbury and they returned him to parliament, though it had been an unpleasant experience, and Disraeli was probably thinking of it when, many years afterwards, he wrote: "Lothair felt nervous; an indefinable depression came over him, as on the morning of a contest when a candidate enters his crowded committee-room." There was a tory majority in the new House, and Peel became Prime Minister. Disraeli felt that his services to the party called for some recognition in the shape of an office however subordinate, and when Peel offered him nothing he wrote to his leader saying that he had struggled against "a storm of political hate and malice which few men ever experienced", that he had only been "sustained under these trials by the conviction that the day would come when the foremost man of this country would publicly testify that he had some respect for my ability and my character", and that he was overwhelmed by this lack of acknowledgment. He concluded by appealing to Peel's justice and magnanimity to save him from "an intolerable humiliation." His chagrin was so extreme that, unknown to him, his wife also wrote to the Prime Minister, enumerating Disraeli's services to the party as well as her own. "Do not destroy all his hopes", she begged, "and make him feel his life has been a mistake." Sir Robert's reply to Disraeli was typically self-righteous: "Your letter is one of many I receive which too forcibly impress upon me how painful and invidious is the duty which I have been compelled to undertake. I am only supported in it by the consciousness that my desire has been to do justice . . ." and so on in the usual parliamentary style.

It is possible that Peel would have done something for Disraeli, but he was doubtless relieved when his Colonial Secretary, Lord Stanley, declared that "if that scoundrel were taken in he would not remain himself." Stanley, who later became the fourteenth Earl of Derby, was to hold the office of Prime Minister three times in the years ahead, with Disraeli as his Chancellor of the Exchequer; and his early prejudice against his future colleague appears to have been purely personal. Disraeli's pique over his leader's failure to acknowledge his services was often cited to explain his later attacks on Peel. But though it may have added gall to those attacks, it was not the cause, as we shall learn. For the time being he went off with his wife to Caen, where his wounds were nursed before, with a fine impartiality, he inflicted more fatal injuries on whigs and tories alike.

Chapter X

THE TRUSTEES OF POSTERITY

IT is important to remember that Peel and his followers were committed to the principle of protecting the country's agriculture, that they were returned to parliament in 1841 as men who could be relied upon to save the British farmer from the possible consequences of Cobden's crusade, Peel, Gladstone and the other tory ministers having given assurances to that effect during the election. At the beginning of his administration Peel reduced the rates of duty on foreign corn but maintained the sliding scale, his policy appealing as little to the farmers as to the Cobdenites, and Disraeli, though he supported the Government, must have echoed the saying "I don't know what effect these men will have on the enemy, but by God! they frighten me." Several M.P.s wanted him to adopt a definite line against the new measures, and the wife of a member tried to draw him. "She was most friendly and particularly disagreeable", he reported. But he would not be drawn, and continued to support Peel for two sessions. On the other hand he wished to make his presence felt in the House, and pitched on a subject that enabled him to attack Palmerston's rule at the Foreign Office while the whigs were in power: the inefficiency of the consular body, which, he said, should be a part of the diplomatic service. He spoke for over two hours and was even congratulated by Cobden. Of course Palmerston was annoyed and insinuated that Dizzy had been disappointed at not receiving a place in the Government, sarcastically hoping that he would obtain one. Disraeli thanked him for his kind wishes, adding that "if to assist my advancement he will only impart to me the secret of his own unprecedented rise, and by what means he has contrived to enjoy power under seven successive administrations, I shall at least have gained a valuable result by this discussion." Much laughter greeted the sally, as it was not easy to score off Palmerston, and

Disraeli sent a full report to his wife at Bradenham, telling her that "the more we are separated the more I cling to you . . . 'Tis your approbation and delight for which I am labouring, and unless I had that stimulus I don't think I could go on."

They spent the winter of 1842–3 together at Paris, again at the Hôtel de l'Europe, and met everyone of note, politicians, ambassadors, peers, financiers, princes and poets. Disraeli himself had many informal talks on politics with King Louis Philippe, who showed him over the Tuileries in company with a few others. "It is rare to make the tour of a palace with a King for the cicerone", he remarked. However stately the dinners at the Tuileries, a huge smoking ham was placed at a certain time before the King, who operated upon it like a conjurer. "The rapidity and precision with which he carved it was a marvellous feat: the slices were vast, but wafer-thin . . . He told me one day that he had learnt the trick from a waiter at Bucklersbury, where he used to dine once at an eating-house for ninepence per head." The Court was in mourning for the King's eldest son, the Duke of Orleans, who had been killed in a carriage accident, and Disraeli was the only stranger to be received, which "causes a great sensation here" he announced with some pride. Mary Anne studied the fashions closely, and "begs you not to have any stays made till she comes home", Dizzy wrote to his sister, "as she can give you valuable information thereon." Their visit closed with a ball at the British Embassy—"a thousand folks and orange-trees springing from the supper-table"—and another at Baron Solomon de Rothschild's, "an hotel in decoration surpassing all the palaces of Munich; a greater retinue of servants and liveries more gorgeous than the Tuileries, and pineapples as plentiful as blackberries . . . The company all the *élite* of Paris."

From these scenes of plenty and splendour he returned to London for the parliamentary session of 1843, and wrestled with the problems of poverty and bread. He was too busy that spring to dine out. "I receive invitations every day, three for tomorrow, but hope to escape them all", he told his sister. "I dine at the House of Commons, over a couple of mutton chops and cayenne pepper." The Cobden creed was gaining new believers with alarming rapidity, and Disraeli made it clear that the preponderance of the landed interest was essential to the country's welfare, and that he could only support Free Trade if it were really free. But the other European states refused to reciprocate, and he proclaimed: "If I saw a prize-fighter encountering a galley-slave in irons, I should consider the combat equally as fair as to make England fight hostile tariffs with free imports." His agricultural constituents at Shrewsbury were getting nervous over Peel's policy, so he went down to steady them, saying that if the Government went back on their pledges and abandoned the landed interest which had put them into power he would vote against them: "I have said this at Westminster, sitting at the back of Sir Robert Peel, alone, and without flinching, and I say it again here." In speaking of the landed interest he was not thinking merely of the squirearchy, but of everything that had been built up on the system: the church, the law, the crown, the estate of the poor in town and country, "the ancient polity of the realm", the alternative to which was "to be turned into a sort of spinning-jenny, machine kind of nation." The Corn Laws, he said, were "the outwork of a great system fixed and established upon your territorial property, and the only object the Leaguers have in making themselves masters of the outwork is that they may easily overcome the citadel." He little realised when he addressed his constituents that he would fulfil his pledge to them within a month. The Government wished to reduce the duty on corn from Canada to a nominal figure, and introduced a Bill to that effect; but it instantly became apparent that, indirectly, corn from the United States could be imported at this preferential rate. Disraeli opposed the Bill, and informed his supporters at Shrewsbury: "I had not the moral courage nor the immoral audacity to say one thing to my constituents, and within twenty-four hours vote diametrically opposite." The twenty-four hours was a piece of Disraelian fantasy, but the vote was factual, and the tory ministers were highly displeased.

Besides, they had other grounds for resentment, for he had become the leader of a small but very vocal group of young men who had been returned to parliament at the recent election in the tory interest, and who seemed to hold strange views on English history. "I already find myself without effort the leader of a party, chiefly of the youth and new members", he told his wife in 1842. The group consisted of George Smythe, Lord John Manners and Alexander Baillie Cochrane, all of whom had been at Eton and Cambridge together and in the interchange of ideas had developed a common viewpoint. They were romantic in spirit and opposed to the utilitarianism of the time with its worship of wealth, its imagination stultified by a love of machines. They believed in monarchy as a principle, not a mere instrument, and wished to restore the throne to its ancient authority. They considered that the church should be independent of state control. They were dissatisfied with the toryism of prerogative and inaction, regarding Pitt and Canning as their party models. They disliked the middle-class; had great sympathy with the labourers, whose natural leaders and protectors they declared the tories to be; and saw no reason why Merry England should not be revived by a harmonious relationship between peers and people.

Disraeli found himself very much in agreement with this group, but watched them with detachment at first. "George Smythe made a most elaborate speech", he noted during the debate on the Corn Laws in '42; "very radical indeed, and unprincipled as his little agreeable self, but too elaborate—his manner affected and his tone artificial, and pronunciation too; but still ability though puerile." A year later the group had won recognition in the House and were called 'Young England'. Disraeli by then was generally accepted as their chief, and Smythe said that they ought to be known as the "Diz-Union'. They attacked Peel's Irish policy and asked a number of pertinent but irritating questions about his foreign policy, the Prime Minister's replies showing that they were getting on his nerves. Sir James Graham, the Home Secretary, believed that if pressure were exerted 'Young England' would treat the Government with more respect; but he did not think anything could be done with Disraeli, whom he described as the ablest man among them, the puppet-master, unprincipled, disappointed, and the only one who was really mischievous: "With him I have no desire to keep terms. It would be better for the party if he were driven into the ranks of our open enemies."

Being no fool, Disraeli must have known of the hostility he had aroused; and when he asked Graham to give an office to one of his brothers, he was probably courting a rebuff. Anyhow he got it, and Graham reported the "impudent" request to Peel, who replied that he was glad it had happened as "It is a good thing when such a man puts his shabbiness on record . . . to ask favours after his conduct last session is too bad. However, it is a bridle in his mouth." Front Bench antagonism went further; and when Disraeli did not receive the usual circular to attend parliament early in '44 he wrote to ask Peel why he had been so treated, at the same time recording his services to the party and complaining of "the want of courtesy in debate which I have had the frequent mortification of experiencing from you since your accession to power." Peel replied that Disraeli's attitude to the Government's policy in the previous session had precluded him "from proffering personally an earnest request for your attendance . . . It gives me, however, great satisfaction to infer from your letter . . . that my impressions were mistaken and my scruples unnecessary." A period of relative calm followed these expressions of enmity veiled in amity. But Disraeli's speeches were making 'Young England' too prominent for the comfort of the Government, and his presence at big social functions was more urgently solicited than that of the tory ministers. We find him at an assembly held by the Duchess of Buckingham, in the company of half a dozen dukes; he was asked by Lady Lyndhurst to meet the King of Hanover, "the second King who has shaken hands with me in six months"; he rubbed shoulders with royalty at a concert, a banquet and a ball given by the Rothschilds at Gunnersbury, where there were military bands, beautiful grounds, temples and illuminated walks; and he addressed a huge meeting on art and literature in the Free Trade Hall at Manchester, his speech being described by the chairman, Charles Dickens, as "very brilliant and eloquent."

He was also writing a book, begun in the autumn of '43 at Deepdene, the home of Henry Beresford-Hope, who shared the aspirations of 'Young England.' He wished to show that Toryism was not a phrase but a fact, and after much consideration resolved to set forth his ideas in a novel, as fiction "offered the best chance of influencing opinion." *Coningsby* appeared in the spring of '44, and established its author permanently as a serious and successful novelist. George Smythe was Coningsby and two other characters were drawn from Manners and Cochrane. But, as usual, the really interesting figure is Disraeli himself, this time thinly disguised as the Spanish-Moslem Jew, Sidonia, the master financier, the power behind all powers, the quiet, self-sufficient, skilful, passionless manipulator and spectator of affairs, one who is "assisted by that absolute freedom from prejudice which is the compensatory possession of a man without a country." People thought it the portrait of a Rothschild, but it was really a fanciful picture of Disraeli in the fortunate ownership of the Rothschild millions. There are good things in the book, which is peppered with epigrams, some of which are still quoted, though their provenance is forgotten:

"There is scarcely a less dignified entity than a patrician in a panic."

"Youth is a blunder; Manhood a struggle; Old Age a regret."

Two persons in the novel might be described as original creations if they had more life; but at least they are original comments on parliamentary life, being typical wire-pullers, place-seekers, time-servers, tuft-hunters, their names Taper and Tadpole:

"'I am all for a religious cry', said Taper. 'It means nothing, and, if successful, does not interfere with business when we are in'."

"'A sound Conservative government', said Taper musingly. 'I understand: Tory men and Whig measures'."

Disraeli is an aphorist, not a novelist. He has not the art of weaving his theme into the texture of the story. Separate chapters are given to the politics of the period; but as he is not stupid enough to think that politics are as interesting as personalities, the gossip of parties is within the endurance of a modern reader. His chief failure in fiction lies in his inability to create vital characters and tell a natural story in a natural manner. His portrait of Monmouth is probably more like the original, Lord Hertford, than Thackeray's Steyne, but there is more genius in a chapter of *Vanity Fair* than in the whole of *Coningsby*, the author of which seldom rises above the capacity to portray stage types and to manufacture novelettes. It has been said that *Coningsby* is the first and best of political novels, and this is certainly true in the sense that it accurately reproduces the flatness and dreariness of political cackle. The lavish style of the narrative was excellently parodied by Thackeray: "Miriam, returning to the mother-of-pearl music stool . . . touched the silver and enamelled keys of the ivory piano." With unconscious humour Disraeli informed a friend that the sustained labour of writing the book was very painful, "and I am daily more convinced that there is no toil like literature." His heroes, when not rich to start with, have a habit of walking into an Ali Baba's cave of wealth when they want to marry and settle down; and Coningsby, whose honesty has resulted in his being disinherited, discovers that in the long run honesty is the best policy and becomes a Croesus. The merit of the novel, as of all Disraeli's best productions, lies in the freedom with which he satirises every shade of opinion, whig, tory, papist, anglican, and the occasional observations of a shrewd spectator of life:

"Talk to a man about himself, and he is generally captivated. That is the real way to win him. The only difference between men and women in this respect is, that most women are vain, and some men are not. There are some men who have no self-love; but if they have, female vanity is but a trifling and airy passion compared with the vast voracity of appetite which in the sterner sex can swallow anything, and always crave for more."

"She indeed generally succeeded in conveying an impression to those she addressed, that she had never seen them before, did not care to see them now, and never wished to see them again. And all this, too, with an air of great courtesy."

" 'I think', said Sidonia, 'that there is no error so vulgar as to believe that revolutions are occasioned by economical causes. They come in, doubtless, very often to precipitate a catastrophe; very rarely do they occasion one'."

Disraeli's recognition of the importance of character and personality in the moulding of events is frequently expressed in his books. "A political institution is a machine", he says; "the motive power is the national character." And with some precognition of his own rise to eminence, he states: "It is the personal that interests mankind, that fires their imagination, and wins their hearts. A cause is a great abstraction, and fit only for students; embodied in a party, it stirs men to action; but place at the head of that party a leader who can inspire enthusiasm, he commands the world." As *Coningsby* was written to advertise the political theories of 'Young England', much stress is laid on the virtues of the immature: "Almost everything that is great has been done by youth." And he was about to proclaim in his next novel: "The Youth of a Nation are the trustees of Posterity."

Chapter XI

TAKE PHYSIC, POMP

THE fame of *Coningsby* crossed the Atlantic, and fifty thousand copies of the book were sold in the United States. Smythe confessed himself "dazzled, bewildered, tipsy with admiration", and congratulations were showered on the lucky author from all quarters. Sydney Smith wished to make his acquaintance and they met at a dinner, their fellow-guests including Lord Melbourne, Greville the diarist and Henry Luttrell. "I sat next to Sydney Smith, who was delightful . . . I don't remember a more agreeable party", recorded Disraeli, quite unaware that nothing so interesting could ever happen to him again, though he was to meet nearly every leading warrior, statesman and monarch of his age.

In the same year that *Coningsby* put him in the front rank of authors he won a place in the front rank of orators. Up to 1844 members of parliament had flocked in to hear him and to laugh at his levity, but now he openly rebelled against the tory leader and spoke in a manner that evoked the admiration as well as the mirth of the Commons. The average speaker who is heard with respect and attention by the House, as Peel and Gladstone were, develops a style that would earn him a reputation as a first-class bore in any other assembly: he is prolix and obscure. Disraeli never entirely mastered the art of saying nothing at great length, though some of his later speeches catch the note of dullness and pseudo-profundity so much admired by lawyers and legislators. But in his attacks on Peel he managed to add solidity to his natural frivolity; and, while his power of ridicule was at its height, he never surpassed the flights of eloquence to which he treated the House from 1844 to the Prime Minister's downfall. They earned him a lasting reputation, and whenever thereafter he rose to his feet the chamber filled up as quickly as members could reach their seats or scramble for standing-room.

His manner as a speaker was as peculiar as his matter was arresting. He had not the apparent spontaneity of the born orator; his voice was clear but low and monotonous; his gestures were calm, untheatrical and uniform; he appeared aloof, disdainful, indifferent. Standing with his hands on his hips or his thumbs in the armholes of his waistcoat, he spoke in a drawl, using no emphasis; and though the words seemed to come without effort, they were uttered as if he were rather bored and not much concerned either with their delivery or with the effect they produced. But this supercilious and undiversified style was carefully cultivated as a striking contrast to the method he employed when making a point. Suddenly he became animated; the tone of his voice changed; an ironic note crept in; the words were enunciated with extreme care and distinctness; their inflection was managed with the utmost nicety; a slight shrug, a quick glance, a fleeting expression of the face, heightened the impression; the House was electrified by the metamorphosis, and waited breathlessly for the issue. It came, with an unerring aim, an icy clarity, an inexorable pungency. Some of his hearers gasped, a few writhed, most were convulsed; and the building echoed with cheers. He took no notice of the outburst, never laughing, never even smiling; the pale face remained immobile, the body motionless; he looked as if he were superior to such human exhibitions, unconscious of the hubbub he had created; and when it died down he continued his speech in the same calm, clear, uninterested, monotonous manner with which he had begun, preparatory to another transition, another taunt, another emotional explosion from his auditors.

Of his real antagonist but nominal leader in those years something must be said. The Duke of Wellington, with his usual perspicuity, hit the nail on the head when he remarked "I have no small talk and Peel has no manners." With good manners Peel would have been Prime Minister until his death, and perhaps the most popular one in English history. But he annoyed many of his followers by his lack of courtesy and he made the fatal error of antagonising Disraeli, the only man in parliament who had the wit to take advantage of that brusque outspokenness which in the northern counties passes for honesty. Sir Robert Peel was a Lancashire man who, though educated at Harrow and Oxford, and occupying important government posts in a parliamentary career of forty years, never got rid of his provincial accent. He was a born business man, had great powers of application, an unusually retentive memory, and knew intuitively the practical way of despatching affairs. Lacking imagination, he was too much under the influence of current theories and therefore over-inclined to change his opinions when contrary views were gaining ground. But he was an unrivalled parliamentarian and could always give a plausible account of his conversion. He also lacked foresight, and so it happened, to quote Disraeli, "that while he always was looked upon as the most prudent and safest of leaders, he ever, after a protracted display of admirable tactics, concluded his campaigns by surrendering at discretion. He was so adroit that he could prolong resistance even beyond its term, but so little foreseeing that often in the very triumph of his manœuvres he found himself in an untenable position. And so it came to pass that Roman Catholic emancipation, Parliamentary Reform, and the abrogation of our commercial system, were all carried in haste or in passion and without conditions or mitigatory arrangements." In each of these cases he started by vigorously opposing the very movement he eventually adopted at a moment's notice, and, as Disraeli said, "no one with all his conservative language more advanced revolution."

By nature Peel was shy, and to cover his early lack of self-confidence he formed an artificial manner when speaking, either frigid or mild to suit the occasion or his mood. He had a fine voice and knew exactly how to clothe what he had to say in words that could be interpreted according to his fancy. Like other specialists in facts and figures, he had no knowledge of human nature; and instead of nursing his party when he came to power, ignored the rank and file and appeared abstracted. He was, in short, an extremely industrious and efficient administrator, mainly interested in finance, hardly at all in his fellow-men, with the result that power brought out his bureaucratic qualities: arrogance, insolence and callousness. It has been said, and repeated *ad nauseam*, that power corrupts; but it would be truer to say that power exhibits corruption, the seeds of which are in a man before power brings them to fruition. The incorruptible man does not seek power and never obtains it. Peel's haughtiness and tactlessness during his last phase were due partly to his popularity at Court, but chiefly to his pride: a belief, instilled in him during years of authority, that no one else could take his place, one of the concomitants of power, due basically to a lack of human sympathy, which leadership had accentuated. As the instrument whereby the rich industrialists of England became fabulously wealthy, it is perhaps significant that he is remembered today, when remembered at all, as the man who established the metropolitan police force in 1829, the members of which were first known as 'Peelers' and are still called 'Bobbies'. Peel was fifty-six years of age, Disraeli forty, when the great duel commenced which drove him from the office which in due time his opponent was to fill.

Early in 1844 Peel's sister wrote to Mary Anne that she wished Disraeli, when next he met the Prime Minister, would shake hands with him. "They are both reserved men", she said, "and one must make the first advance; the other would accept it most gladly." Apparently each of them was too reserved to make the first advance, and in any case it would have been like the handshake of a pair of pugilists before the battering began. Although Disraeli had frequently criticised and voted against Peel, receiving imperious reproofs for his behaviour, he made the first step of naked rebellion in June '44 over the sugar duties, which Peel wished to reduce. A small section of tories, with the help of the Opposition, carried an amendment against the Government in favour of British free-grown, as against foreign slave-grown, sugar. Peel was angry, summoned a meeting of his party, and practically ordered them to support him. Disraeli declined to be bullied into subjection, and declared in the Commons that Peel's well-known dislike of slavery was not extended to his own followers on the benches behind him: "There the gang is still assembled, and there the thong of the whip still sounds." His speech would have resulted in the resignation of the Government if Stanley had not saved his side by appealing to tory sentiment, and Peel got a majority of twenty. After which Disraeli visited Shrewsbury to explain his conduct to his constituents. This he did to their satisfaction, and in the course of a speech made one of those personal confessions which are like draughts of clean air in the foggy atmosphere of cant and humbug enveloping politics and public life generally: "There is no doubt, gentlemen, that all men who offer themselves as candidates for public favour have motives of some sort. I candidly acknowledge that I have, and

I will tell you what they are: I love fame; I love public reputation; I love to live in the eyes of the country; and it is a glorious thing for a man to do who has had my difficulties to contend against."

Accompanied by his wife he then went to Manchester for a meeting at the Athenaeum, at which he took the chair and 'Young England' made speeches. The Duke of Rutland, father of John Manners, and Lord Strangford, father of George Smythe, were extremely annoyed by the association of their sons with Disraeli. "I lament", wrote the Duke to Strangford, "the influence which Mr Disraeli has acquired over several of the young British senators, and over your son and mine especially. I do not know Mr Disraeli by sight, but I have respect only for his talents, which I think he sadly misuses." Strangford was incensed because he hoped to restore his fortune by currying favour with Peel, and his chances of doing so lessened every time his son voted with Disraeli against their chief. The speeches of the Young Englanders on this occasion were widely reported, and their publication in a pamphlet cannot have helped to reconcile the young men's parents to their misleader.

Disraeli spent some time in the north, because he was writing a novel dealing with the condition of the poor which he wished to study at first hand. He felt more strongly on this subject than on any other, and many of his speeches dealt with the vast accumulation of wealth by one section of society and the filthy degradation of poverty among the real creators of that wealth. He had attacked the new Poor Law, which was a characteristic production of the rich, and he supported Lord Ashley (afterwards Shaftesbury) in his attempts, eventually successful, to get a Ten Hours Factory Bill through parliament, attempts that were opposed by Cobden and Bright, the two great 'progressive' spirits of that age. Disraeli did not take sides in the dispute between the manufacturers and the landowners, because he knew that the farm hands were as badly off as the factory hands; but he asserted that "the rights of labour are as sacred as those of property", and that "the social happiness of the millions should be the first object of a statesman", neither of these remarks appealing to the whigs and tories, most of whom represented one or other of the rich and interested classes. He was not therefore a supporter of protection or free trade on principle, regarding both as expedients, not panaceas; but he was determined to hinder the endeavours of the growing middle-classes to increase their wealth at the cost both of the toilers and the farmers. "The privileges of the multitude and the prerogatives of the Sovereign had grown up together, and together they had waned", he declared, and he wished to see both rescued from the greedy oligarchy of landowners that had seized them and the avaricious middle-class of manufacturers that were now taking possession of them.

Perceiving that his more fortunate fellow-countrymen knew nothing of the plight of the field labourers and factory toilers, he decided to expose it; and his propaganda appeared in the form of a novel called *Sybil*, which came out in the spring of '45. Its sub-title was "The Two Nations", these being the rich and the poor, and it was dedicated "to one whose noble spirit and gentle nature ever prompt her to sympathise with the suffering; to one whose sweet voice has often encouraged, and whose taste and judgment have ever guided, its pages; the most severe of critics, but—a perfect Wife!" It was finished under difficulties: "The printers were on my heels, and have been for the last month . . . What with the House of Commons, which was itself quite enough for a man, and writing 600 pages, I thought sometimes my head must turn." It is improbable that he remembered one whose head had really turned, but King Lear's words should have been the epigraph of his book, for they are the text from which he unconsciously preached:

> Take physic, pomp;
> Expose thyself to feel what wretches feel,
> That thou mayst shake the superflux to them
> And show the heavens more just.

The descriptions of working-class conditions in *Sybil* are founded on first-hand or authentically documented evidence, and there is no better account of the circumstances that produced chartism. Disraeli suppressed the more horrible examples of cruelty, poverty and serfdom, because he knew that his readers would not believe them and their inclusion would only give the book an air of improbability; but on the employment of children in factories he had this to say: "Infanticide is practised as extensively and as legally in England as it is on the banks of the Ganges;

a circumstance which apparently has not yet engaged the attention of the Society for the Propagation of the Gospel in Foreign Parts." The hideous lives of miners and colliers had also, he declared, "escaped the notice of the Society for the Abolition of Negro Slavery." We learn that "the people were better clothed, better lodged, and better fed just before the War of the Roses than they are at this moment", that "the average term of life in this district among the working-classes is seventeen", and that "we have more pestilence now in England than we ever had, but it only reaches the poor." He refers to the age as one of political materialism, aspiring only to wealth because it has faith in no other accomplishment, "as men rifle cargoes on the verge of shipwreck", and he looks back nostalgically to the pre-Reformation age when the Church protected the poor, sardonically wondering whether the workhouses would be adequate substitutes for the monasteries.

It is a grim picture that he paints, true according to the Blue Books but imaginatively undigested and so without the compelling artistic quality of Dickens's work in the same field. Yet it says much for Disraeli that he was constrained to produce it, for the governing classes, whether rich or getting rich, whether whig, tory or radical, were wholly unattuned to it. Peel, of course, earns a few well-merited kicks, and we are ironically informed that his great measures have produced "three good harvests." He is politely introduced as "a gentleman of Downing Street", who advises his faithful functionary, Mr Hoaxem, to be "frank and explicit" when addressing a deputation of manufacturers: "that is the right line to take when you wish to conceal your own mind and to confuse the minds of others. Good morning!"

Along with the scenes of violence and misery among the destitute and disinherited, we are given the usual Disraelian glimpses of high life, which prove that he could portray loungers better than labourers, and a love-story that reminds us that all his novels are fairy-tales. The heroine Sybil is simply his variation of Cinderella, with the hero Egremont, first of all disguised as an ordinary person, as the prince; but his Cinderella, as we might expect, turns out to be of noble blood and vast fortune, while his prince, unable in Victorian England to become a king, has to be contented with an earldom. There are not perhaps so many pithy sayings scattered over the book as in his earlier works, but a few are still quoted:

"To be conscious that you are ignorant is a great step to knowledge."

"Little things affect little minds."

"The Duke of Wellington brought to the post of first minister immortal fame; a quality of success which would almost seem to include all others."

" 'I rather like bad wine', said Mr Mountchesney; 'one gets so bored with good wine'."

In adapting a remark that Dr Johnson made in the eighteenth century, Disraeli showed that it would have a wider application in the twentieth: "Mr Kremlin himself was distinguished for ignorance, for he had only one idea, and that was wrong."

Chapter XII

PEEL REPEALS

'YOUNG England' had served its turn as a sort of guerilla movement in politics and had produced its text-books in *Coningsby* and *Sybil.* But Disraeli was not content to be the captain of a clique or to embalm their dreams in fiction. He wished and intended to be Prime Minister of England, and he commenced operations to that end by launching a devastating attack on the Prime Minister of the moment, the most powerful and popular politician both in the country and in the Commons. In the uproar thus caused 'Young England' was forgotten and its ideals were filed for reference. Yet the moment seemed inauspicious for political upheavals; railway development and several good harvests had given the country an appearance of prosperity, and at the beginning of '45 it looked as if Peel's Government would last for ever. Early that session there was a pleasant prelude to the coming clash. Peel had shown some warmth during a debate, and Disraeli commented on it, saying that "in a popular assembly it is sometimes expedient to enact the part of the choleric gentleman", but telling the younger tories not to be alarmed as Peel's emotion had been simulated. Upon which Peel got up and made what everyone thought a withering retort: "He undertakes to assure the House that my vehemence was all pretended . . . I on the contrary will do him entire justice; I do believe that his bitterness was . . . entirely sincere. The hon. gentleman has a perfect right to support a hostile motion . . . but let him not say that he does it in a friendly spirit:

> 'Give me the avowed, the erect, the manly foe,
> Bold I can meet—perhaps may turn his blow!
> But of all plagues, good Heaven, thy wrath can send,
> Save me, oh, save me from the candid friend!' "

It took more than a convenient quotation to wither Disraeli, who moreover perceived that Peel had laid himself open to a deadly thrust, because, as a one-time friend and colleague, he had treated the author of those lines, George Canning, in a very scurvy manner, even his friends being unable to make much of a case for him. A lesser man than Disraeli would have missed his real chance by indulging in a quick riposte; but Dizzy went home to brood, and a week later, speaking on a different subject, delivered his blow well and truly. After explaining that Peel had nothing to fear from the Opposition—"the right hon. gentleman caught the Whigs bathing, and walked away with their clothes"—and saying that, in reproving his own followers, his quotations were more effective than his imputations, Disraeli went on:

The right hon. gentleman knows what the introduction of a great name does in debate—how important is its effect, and occasionally how electrical. He never refers to any author who is not great, and sometimes who is not loved—Canning, for example. That is a name never to be mentioned, I am sure, in the House of Commons without emotion. We all admire his genius. We all, at least most of us, deplore his untimely end; and we all sympathise with him in his fierce struggle with supreme prejudice and sublime mediocrity—with inveterate foes and with candid friends. (*Loud cheering.*) The right hon. gentleman may be sure that a quotation from such an authority will always tell. Some lines, for example, upon friendship, written by Mr Canning, and quoted by the right hon. gentleman. The theme, the poet, the speaker—what a felicitous combination! (*Loud and long-continued cheers.*) Its effect in debate must be overwhelming; and I am sure, if it were addressed to me, all that would remain would be for me thus publicly to congratulate the right hon. gentleman, not only on his ready memory, but on his courageous conscience.

The effect of these words on the House was tremendous; the cheers, mingled with shouts of laughter, rose and fell and rose again. The Home Secretary, Graham, got up to reply, but his words were lost in the din. When he could be heard he was expressing his joy that the member for Shrewsbury had exchanged avowed rebellion for covert mutiny. "As for Peel", recorded Disraeli, "he was stunned and stupefied, lost his head, and, vacillating between silence and spleen, spoke much and weakly. Never was a greater failure! Assuring me that I had not hurt his feelings, that he would never reciprocate personalities again, having no venom . . ." It could scarcely be said that Dizzy had no venom, though he managed to conceal it under banter. But his was not the spite of a man who hates a religion or a party because he has once belonged to it, who detests another man because he has once been influenced by him. Nor was it the spite of jealousy or a feeling of inferiority. It was simply the enmity felt by an ambitious man against anyone who stood in his way and hindered his progress. This purely personal feeling was reinforced by a conviction that Peel was ratting; and so Dizzy's rancour and rectitude were in harmony. But irony, not invective, was his weapon, and when next he attacked Peel he wielded it so effectively that the scene which followed was unique in the memory of the oldest members.

No other countries having made reciprocal offers of free or preferential trade, Peel was now toying with the idea of free imports for Great Britain, whatever the taxes imposed by foreign countries on British exports. In other words he had accepted Cobden's theories holus-bolus, though they were originally advanced in the belief that the rest of the world would follow England's lead in free trade, and Disraeli reminded the House of Peel's protectionist principles before he became Prime Minister:

There is no doubt a difference in the right hon. gentleman's demeanour as leader of the Opposition and as Minister of the Crown. But that's the old story; you must not contrast too strongly the hours of courtship with the hours of possession. 'Tis very true that the right hon. gentleman's conduct is different. I remember him making his protection speeches. They were the best speeches I ever heard. It was a great thing to hear the right hon. gentleman say: 'I would rather be the leader of the gentlemen of England than possess the confidence of Sovereigns.' That was a grand thing. We don't hear much of 'the gentlemen of England' now. (*Great cheering.*) But what of that? They have the pleasures of memory—the charms of reminiscence. They were his first love, and, though he may not kneel to them now as in the hour of passion, still they can recall the past; and nothing is more useless or unwise than these scenes of crimination and reproach, for we know that in all these cases, when the beloved object has ceased to charm, it is in vain to appeal to the feelings. (*Great laughter.*) . . . And that, sir, is exactly the case of the great agricultural interest—that beauty which everybody wooed and one deluded. There is a fatality in such charms, and we now seem to approach the catastrophe of her career . . . For my part, if we are to have free trade, I, who honour genius, prefer that such measures should be proposed by the hon. member for Stockport [Cobden] than by one who through skilful parliamentary manœuvres has tampered with the generous confidence of a great people and a great party. For myself, I care not what may be the result. Dissolve, if you please, the Parliament you have betrayed, and appeal to the people, who, I believe, mistrust you. For me there remains this at least—the opportunity of expressing thus publicly my belief that a Conservative Government is an organised hypocrisy.

This definition of a Conservative Government was received with frantic delight by the whigs, and has since been quoted, carefully disjoined from its context, by many liberals and socialists, all of them naïvely oblivious that the same phrase applies equally to every sort of government; but such was the feeling aroused by his speech that even the tory rank and file cheered, if somewhat shamefacedly, the ministers alone exhibiting no sign of enthusiasm.

From now onwards Disraeli held the House completely in his power. If it were known that he was going to speak, members would endure the boredom of debate so as to be in their places when he rose to his feet. The assembly fluttered with excitement as he got up and was thrilled to silence as the measured tones began to work their spell. The eyes of all continually shifted from the speaker to his victim, noting the deliberate gestures of the first, the nervous twitches of the second. It is not easy to maintain an air of complete sang-froid when a gathering in which you are the leading figure is laughing deliriously over a drollery at your expense. Peel, who for years had been the master of the House, to whom nothing but deference had been paid, was quite unequal to the contest. Not only did he fail utterly on the one occasion when he attempted to reply, but he was quite incapable of concealing his wrath and mortification when the House rocked with mirth; and so self-confident, nonchalant and skilful was Dizzy that no one dared come to Peel's rescue. The lack of proper Opposition in the Commons was a constant theme of Disraeli's, for the whigs had nothing to offer in place of Peel's policy and the tories were being duped by the man they trusted, with the result that Peel had become a parliamentary middleman, who "bamboozles one party and plunders the other, till, having obtained a position to which he is not entitled, he cries out 'Let us have no party questions, but fixity of tenure.' I want to have a commission issued to enquire into the tenure by which Downing Street is held. I want to know whether the conditions of entry have been complied with, and whether there are not some covenants in the lease which are already forfeited." What they should do, Dizzy declared, was to bring back to the House "the legitimate influence and salutary check of a constitutional Opposition . . . Let us do it at once in the only way in which it can be done, by dethroning this dynasty of deception, by putting an end to the intolerable yoke of official despotism and parliamentary imposture." Peel, an onlooker tells us, changed colour, dropped his head, and pulled his hat over his eyes.

Disraeli's efforts in the session of '45 exhausted him, and he went with his wife to Cassel in French Flanders for rest and seclusion, seeing no one, hearing from no one except his sister, getting up at 5.30 in the mornings, going to bed at 9.30 in the evenings, taking pleasant walks in a rich rural landscape, enjoying panoramic views, and writing his next novel. "My wife walked 300 miles in two months, of which she is very proud", and their greatest adventure was the occasional discovery of a village. They were in Paris by the end of the year, and again he had a long talk with Louis Philippe at St Cloud. He also met Washington Irving, whom he thought "vulgar and stupid."

While they were away, news came that the potato crop in Ireland had failed, and this mysterious sickness of a single root, he later asserted, was to change the history of the world. At any rate it gave Peel the excuse for which he had been waiting. Ireland must be saved by the introduction of tax-free corn. Lord John Russell, leader of the Whig Opposition, issued a statement that he favoured the total repeal of the Corn Laws; and Peel called a meeting of the cabinet on December 4th with that in view. But his chief supporter, Stanley, now in the Upper House, would only agree to a temporary suspension of the Laws to meet an emergency, and Peel resigned from office. The Queen sent for Russell, who first undertook and then abandoned the task of forming a government, probably from fear, because he gave the feeble excuse that one of his new ministers would refuse to serve if another were in the cabinet. So Peel was asked to carry on, and this time he ignored Stanley's opposition, appointing Gladstone in his place. It was soon discovered that the potato famine in Ireland had been exaggerated; but in any case a temporary suspension of the Corn Laws would have met that difficulty. Wellington said that rotten potatoes had "put Peel in his damned fright", but, as we now know, he had been wholly converted to Cobden's theories, and the Irish situation merely gave him the cue. It is just possible that if he had called a meeting of his party, explained the position of affairs, and asked for their confidence, he would have carried them with him; but he had reached the swollen-headed condition of all autocrats and would not condescend. His action over the Corn Laws was criticised by opponents and accomplices alike. "Ma'am, it's a damned dishonest act!" said Melbourne to Queen Victoria; and even Cobden thought he did wrong to ask his party to repudiate their pledges; but he was in that state of emotional excitement which converts to a belief so frequently exhibit, and he suffered from the megalomania of one who feels himself the instrument whereby great issues are to be guided.

Even so he might have passed the measure through the House with some degree of credit to himself if it had not been for Disraeli. When parliament met in January '46, Peel did a clever thing. Knowing that everyone was on tip-toe to hear about the crisis, he lowered the temperature of the House by talking at great length about the prices of beef, flax, wool and lard, by prosing about the duty of statesmen to posterity, and boasting that his Government had put down sedition and silenced agitation. Russell followed him with another rambling speech, and it seemed as if the evening would pass off in an atmosphere of inertia and despondency, everybody bored into acceptation of whatever the Government might propose. Disraeli saw the danger, and rose to reanimate the House:

Sir, there is a difficulty in finding a parallel to the position of the right hon. gentleman in any part of history. The only parallel which I can find is an incident in the late war in the Levant . . . I remember when that great struggle was taking place, when the existence of the Turkish Empire was at stake, the late Sultan, a man of great energy and fertile in resources, was determined to fit out an immense fleet to maintain his empire. Accordingly a vast armament was collected. The crews were picked men, the officers were the ablest that could be found, and both officers and men were rewarded before they fought. (*Much laughter.*) There never was an armament which left the Dardanelles similarly appointed since the days of Solyman the Great. The Sultan personally witnessed the departure of the fleet; all the muftis prayed for the expedition, as all the muftis here prayed for the success of the last general election. Away went the fleet, but what was the Sultan's consternation when the Lord High Admiral steered at once into the enemy's port. (*Loud laughter and cheers.*) Now, sir, the Lord High Admiral on that occasion was very much misrepresented. He, too, was called a traitor, and he, too, vindicated himself. 'True it is', said he, 'I did place myself at the head of this valiant armada; true it is that my Sovereign embraced me; true it is that all the muftis in the empire offered up prayers for the expedition; but I have an objection to war. I see no use in prolonging the struggle, and the only reason I had for accepting the command was that I might terminate the contest by betraying my master.' (*Tremendous tory cheering.*)

As for Peel's claim that he had destroyed agitation, when it was perfectly clear that he was acting under the influence of the agitation by the Anti-Corn-Law League, Disraeli quickly disposed of it:

But, really, when he told us that his Conservative administration had put down agitation, when he said this in the face of the hon. member for Stockport [Cobden], in the face of the hon. member for Durham [Bright]—then, sir, I confess that the right hon. baronet did manage to achieve the first great quality of oratory, that he did succeed in making an impression on his audience! Put down agitation! Will he rise and deny that he is legislating or about to legislate with direct reference to agitation? (*Loud cheers.*) What other excuses has he, for even his mouldy potatoes have failed him . . .?

Peel had given the assurance that he and his colleagues were only thinking of the future. "Who can doubt it?" asked Disraeli. "Look at them. Throw your eyes over the Treasury bench . . . They are just the men in the House you would fix upon as thinking only of posterity. The only thing is, when one looks at them, seeing of what they are composed, one is hardly certain whether 'the future' of which they are thinking is indeed posterity or only the coming quarter-day." As the whig leader, Lord John Russell, had recently announced his conversion to Cobdenism, Disraeli's references to the general abandonment of protection, though they convulsed the House, brought no gleam of gladness to the faces of its leaders on either side:

We accepted him [Peel] for a leader to accomplish the triumph of protection, and now we are to attend the catastrophe of protection. (*Loud laughter.*) Of course the Whigs will be the chief mourners. (*Loud laughter.*) They cannot but weep for their innocent, although it was an abortion (*loud cheers and laughter*); but ours was a fine child. Who can forget how its nurse dandled it, fondled it? (*Loud laughter.*) What a charming babe! Delicious little thing! so thriving! (*Loud laughter.*) Did you ever see such a beauty for its years? This was the tone, the innocent prattle; and then the nurse, in a fit of patriotic frenzy, dashes its brains out (*loud laughter*) and comes down to give master and mistress an account of this terrible murder. The nurse, too, a person of a very orderly demeanour, not given to drink, and never showing any emotion, except of late, when kicking against protection.

To support Peel's free trade policy when he had been elected to support protection was not fair to the people of England, said Disraeli, who concluded on a note of warning which has never been heeded:

While we are admitting the principles of relaxed commerce, there is extreme danger of our admitting the principles of relaxed politics. I advise, therefore, that we all—whatever may be our opinions about free trade—oppose the introduction of free politics. Let men stand by the principle by which they rise, right or wrong. I make no exception . . . Do not, then, because you see a great personage giving up his opinions—do not cheer him on, do not give him so ready a reward to political tergiversation. Above all, maintain the line of demarcation between parties, for it is only by maintaining the independence of party that you can maintain the integrity of public men, and the power and influence of Parliament itself.

When Disraeli resumed his seat, he was cheered for several minutes; and indeed he had done an unprecedented thing. Before this speech he had spoken for himself, or at most for a very small group of independent tory members. After it he was to speak for the agricultural interest in parliament, which under his influence grew until it became a new and vital Tory party recreated and led by himself.

What he knew was going to happen was soon made known to the rest of the world. Naturally Peel did not break the news too suddenly. When he rose to outline his scheme he began with a dissertation on candles, soap, shoe-leather, sugar, brandy and other commodities, the taxes on which were to be reduced. Having got the House into a proper frame of mind, he quietly announced the total repeal of the Corn Laws at the end of three years, and rapidly went on to the question of compensation for farmers, which, though broached in magniloquent fashion, remained dubious. The representatives of the agricultural constituencies were unimpressed, and the movement to form a third party quickly grew. The leading rebel was Lord George Bentinck, second son of the Duke of Portland, who had been one of Peel's strongest supporters, believing in him so devoutly that, when Disraeli prophesied Peel's defection in 1845, Bentinck had no adequate words for so dastardly a libel on an honourable man. He had therefore held aloof from Disraeli, and they only became acquainted during the session of '46. Bentinck was mad on horses, racing and hunting, and though he had sat in eight parliaments for eighteen years he had scarcely opened his mouth during the debates, sometimes attending them in a white greatcoat which scarcely concealed his scarlet hunting coat. Trained as a soldier, he kept some of the rigidity picked up on parade; but he also possessed a soldier's best qualities, honesty, simplicity and courage. Deception and treachery were not within his comprehension, and when Peel displayed these characteristics the effect on Bentinck was sufficient to turn a first-class sportsman into a vigorous statistician. "I keep horses in three counties", he said, "and they tell me that I shall save fifteen hundred a year by free trade. I don't care for that: what I cannot bear is being sold." All the energy that had once been devoted to hunting and the turf was now thrown into the business of organising an anti-Peel party; but when it was suggested that he should be the leader of it, he remarked "I think we have had enough of leaders; it is not in my way; I shall remain the last of the rank and file."

Nevertheless he could not help being acknowledged as head of the new protectionist party, and as Disraeli virtually became its brains everything promised well for its survival. As we know, Disraeli from youth had the remarkable faculty of gaining the confidence of others and working his will through them; and the stronger the character of the intermediary the more successfully he exercised his power, for his tact in management and his knack of self-suppression reached their highest manifestation when the force and enthusiasm of the subject were adequate to his purpose. And since he was as free from jealousy as an ambitious man can be, their collaboration, though Bentinck was naturally vehement and quarrelsome, ran smoothly from first to last. They managed, by successive speakers, to draw out the first debate on the Corn Laws for a period of three weeks, and when the House divided only 112 tories voted for Peel, 242 against him, his majority of 97 being obtained by the support of his political opponents. In the course of this debate Disraeli spoke of "the school of Manchester", and the phrase passed into general currency as "the Manchester school" to denote Cobden's free-trade party. Later he said that "there is no greater opponent of real democracy than a modern liberal; and as to popular principles, I believe they are never in more danger than when they are professed by political economists", a truth which the passage of a century has helped to clarify.

Both Bentinck and Disraeli worked indefatigably, speaking regularly, keeping their party up to scratch, and increasing it. Bentinck even forewent his meals, eating nothing till the House had adjourned for the night, because he found that food made him lethargic. At the second reading of the Bill to repeal the Corn Laws, the Government's majority dropped to 88. Needless to say, there was much intrigue, and at one moment it seemed that the Irish members would vote with the tory secessionists if the latter would oppose the Irish Coercion Bill which the Government were trying to force through parliament at the same time. This brought Cobden to his feet, and he threatened the intriguers with dissolution if the repeal were held up. "There are the people of England", he stormed—"I don't mean the country party, but the people living in the towns, and who will govern this country." Peel appeared to cheer the statement, and Disraeli commented on the fact that he had done so, though he had once prided himself on being the head of the gentlemen of England. Peel instantly jumped up and hotly denied that he had cheered Cobden's phrase. "If he means to say that anything I stated is false, of course I sit down", returned Disraeli. Peel was silent while everyone started arguing with everyone else; but when he explained that he had cheered Cobden generally, not that particular definition, the atmosphere became calm and the House proceeded with the business of the country. The Prime Minister's brother, however, Colonel Peel, feeling that honour had not been satisfied, went up to Disraeli and said: "There shall be no doubt as to what *one* person thinks of your assertion, and *I* say it *is* false." The time had not yet passed when an insult could only be washed out with blood, and seconds were duly appointed, Bentinck acting for Disraeli, who retired to bed under the impression that he would visit a quiet spot at Wormwood Scrubbs with a brace of pistols early the following morning. But the seconds conferred at White's Club late that night, as a result of which Colonel Peel withdrew his offensive expression and offered an apology. Disraeli was destined only for duels of a verbal nature. His attacks on Peel made that statesman curiously distrait, for on an occasion about this period, possibly the one just described, the minister remained in his seat after the House had emptied, "plunged in profound and perhaps painful reverie", and was roused by the clerk whose duty it was to examine the chamber before the lights were extinguished.

The Corn Bill was read for the third time on May 15th and carried by a majority of 98, Disraeli making a speech which lasted for three hours, in the course of which he described Peel's life as "a great appropriation clause. He is a burglar of others' intellect . . . there is no statesman who has committed political petty larceny on so great a scale." Disraeli also had something to say about the 112 tories who had voted for the repeal:

Why, what a compliment to a Minister—not only to vote for him, but to vote for him against your opinions (*much cheering*), and in favour of opinions which he had always drilled you to distrust. (*Loud cheers.*) That was a scene, I believe, unprecedented in the House of Commons. Indeed, I recollect nothing equal to it, unless it be the conversion of the Saxons by Charlemagne, which is the only historical incident that bears any parallel to that illustrious occasion. (*Great cheers and laughter.*) Ranged on the banks of the Rhine, the Saxons determined to resist any further movement on the part of the great Caesar; but when the Emperor appeared, instead of conquering he converted them. How were they converted? In battalions and baptised in platoons. (*Roars of laughter.*) It was utterly impossible to bring these individuals from a state of reprobation to a state of grace with a celerity sufficiently quick. When I saw the hundred and twelve fall into rank and file, I was irresistibly reminded of that memorable incident on the banks of the Rhine. (*Loud cheers.*)

After referring to "this huckstering tyranny of the Treasury bench—these political pedlars that bought their party in the cheapest market, and sold us in the dearest", Disraeli brought his speech to a close with a prophecy which was to be fulfilled a generation after his death, when the principle of getting rich quick had yielded in the wastage of war to the operation of getting poor quicker, and the abandonment of the country's agriculture had nearly caused the surrender of England and the end of freedom:

> I know that the public mind is polluted with economic fancies—a depraved desire that the rich may become richer without the interference of industry and toil. I know, sir, that all confidence in public men is lost. (*Great cheering.*) But, sir, I have faith in the primitive and enduring elements of the English character. It may be vain now, in the midnight of their intoxication, to tell them that there will be an awakening of bitterness; it may be idle now, in the springtide of their economic frenzy, to warn them that there may be an ebb of trouble. But the dark and inevitable hour will arrive. Then, when their spirits are softened by misfortune, they will recur to those principles that made England great. (*Prolonged cheers.*) Then too, sir, perchance they may remember, not with unkindness, those who, betrayed and deserted, were neither ashamed nor afraid to struggle for the 'good old cause' —the cause with which are associated principles the most popular, sentiments the most entirely national, the cause of labour, the cause of the people, the cause of England!

The speech was received with tumultuous cheers, the like of which in volume and duration had not been heard before. Peel looked wretched, his brother more so, and Russell, the next speaker, was unable to proceed; for whenever he opened his mouth as each cheer began to die down, a fresh outburst silenced him before he had got beyond a sentence. Peel was completely knocked over, and when, later that evening, he was received with shouts of derision in a place where he had always been treated with veneration, he lost his self-possession and it seemed for a moment as if he would weep. But he felt murderous as well as miserable and in his speech implied that Disraeli had asked for office in the early days of his administration. For once in a way Dizzy, too, lost his self-possession, and instead of frankly admitting that he had done so, while making it clear that he would have resigned office the moment Peel ratted over protection, he calmly lied, saying that it was totally foreign to his nature to apply for a place. It was a risky thing to do, and lucky for him that Peel, after a careful search, had failed to find his letter. But few men in Dizzy's place, certainly no politician, would have told the truth at such a moment.

With the third reading of the Corn Bill in the Commons "the field was lost", wrote Disraeli, "but at any rate there should be retribution for those who had betrayed it"; and when the Bill passed the Lords on June 25th, the Government was defeated in the House of Commons on the Irish Coercion Bill, largely as a result of Bentinck's strategy and Disraeli's tactics, and vengeance had overtaken the traitor, as Bentinck called his former leader. Since every tory had previously supported the Coercion Bill, it was a fearful shock to Peel when he saw "the gentlemen of England" trooping past him into the hostile lobby. "It was impossible that he could have marked them without emotion", wrote Disraeli some years afterwards: "the flower of that great party which had been so proud to follow one who had been so proud to lead them. They were men to gain whose hearts and the hearts of their fathers had been the aim and exultation of his life. They had extended to him an unlimited confidence and an admiration without stint. They had stood by him in the darkest hour, and had borne him from the depths of political despair to the proudest of living positions. Right or wrong, they were men of honour, breeding, and refinement, high and generous character, great weight and station in the country, which they had ever placed at his disposal. They had been not only his followers but his friends; had joined in the same pastimes, drank from the same cup, and in the pleasantness of private life had often forgotten together the cares and strife of politics."

Peel resigned, though his policy triumphed for two generations during the industrial expansion of Great Britain. But covetousness must be paid for sooner or later; and when the greedy, sordid, glittering days were over, people began to wonder whether the creation of cotton millionaires and the conversion of England's green and pleasant land into vast slum areas were fitting recompense for the ruin of the country's rural life and the loss of individual character among its inhabitants. Disraeli foresaw the event, and did not wonder. But he never suffered from self-righteousness, nor felt personally aggrieved when he had caused a grievance. Having driven Peel from office, he was content, showed no further sign of hostility, and might have adapted Prospero's words to the occasion:

he being beaten,
The sole drift of my purpose doth extend
Not a frown further.

Besides, he had become a big figure in the political world, and those who had recently distrusted him now did him honour. In August '46 he and Bentinck, the Marquis of Granby and the Duke of Richmond, were staying with the Duke of Rutland at Belvoir Castle, which was exactly like the Coningsby Castle of Dizzy's novel. "Granby and myself arrived here in a fly on Thursday, and were received by two rows of servants, bowing as we passed, which very much reminded me of the arrival of Coningsby himself." At last his dreams were being realised.

II

Chapter XIII

LEADERSHIP

WHILE Disraeli's dreams were coming true, Bentinck's were dissolving. At the Goodwood races in July '46 his horses were very successful and he appeared as much absorbed in the sport as ever. His racing stud was the finest in the country, and it seemed almost certain that in a year or two he would achieve the ambition of his life and win the Derby. After the third day's racing at Goodwood, he asked in a sleepy manner during dinner "Will any of you give me £10,000 for all my lot, beginning with old Bay Middleton and ending with little Kitchener?" As he was sober and not subject to joking on sacred matters, everyone thought that politics had affected his brain; and they were right; for he had determined to abandon sport entirely and devote himself to his duties in parliament. His horses were sold that year; but he did not fully realise the sacrifice he had made until May, 1848, when the Derby was won by his horse Surplice, which had gone with the rest. Disraeli met him in the House of Commons library on the day after the Derby had been run, and gave an account of what passed between them: "He was standing before the bookshelves, with a volume in his hand, and his countenance was greatly disturbed . . . He had nothing to console him, and nothing to sustain him except his pride. Even that deserted him before a heart which he knew at least could yield him sympathy. He gave a sort of superb groan." And then he spoke:

"All my life I have been trying for this, and for what have I sacrificed it!"

Disraeli tried to comfort him, but "You do not know what the Derby is", moaned Bentinck.

"Yes, I do", said Dizzy, who also knew how to coin a phrase: "it is the blue ribbon of the turf."

"It is the blue ribbon of the turf", Bentinck slowly repeated as he sank into a chair. Then, turning to the table, he buried himself in a folio of statistics.

With the resignation of Peel, a whig cabinet was formed with Lord John Russell as Prime Minister and Palmerston again at the Foreign Office. The whigs were in a minority and depended on Peel's followers for getting their Bills through parliament, Peel being determined to keep the protectionists, and especially Disraeli, out of power. Bentinck remained the nominal leader of the new group in the Commons, but insisted that Stanley, in the Upper House, was the real leader of the whole party. After the Corn Laws the question of sugar engrossed the attention of the people's representatives on and off for several years; but it need not engross ours longer than it takes to overhear Dizzy musing on the subject: "Strange that a manufacture which charms infancy and soothes old age should so frequently occasion political disaster." In the autumn of '46 he and his wife were at Bradenham, where he worked hard on his next novel. He experienced, what became a regular occurrence with him, a curious lassitude immediately after exchanging the energetic life of the capital for the restful ease of the country. He had, as it were, to become acclimatised to pure air. It usually took him a fortnight to get seasoned to the change, after which he did not think it possible that he could ever live anywhere except "among the woods and turfy wildernesses of this dear county, which, though it upset Charles I, so exhausted its progressive spirit in 1640, that it has now neither a town nor a railroad." He loved what he called "those beechen groves of Bucks which even Julius Caesar could not penetrate", and he liked to think that every great name in English history was in some way connected with the county of his adoption.

With the opening of the 1847 parliamentary session Disraeli took his seat in the House on the front bench, sitting in rather awkward proximity to Sir Robert Peel, seldom more than two members between them. Dizzy never allowed his head to be affected by his worldly success or position; but he was now playing an important part in the political drama, and his speech no less than his costume had to be in accordance with his new rôle. His oddities of dress were abandoned; the rings and ruffles and coloured waistcoats disappeared, giving way to "customary suits of solemn black." His tone of speech altered; frivolity vanished with his frills; and henceforth even his humour was liable to be a little heavy. He was clearly thinking of himself when he wrote in *Endymion*: "There is a tone of levity about him which is unfortunate. Men destined to the highest places should beware of badinage . . . an insular country subject to fogs, and with a powerful middle class, requires grave statesmen." The country party which he represented also required grave landowners to speak for them, and he decided to buy an estate. It was not easy. Already his wife had paid £13,000 towards the liquidation of his debts, and was prepared to pay as much again. But his father was anxious to see him as a Buckinghamshire squire, and put up £10,000 towards the purchase of Hughenden Manor, near Bradenham and High Wycombe. It was some time before the place became his, because another £25,000 was required to complete the purchase; but the Bentincks advanced the necessary balance, and in September '48 he was able to announce to his wife "It is all done, and you are the Lady of Hughenden." The estate consisted of some 750 acres, which Disraeli increased to 1400 before his death.

There was yet another position he coveted, and that too was to be his in the General Election of '47, which resulted in a continuance of Russell's ministry, but only with the support of the Peelites. At this election Disraeli was returned unopposed for the county of Buckingham, which he continued to represent for the remainder of his career in the House of Commons. He had come to the conclusion that free-trade must be given a fair trial, and all his future efforts were confined to the improvement of agricultural conditions by tax-reduction. His method of imparting this conclusion to his new constituents was typical: "You are in the position of a man who has made an improvident marriage. You have become united to Free Trade, and nothing can divorce you except you can prove the charmer to be false. Wait, then, till that period has arrived; when you find that you have been betrayed, then will be the time to seek a divorce from that pernicious union." He hoped the time would come when every commodity from her colonies would enter England free, and foreign produce alone would be taxed. Had the election been postponed till the autumn of '47, the free-traders might have been swept out of office by the financial panic, due to railway speculation, which resulted in the bankruptcy of many leading firms throughout the country. The Government had been advised by Bentinck and Thomas Baring to suspend the Bank Charter Act which limited the issue of banknotes; but it was not until much havoc had been done, and the Governor of the Bank of England had warned Russell that the position was desperate, that the Government licensed the Bank to issue the necessary credits, and the panic instantly ceased. Disraeli provided an apt analogy in his speech criticising the Government's delay:

I scarcely know to what to compare their conduct, except something that occurs in a delightful city of the South . . . There an annual ceremony takes place, when the whole population are found in a state of the greatest alarm and sorrow. A procession moves through the streets, in which the blood of a saint is carried in a consecrated vase. The people throng around the vase, and there is a great pressure—as there was in London at the time to which I am alluding. This pressure in time becomes a panic—just as it did in London. It is curious that in both cases the cause is the same: it is a cause of congealed circulation. Just at the moment when unutterable gloom overspreads the population, when nothing but despair and consternation prevail, the Chancellor of the Exchequer—I beg pardon, the Archbishop of Tarento—announces the liquefaction of St Januarius's blood, as the Chancellor of the Exchequer announced the issue of a Government letter; in both instances, a wholesome state of currency returns; the people resume their gaiety and cheerfulness, the panic and the pressure disappear, everybody returns to music and macaroni—as in London everybody returned to business; and in both cases the remedy is equally efficient and equally a hoax.

Both Bentinck and Disraeli became very unpopular with their followers at the close of '47, because they supported Russell's motion for the removal of the civil and political disabilities under which the Jews laboured. What brought this up was the election of Baron Lionel de Rothschild, head of the famous financial house, to represent the City of London in parliament. Rothschild would not take the oath "on the true faith of a Christian", but the Tory party as a whole considered that no one should sit in parliament who did not accept the divinity of Christ. Bentinck simply believed in toleration for all religions, and supported Russell's motion for that reason. But Disraeli's support was founded on his conception of the Jews as the spiritual predecessors of Christianity. He said that the doctrines of Jesus were the completion, not the change, of Judaism; that Jesus, the Apostles, the Evangelists, and all the early Christians, were Jews; that "the infallible throne of Rome" was established by a Jew; that the Jews, as the guardians of religious revelation, were a highly privileged race; and that England would not be a Christian country if it had not been for a Jew. "Where is your Christianity if you do not believe in their Judaism?" he asked the House. His speech was constantly interrupted, and he became a little heated, telling his party that it was "influenced by the darkest superstitions of the darkest ages that ever existed in this country", and closing with the statement: "Yes, it is as a Christian that I will not take upon me the awful responsibility of excluding from the legislature those who are of the religion in the bosom of which my Lord and Saviour was born." For the first time since he first rose in the House, his speech was received without a sign of approval, and the whole of their party voted against Bentinck and Disraeli on this question. Russell's motion was carried in the Commons but defeated in the Lords, and the controversy lasted until 1858, each Bill brought forward by Russell being supported by Disraeli, approved by the Commons and rejected by the Lords. At length, under Disraeli's leadership, a measure was passed giving each House the power to alter its own form of oath, and soon after that Jews were enabled to sit in the Commons without swearing as Christians.

Disraeli's attitude from the first was consistent and plucky. He had everything to lose by voting against his own side, and his opinions concerning the historical mission of the Jews were not shared by another member of the House. His leader in the Lords, Stanley, was in the opposite camp and was largely instrumental in getting the Bills rejected. Except Bentinck, all his important colleagues, whom he had done so much to conciliate, and all the country gentlemen, whose mouthpiece he had become, were violently opposed to the alteration of the oath. Yet at regular intervals for ten years his honesty compelled him to irritate and antagonise the very people on whose support he counted for the furtherance of his ambition; and knowing that the politics of Rothschild and the other leading Jews were not his, he was well aware that the removal of the disqualification would merely increase the votes against his party. But, as he told his constituents, "Independence is the necessary, the essential element of my political position . . . I cannot take a seat in the House of Commons if I am not the master of my political destiny."

His courage was further attested by the appearance of a novel called *Tancred* in the spring of '47. It was the final instalment of the trilogy which dealt, first with politics in *Coningsby*, next with social conditions in *Sybil*, and now with religion in *Tancred*. He probably intended to show the spiritual value of the Church of England in the fabric of the constitution; but a glance at the Christian hierarchy did not give him a feeling that salvation lay in the West, one eminent churchman being thus designated: "The bishop, always ready, had in the course of his episcopal career placed himself at the head of every movement in the Church which others had originated, and had as regularly withdrawn at the right moment, when the heat was over, or had become, on the contrary, excessive." Also the attitude of the clergy to their Roman Catholic neighbours proved that they were in need of enlightenment: "It was then an established doctrine that all that was necessary for Ireland was more Protestantism, and it was supposed to be not more difficult to supply the Irish with Protestantism than it had proved, in the instance of a recent famine, to furnish them with potatoes. What was principally wanted in both cases were subscriptions." In short the West had surrendered to the gospel of materialism: "The European talks of progress, because, by an ingenious application of some scientific acquirements, he has established a society which has mistaken comfort for civilisation." Tancred, therefore, goes to the cradle of the creeds in search of a fresh revelation, and in the East he discovers, what his creator already believes, that Christianity is the inevitable development of Judaism, and that the English owe their emergence from barbarism to Syrian inspiration, which had provided them with everything, from the Saviour to the Sabbath, from the Decalogue to the Atonement, a conclusion that comforted Disraeli but did not appeal to the Tory party. In effect the novel is a sermon against materialism, and suggests that the author was passing through a phase of aversion from politics and avidity for mysticism. He was always conscious of his intellectual superiority to the men about him, though he could not help admiring many of their less aesthetic qualities. The book reflects Disraeli's pride in his Jewish origin and his desire to lead a modern crusade. Europe, he thinks, is miserable because it has lost belief in God, and he pictures its inhabitants as weary, cynical, disillusioned and irreligious; which is rather as we see ourselves nowadays, not as we see the Victorians, whose age appears relatively stable, enthusiastic, energetic and credulous. But it is the mark of a civilised people that they have a poor opinion of themselves.

In the Holy Land our hero meets Eva, the daughter of a banker, and she represents the genius of Judaism. Tancred says that her race must come to the rescue of unhappy Europe: "Send forth a great thought, as you have done before, from Mount Sinai, from the villages of Galilee, from the deserts of Arabia, and you may again remodel all their institutions, change their principles of action, and breathe a new spirit into the whole scope of their existence." Eva objects: "No, no, it is impossible. Europe is too proud, with its new command over nature, to listen even to prophets. Levelling mountains, riding without horses, sailing without winds, how can these men believe that there is any power, human or divine, superior to themselves?" But Tancred assures her that "Europe is not happy. Amid its false excitement, its bustling invention, and its endless toil, a profound melancholy broods over its spirit and gnaws at its heart. In vain they baptise their tumult by the name of progress; the whisper of a demon is ever asking them 'Progress, from whence to what?' . . . Europe, that quarter of the globe to which God has never spoken, Europe is without consolation."

Though Tancred finds a female in Palestine, he fails to find a faith; and as his creator is unable to conceive how such a quest can fruitfully end, he brings the curtain down when Tancred's mother and father arrive in Jerusalem to fetch him home. We may be grateful to Disraeli for not discovering a new creed for the modern world; but filial obedience seems rather a puerile substitute for his Messianic dreams. Nevertheless the author preferred it to all his other novels, and he once said that he re-read it whenever he wanted to refresh his knowledge of the East. It did not sell as well as its two predecessors, and it must have done him considerable harm with the orthodox folk whom he most wished to propitiate. Indeed his whole career was a long fight to cover up his indiscretions, which something in his nature incited him to go on committing. His candid speeches in parliament on Jews and Christians, together with *Tancred*, mainly account for the difficulties he was about to encounter.

Near the end of his life Disraeli said to a Jewish boy who had been presented to him: "You and I belong to a race which can do everything but fail." He believed in the paramount importance of race. "Progress and reaction are but words to mystify the millions", he wrote. "They mean nothing, they are nothing, they are phrases and not facts. All is race. In the structure, the decay, and the development of the various families of man, the vicissitudes of history find their main solution." This doctrine was opposed to such tenets as the equality of man, which, he asserted, had destroyed ancient society without creating a satisfactory substitute. Men were only equal in relation to their Creator; all other equality was absurd; but faith was essential; and spiritual, not material, values were all that mattered. Such was his creed, and it explains his belief in an aristocracy that should lead, guide and enlighten, soften vulgar prejudices and encounter popular passions. But his doctrine does not take account of individual genius, which, in literature and action, has had more effect on the world than race; and it does not do justice to his own remarkable achievement, which was as unique as himself, and due to the peculiarities of his nature, not to his racial characteristics. It is true that his origin was against him, true also that his chief racial quality, patience, was in his favour; but what ultimately made him leader of a party whose components were radically antipathetic to his derivation, his manners, his mentality, his habits, his personal appearance, and indeed everything about him, was the compelling force of his personality; in a word, his genius.

When Lord George Bentinck spoke and voted for the abrogation of Jewish disabilities, he was told that his attitude displeased his supporters, and, with a sigh of relief, he retired from the nominal leadership of the party in the Commons, having undermined his constitution and shortened his life by the immense labour of the previous two years. There was no one to take his place except Disraeli; but Stanley, the real leader of the party, distrusted him, and, according to Greville, the rest of the party detested him. Apparently there had been no personal relationship between himself and Stanley, and in the recent election he had stated that, though he respected their leader in the Upper

House, he would not "pin his faith and his political creed to the robe of any senator, however exalted." The ticklish question Stanley had to decide was whether he could ask Disraeli, without offending him, to give his full support to someone the party would accept, however inferior in capability to himself. All the able tories who had occupied governmental posts were Peelites; there were scarcely half a dozen protectionists fit to take Bentinck's place, and none of them was anxious to do so. Apart from the general suspicion aroused by Dizzy's foreign and mysterious manner, his attitude to the Jewish claims even more than Bentinck's had irritated their followers, and the editor of *The Morning Herald*, Samuel Phillips, had started a campaign against him, which annoyed Bentinck so much that he wrote to Stanley on February 9th '48, the day before the party met to elect a new leader, criticising him severely for taking any notice of Phillips and saying that "none of all this could have happened, had you played a generous part." Bentinck also told J. W. Croker that Disraeli, in spite of Stanley, Phillips and the rest, would be the chosen leader of the party before two sessions were out. "He cuts Cobden to ribbons; and Cobden writhes and quails under him just as Peel did in 1846."

When parliament reassembled the party had no leader, but that did not prevent Disraeli from continuing his attacks on the Manchester school of economics, with its reiterated belief in certain abstract qualities not wholly unfamiliar to us at the present time: "Competition is always at the head of the list; then follow, you may be sure, energy and enterprise. These remedies are not facts—they are only phrases. What is this competition, of whose divine influence we hear so much? Define it, tell us its sex and character. Is it a demigod or a nymph? It inspires all their solutions of economical difficulties. Is the shipping interest in decay? Competition will renovate it. Are the Colonies in despair? Energy will save them. Is the agricultural interest in danger? Enterprise is the panacea." The commercial principle now ruled the country, he added, "but you may rest assured that, if you convert the senate into a counting-house, it will not be long before the nation degenerates into a factory." Throughout '48 he led the party in all but name, his contributions to the debates being incomparably the best from whichever side of the House, and Stanley could no longer ignore his pre-eminence, asking him to make a speech at the close of the session summarising the ministerial failures. This he did with great success, and he afterwards declared that it had made him the leader of the party; but much intrigue was to take place, and considerable vacillation was to be exhibited by Stanley, before he was acknowledged as such.

With the rising of parliament Bentinck went to his father's home, Welbeck Abbey. On September 21st he started to walk through the woods to Thoresby, about five miles distant, where he was going to stay for two days with Lord Manvers. He did not arrive; a search was made; and he was found, lying on his face, about a mile from the Abbey. His heart, strained by overwork, had failed, and he had been dead some hours. "It is the greatest sorrow I have ever experienced", wrote Disraeli to Bentinck's brother. "A peculiar and unparalleled spirit has departed: at all times a loss; in an age of degeneracy, an irreparable one . . . I can neither offer, nor receive, consolation." This tragedy quickened the efforts of Disraeli's adherents to establish him as leader of the party in the Commons; and incidentally sharpened Disraeli's own efforts, for he made friendly advances to Phillips of *The Morning Herald* and spent some weeks in London cautiously canvassing influential people. But Stanley remained hostile to the project. It was generally agreed that no one but Disraeli had the ability to captain the side, and as generally agreed that he could not be trusted to do it. No one was able to give a reason for the want of confidence; yet, apparently, nearly everyone thought that confidence was wanting. It was of course the perennial distrust of genius by mediocrity, strongly felt, inarticulately expressed, the one fixed emotion in a fluid organism.

At last Stanley mustered up the courage to write Disraeli a long letter, which, shorn of its rigmarole and its compliments, stated that his appointment to the post of leader would not meet "with a general and cheerful approval" and asked whether he would support someone "of abilities inferior to your own, who might command a more general feeling in his favour." But Disraeli was not the man to serve under a nonentity, and made it clear in his reply that he was "no longer disposed to sacrifice interesting pursuits, health, and a happy hearth, for a political career which can bring one little fame", and that he could do the cause more good "by acting alone and unshackled, than if I fell into the party discipline which you intimate." He was in fact thoroughly disgusted and depressed by Stanley's letter, telling a friend that "the summit of Heaven's bliss was to be possessed of £300 a year, and live a retired life amongst books." Stanley was perturbed by the line Disraeli had taken, and wrote again begging him to reconsider the question, and even implying that he was in the running for the leadership.

Meanwhile a group of Disraeli's friends petitioned and interviewed Stanley, and, following his spasm of distaste for politics, or rather politicians, Disraeli himself pulled as many wires as he could without showing his hand. "I am not a candidate for the leadership", he informed Lord John Manners, "tho' I am prepared to undertake the task at the unequivocal desire of the party." His opponents were powerful, including the party Whips, and his existence was ignored by the leading organ of Toryism, *The Quarterly Review*, run by Murray and Croker, both of whom had a personal grudge against him. But the persistence of his friends had some effect on Stanley, who at length proposed that the leadership should be a triumvirate: Disraeli, Lord Granby, and a one-time Chancellor of the Exchequer and War Secretary named J. C. Herries. Without actually approving the plan, Disraeli temporarily fell in with it, knowing quite well what would happen. The government of three lasted for three weeks, and on February 22nd '49 Disraeli wrote to his sister: "After much struggling, I am fairly the leader." One is reminded of another triumvirate, which consisted of the abbé Sieyès, Roger Ducos, and Napoleon Bonaparte; but Sieyès and Ducos had a longer innings than Granby and Herries.

Chapter XIV

AT HOME

THE soul hankers after what the mind knows to be futile. Disraeli was only quite happy at home with his wife; yet, such was the necessity of his nature, he would not have been happy at home if he had not been busy in the world. In the early days of his leadership he wrote to Lady Londonderry that he was absorbed in the strange profession of his choice, and that though he wondered how a man could embark on such a career of sacrifice, with its ceaseless worries and labours, he was quite unable to give it up. He was devoted to his family, but his father, his sister and his wife meant less to him than his ambition.

Like so many people who are not wholly indigenous, Disraeli was fonder of England and the English way of life than were the natives of the island. His letters display a keen appreciation of the scenery and the great country-houses, though the average Englishman may have felt that his estimates were expressed too ornately. "Good-bye, my dear Lord", he once said after a visit to Lord Shaftesbury. "You have given me the privilege of seeing one of the most impressive of all spectacles: a great English nobleman living in patriarchal state in his own hereditary halls", a remark that conjures up the Caliph of Bagdad rather than Sir Roger de Coverley. He was on pleasant terms with the farmers, publicans and rustics in his own neighbourhood, and though they were inclined to treat him with jocularity, especially at political meetings, they were proud of him.

His opponents seldom missed an opportunity of heckling him. At Aylesbury his radical antagonist, a man of notoriously profligate life, produced Disraeli's own radical manifesto of some years before and asked him what he had to say about it. "I say that we all sow our wild oats", replied Dizzy, "and no one knows the meaning of that phrase better than you." In delivering a speech he invariably began slowly and quietly. "Speak up! I can't hear you", shouted someone at a Newport Pagnell meeting in December '49. Back came the answer: "Truth travels slowly, but it will reach even you in time." The landlord of the Greyhound at Aylesbury, Joe Ivens, had another complaint. "Speak quick", he called out. "It is very easy for you to speak quick, when you only utter stupid monosyllables", returned Disraeli, "but when I speak I must measure my words. I have to open your great thick head. What I say is to enlighten you. If I bawled like you, you would leave this place as great a fool as you entered it." Needless to say, he was on excellent terms with Mr Ivens. Sometimes the political hostility took more personal forms. During a dinner at the George, Aylesbury, an elector informed the assembly that Disraeli's wife had picked him out of the gutter. "My good fellow", drawled Dizzy, "if you were in the gutter nobody would pick *you* out." But as a rule the people were so anxious to hear him that they shouted down the interrupters, and once, at Newport Pagnell, the crowd, standing in the yard of the inn outside the room, broke every pane of glass in order to listen to his speech. He promptly thanked them for giving him a larger audience and thenceforth addressed himself both to those in the room and to those outside. His wife often attended his meetings, and when a friend expressed indignation at certain offensive sallies to which Dizzy had been subjected she said "Oh, it's nothing; *he* doesn't care; he's a match for them all."

On the subject of his wife no one was allowed to joke except himself, and he sparingly indulged the luxury. "She is an excellent creature, but she never can remember which came first, the Greeks or the Romans", he said. Her quaint remarks about him were much relished in social circles. This for instance: "Dizzy has the most wonderful moral courage, but no physical courage. When he has his shower-bath, I always have to pull the string." She was fairly generally regarded as a figure of fun; but not by her husband, who listened to her drollest comments with an air of gravity, compelled everyone by his manner to treat her views with respect, and constantly brought her into conversations where she seemed out of her depth by tactfully quoting what she had said on this or that point and requesting her opinion on the subject under discussion.

He was more than ever dependent on her when his parents died and the Bradenham home was broken up. His mother, of whom he appears to have been fond, had little effect on his life, and her only recorded comment on his career was made about a month before her death, when she confessed that a speech of his in the Commons was equal to anything of Pitt's. She died, at the age of 71, on April 21st, 1847. His father, whom he loved and admired, was blind during the last eight years of his life, but bore his fate with cheerfulness and with the help of his daughter Sarah contrived to finish a long book on English literature and to revise his work on the Life and Times of Charles I. He died on January 19th, 1848, nine months after his wife, at the age of 82. Disraeli once informed his constituents that he would not exchange his father for any duke alive or dead, and in a Memoir which he wrote for a new edition of Isaac's *Curiosities of Literature* his pride in the old man is manifest. The library of 25,000 volumes which his father had collected was mostly sold, but Benjamin transferred a number to Hughenden. The family were scattered, Sarah eventually settling down at Twickenham. We hear little of Benjamin's two brothers, and it is clear that he exhausted the genius of the family as well as the interest of his father; but he was able to do something for both of them, Ralph getting a clerkship in Chancery at £400 a year and then becoming clerk-assistant in the House of Lords, James, after an attempt to farm lands at Bradenham, obtaining a small post in the Treasury and ultimately a commissionership of Inland Revenue.

Disraeli's home life was almost restricted to Hughenden. When in London he was always busy or dining in with a number of guests or dining out as one of a number. The house in Park Lane appears to have been decorated in what we would now consider faultless bad taste. The vestibule leading to the drawing-room was enclosed in the form of a Persian tent with hangings of rose-coloured silk, and the drawing-room itself was crowded with bric-à-brac, ornamented in gilt, the walls draped in places and covered elsewhere with oriental curiosities. But at Hughenden a more Victorian note prevailed, so that visitors did not seem to be stepping straight from an English park into an Egyptian bazaar. One asiatic touch was provided by the peacocks on the terrace. "My dear lady, you cannot have terraces without peacocks", said Dizzy to a guest; and certainly he could not. Perhaps the only other hint of the East came from the host himself, whose clothes were not those of a typical British squire.

The fancy waistcoats that had been abandoned in London reappeared in the country, looking even more remarkable by contrast with a black velveteen jacket and a Tyrolese hat. A rumour reached his friend Beresford in December 1850 that he was growing a fierce pair of moustaches. "Now this is very sad", wrote Beresford to Stanley, "for he is not the person who ought to attract attention by *outré* dress and appearance, but by his talents. I do trust that this style is only assumed while he is rusticating . . ." Apparently it was.

In spite of his oddities, or because of them, his tenants and workmen liked him, and he attended to their wants. He enjoyed talking to them, finding their conversation racy, their manners restful and agreeable. He particularly liked the society of woodmen, whose knowledge, speech, quick observation and common sense appealed strongly to him, so different from the humbug, stupidity and pretentiousness of politicians. "Nature whispers to them many of her secrets", he noted. "A forest is like an ocean, monotonous only to the ignorant. It is a life of ceaseless variety." He admired the way in which his head-woodman felled a tree; it was all done as easily as falling off one; "no bustle, no exertion, apparently not the slightest exercise of strength."

He loved his trees and was constantly planting new ones, especially cedars, firs and pines: "I have a passion for books and trees. I like to look at them. When I come down to Hughenden I pass the first week in sauntering about my park and examining all the trees, and then I saunter in the library and survey the books. My collection is limited to Theology, the Classics, and History." He had a favourite beech walk at the bottom of his garden, and what he called a German Forest up the hill behind the house, through which paths were cut and rustic benches placed where he could enjoy the views. There were trees wherever he looked, and the woods of Wycombe Abbey could be seen from his terrace. "I am not surprised that the ancients worshipped trees", he said. "Lakes and mountains, however glorious for a time, in time weary; sylvan scenery never palls." And in his will he stated that the trees of the estate were not to be cut down. Largely because Queen Victoria sent a wreath of primroses for his grave with the inscription "His favourite flowers", they became associated with his name, and his political opponents, such as Gladstone, were scornful of the notion that such an orchidaceous personality should have loved a simple English plant, recalling that in his novel *Lothair* one of the characters remarks "They say primroses make a capital salad." But apart from the fact that a capital salad would add to one's liking of its ingredients, we have the evidence of Disraeli's land-agent that the woodmen at Hughenden had special orders to protect primroses, large numbers of which were cultivated all over the estate. This of course does not rule out the possibility that he liked lilies, which Gladstone seemed to think were more expressive of his nature. The truth is that he loved the country and everything in it, and would have liked to live there, as he said, from the first note of the nightingale till the first note of the muffin-bell.

The church was in his grounds, and he was a regular attendant as well as a constant communicant. In those days it was considered wicked to travel on Sundays, and when, soon after his arrival at Hughenden, Disraeli had to leave for London at the conclusion of a morning service, the vicar admonished him for breaking the Fourth Commandment. He replied that urgent and important public affairs had necessitated a journey causing him great personal annoyance and inconvenience, and that the vicar had acted intemperately, precipitately and indelicately. The vicar did not stay there for long, and Disraeli appointed a new and more harmonious one, who recognised that the Sabbath was made for man.

The Disraelis did a certain amount of entertaining at Hughenden, but the older he grew the less pleasure he derived from the social give-and-take. He was Deputy-Lieutenant of his county from 1845, and as such had to receive a number of guests he would otherwise have avoided. His feeling about these functions appeared in a letter to his sister, in which he gave a list of the dukes and lords present at a county dinner in Sussex, adding "The best guests, however, were turtle, whitebait, venison, and burgundy." As leader of the Opposition he was a regular visitor at all the big tory houses, Belvoir, Welbeck, Wimpole, Burghley, Hatfield, etc. "We live in the state rooms, brilliantly illuminated at night", he wrote from Belvoir in January '50. "A military band plays while we are at dinner, and occasionally throughout the evening. Dinner is announced to the air of 'The Roast Beef of Old England' . . . Almost all the gentlemen being members of the famous Belvoir hunt . . . wear scarlet coats in the evening, which adds greatly to the gaiety and brilliancy of the scene." He adored instrumental music, but did not care for singing. A little later he was enjoying the wonders of Burghley, with its fantastic exterior, vast park, gigantic oaks, and "the history of England in the golden presents from every sovereign, from Elizabeth and James I to Victoria and Albert." There were "great battues every day; five hundred head slaughtered as a matter of course."

Then he had to attend the annual banquets of the Royal Academy; but as a political figure of consequence in 1850 "they took me out of the wits, among whom I sat last year, and which were represented this by Rogers, Hallam, Milman, Thackeray, Lockhart, and placed me among the statesmen. I sat within two of Peel, and between Gladstone and Sidney Herbert. A leader of Opposition, who has no rank, is so rare, if not unprecedented an animal, that the R.A.s were puzzled how to place me; and though they seem to have made somewhat of a blunder, it went off very well, Gladstone being particularly agreeable." He had to be present, too, at ambassadorial receptions, and we are reminded of certain episodes in Dickens's novel *Martin Chuzzlewit* by his report of the first assembly given by Mrs Abbot Lawrence, wife of the American Minister: "There were a good many Americans, among them the Peabody family—great people. As Mrs Lawrence says, 'the Peabodys are the Howards of America.' The chief Peabody was presented to me, and he remarked of the Duke of Wellington who was near, 'The two hemispheres can't show a man like that, sir'."

The sudden surges of eloquence which amazed people who met him before he became a power in politics were scarcely ever heard now. He had fixed on the character he was henceforth to assume in public, and always appeared calm, dignified, mysterious, solemn, only his dark flashing eyes giving life to his face, his talk being measured, grave, epigrammatic, and delivered in a deep equable tone. Such remarks as these, spoken in an oracular manner, seemed perhaps more significant than they were:

"All the great things have been done by the little nations."

"Reaction is the law of society; it is inevitable. All success depends upon seizing it."

"I do not believe in national regeneration in the shape of a foreign loan."

"Passion is the ship, and reason is the rudder."

"Depend upon it, when a man or a phrase is much abused, there is something in both."

"A man can only be content when his career is in harmony with his organisation."

"What we want is to discover the character of a man at his birth, and found his education upon his nature."

Disraeli's temperament was theatrical, but it was that of an impresario, not an actor: he did not care about making a hundred different effects; he wanted to make a single definite effect. It was broadly the difference between the man of affairs and the man of ideas, the organiser and the artist. But what makes him an exceptionally interesting figure is that, though well aware that action was his true *métier*, he had a strong predilection for art, and knew intuitively that the poet was more important than the politician, a perception that places him spiritually above the other leading statesmen of our history. He was also gifted with more imagination than the rest, an imagination that found admirable expression in occasional sentences and sometimes in more extended passages. Many of his apothegms are first-rate, and he was a master of picturesque and pithy phrases. Some years before they were forced into association, he described Stanley as "the Prince Rupert of parliamentary discussion; his charge is resistless; but when he returns from the pursuit he always finds his camp in the possession of the enemy." Stanley was thereafter known as "the Rupert of debate." Again, when someone complained of the bitter invective in Dizzy's attacks on Sir Robert Peel, he replied in a speech at High Wycombe during the 1847 election that "Revolutions are not made with rose-water", which immediately became a familiar quotation. Both these remarks were appropriated by Bulwer Lytton, who is still given the credit for the second in *The Oxford Dictionary of Quotations*.

But Disraeli, who by the way pronounced his name Disreli, was not imaginative enough to idle for more than a week. He could not

> Under the shade of melancholy boughs,
> Lose and neglect the creeping hours of time.

When resting from one kind of work, he occupied himself with another; and he did not really relax even at Hughenden. If not writing letters, he was writing something else; and in the autumn of 1850 he began a Life of Lord George Bentinck. For a man in his position it was a big undertaking, and he anticipated "enormous labour, which nothing but solitude, study, and abstinence can beat down, if indeed they can." But the Bentinck family said that he alone could and must do it, and the Duke of Portland sent him two huge chests of papers. "I am getting on pretty well with my work", he wrote after some six weeks of it, "though tired of this life of everlasting labour." He was able to deal fairly freely with the great Corn Law debates, because Peel had fallen from his horse that summer on Constitution Hill and had died within four days; and as the book dealt with "every topic of present interest in the political world", he was well abreast of his subject; but progress was slow, and, as he put it, "the pen often pauses to think." After the parliamentary session of '51 he returned to his labours, and in November of that year, though the weather was delightful, he stuck to his job: "From seven to two o'clock Hughenden looks like summer, but when I get out the owls are stirring." On December 7th he was able to report "I finished the last line of the last chapter last night, and never in my life felt more relieved, not having had a moment's ease the whole autumn."

The chief criticism to be made of the book is that it is not primarily a biography, but a history. The author had once written in *Contarini Fleming*: "Read no history, nothing but biography, for that is life without theory"; and it is a pity he did not heed his own advice. To those who are interested in human beings, the story of humanity is tedious and depressing, because repetitive. Individuals vary; humanity is always the same. The only thing that brings old movements, far-off politics and battles long ago to life is the participation in them of a remarkable personality; and in this case the vivifying personality was Disraeli, who could not very well exhibit himself in the biography of someone else. Even so, Bentinck was sufficiently out of the common to make his portrait worth painting; but his biographer was too much concerned over the events to give us the man, and his work, though it sold well enough at the time, would now appeal only to a historian. Disraeli described his undertaking as "a mournful office, like commemorating the exploits of the Grand Army at St Helena." That was his error; he should have summarised the exploits and concentrated on the hero.

The book's main interest for us is the proof it gives of the author's courageous attitude to current affairs and his indifference to the prejudices of the time. There is a chapter to the glory of Judaism, his praise of which had already harmed him greatly with his party; and nothing could have irritated the sentiment of the age so effectually as his statement "The movement of the middle classes for the abolition of slavery was virtuous, but it was not wise", which was followed by this declaration: "The history of the abolition of slavery by the English and its consequences, would be a narrative of ignorance, injustice, blundering, waste, and havoc, not easily paralleled in the history of mankind."

As, further, it almost ignores Stanley's contributions to the cause for which Bentinck fought, the biography was another of those obstacles which the tireless Dizzy placed in his own path to power.

Chapter XV

IN AND OUT

WE must telescope the years. From 1846 to 1851 Disraeli's job as leader of the Opposition was mainly the twofold one of making his party, and especially his chief in the Lords, take a practical view of the free-trade question, and of criticising the whig foreign policy under Palmerston. The first was the more difficult of the two. The country as a whole accepted Free-Trade as a social and political panacea, and as every business except that of agriculture was thriving Disraeli did not wish his party to waste its energies in trying to force the unpopular doctrine of Protection on the electorate, his object being to benefit the farmers by reducing taxation on land and other local burdens. His relations with Stanley remained uneasy, because the latter was an uncompromising protectionist and criticised every attempt to adapt his principles to the exigency of the situation. Disraeli was wonderfully patient, making the protectionists move inch by inch towards his common sense view that "we cannot pretend to disturb *un fait accompli*", and keeping the question of rural distress constantly before the House. But if he had not been by general consent the brains of the party and their only possible leader in the Commons, he could never have made them see reason. "They are evidently much more afraid of losing me, than I them", he told his wife; and being convinced that "Protection is not only dead but damned", he addressed himself to the conversion of his followers with tact, skill and persistence. It took some years, but at last he was able to claim: "By a series of motions to relieve the Agricultural Interest . . . I withdrew the Tory party gradually from the hopeless question of Protection, rallied all those members who were connected either personally or by their constituencies with the land, and finally brought the state of parties in the House of Commons nearly to a tie."

Meanwhile, he was keeping an eye on Palmerston, whose successful attempts to maintain England's power and prestige on the continent were accompanied by a dangerous policy of sympathising with movements of disruptive tendencies, until Disraeli declared that Great Britain was generally recognised as the handmaid and colleague of the discontented in every country. Palmerston had been War Secretary under various Prime Ministers for some twenty years, and Foreign Secretary for about ten, before his reappearance in the latter office under Russell in 1846. He was a man of great personal charm and exceptional ability, perhaps the only member of the House whose brain Disraeli respected. There is an admiring portrait of him as 'Lord Roehampton' in *Endymion*, from which we learn that he was tall and had a stately presence, a musical voice, an impressive countenance and an Olympian brow: "The lower part of the face indicated, not feebleness but flexibility, and his mouth was somewhat sensuous. His manner was at once winning, natural, and singularly unaffected, and seemed to sympathise entirely with those whom he addressed." All the ladies admired him, we are told, and he admired all the ladies. He was something of a Don Juan, an aspect suggested in the novel by his comment on the remark "I cannot imagine a position more unfortunate than that of an exiled prince", to which he replies: "I can. To have the feelings of youth and the frame of age." He was destined to prevent the realisation of Disraeli's ambition for many years; and once a youthful enthusiast, who had taken much trouble to collect evidence of a furtive love-affair in which Palmerston had been engaged, placed it before Disraeli with the suggestion that its publication would discredit Palmerston in a coming election. "Palmerston is now seventy," said Disraeli. "If he could provide evidence of his potency in his electoral address, he'd sweep the country." In fact Palmerston brought more than a whiff of the eighteenth century into the nineteenth, and if he had not been so much of a John Bull he would have been out of place in the England of Victoria and Albert. But his policy of safeguarding Britons in remote lands, and of advising other countries to model their institutions on those of Great Britain, made him extremely popular with the middle classes at home. Unfortunately he went further, and threatened despotic governments with his support of subversive elements if they did not mend their ways. One cannot say to what extent his attitude influenced the outbreak of revolution throughout Europe in 1848, but there is little doubt that the revolutionists were encouraged by his sympathy with insurrection, and no doubt at all that they were assured of a safe asylum in England if their actions miscarried.

Thrones began to topple early in '48. The first to suffer was Disraeli's friend, Louis Philippe, who with his Queen found sanctuary in England. Disraeli went to see the fallen monarch at Claremont, and after talking without pause for an hour Louis went into hysterics, greatly to his visitor's distress. Austria and Prussia followed France, and Disraeli had some long and interesting talks with Metternich, temporarily exiled on Richmond Green. It was not Palmerston's fault that Spain did not follow suit, since he lectured the Queen, through the British ambassador, on the advantages of a constitutional monarchy. The Pope also aroused hostile comment in the House of Commons, upon which Disraeli remarked that he had less fear of seeing red stockings in England than blue. He also perceived that all the "dreamy and dangerous nonsense" talked by German nationalists was an excuse for Prussian predominance, and he prophesied that the German desire to take Schleswig would result in a maritime power rivalling England's in the North Sea. He never ceased to criticise Palmerston's policy of encouraging the rise of so-called nationalism under the pretext of liberal and progressive idealism:

> You could not find a country governed by an absolute form without telling it that the only way to be happy and prosperous was to have a House of Lords and a House of Commons, and an English treaty of commerce. All this ended in confusion. All that was practical you never obtained. You never obtained the treaty of commerce, but you fostered confusion and convulsion. By lending all the aid of a great country like England to some miserable faction, you created parties in domestic policy in every country, from Athens to Madrid, deteriorated the prosperity and condition of the people, and laid the seeds of infinite confusion. The noble lord opposite proceeded in this course—the great prophet of Liberalism in foreign affairs.

Disraeli was the first to recognise the existence and danger of the secret societies which covered Europe like net-work, and which, taking advantage of sudden uprushes of popular feeling, would end by destroying the social structure. "It is the manœuvres of these men", he wrote, "who are striking at property and Christ, which the good people of this country, who are so accumulative and so religious, recognise and applaud as the progress of the Liberal cause." It was generally thought that he had a bee in his bonnet on the subject of these societies, the existence of which was denied; but we can now see them as the seeds of a movement which, having found a formula, fused and festered into Communism. He described certain early manifestations of such destructive doctrines in action as "the system that commences with 'fraternity' and ends with assassination . . . the system that begins by preaching universal charity, and concludes by practising general spoliation."

But England was busy "shooting Niagara" and nothing could shake Palmerston's popularity, which reached a new peak after the Grecian affair in 1850. Several British subjects who had grounds for complaint against the Greek Government, their property having been expropriated or damaged, appealed to Palmerston, who promptly despatched a fleet to the Piraeus. The admiral in command seized some Greek vessels, and protests against these arbitrary proceedings were made by Russia and France. There was a debate in the House, and Palmerston spoke for five hours, closing with a sentence which rang like a clarion through the country: "As the Roman, in the days of old, held himself free from indignity, when he could say *Civis Romanus sum*, so also a British subject, in whatever land he may be, shall feel confident that the watchful eye and the strong arm of England will protect him against injustice and wrong." At heart Disraeli was in sympathy with this sentiment, and, not caring for the job of critic, made a feeble summary of the case for the Opposition. It annoyed him that a man who could speak so well for England on such occasions should do so much harm to Europe by fostering anarchy disguised as reform.

British patriotism took a new turn in the autumn of '50, when the Pope issued a Bull establishing a Romish hierarchy in England, Cardinal Wiseman being appointed Archbishop. Nowadays only a case of murder would arouse so much public excitement. The Prime Minister, Lord John Russell, whose party was losing ground, made a bid for popularity by denouncing Papal aggression. Instantly the Protestant feeling in the country manifested itself in meetings, memorials, pronouncements, appeals, accusations, and general hysteria. "Even the peasants think they are going to be burned alive and taken up to Smithfield instead of their pigs", wrote Disraeli, who, not caring to let his opponents reap all the benefit of the mass emotion, played the relatively safe game of reprobating the so-called Romish aggression, while criticising the Government's measures to meet it. Gradually the turmoil subsided, and by the time Russell brought in his Bill, which prohibited the adoption of territorial titles by Roman Catholics within the realm, and nullified bequests and donations made to them under such titles, members of parliament were beginning to perceive that the Prime Minister had acted too rashly. The greater part of the 1851 session was squandered on the measure, which, though passed, was never enforced, and about twenty years later was peacefully revoked.

While this agitation was in process the Government were defeated on a motion by a private member to extend the franchise, Disraeli and his party not voting, and Russell resigned. The Queen sent for Stanley. After an abortive attempt to set up a Coalition, Stanley said that he would try to form a Government out of his party. The Queen asked who would be leader in the Commons. Stanley mentioned Disraeli. "I do not approve of Mr Disraeli", said Her Majesty. "I do not approve of his conduct to Sir Robert Peel." Stanley replied: "Madam, Mr Disraeli has had to make his position, and men who make their positions will say and do things which are not necessary to be said or done by those for whom positions are provided." The Queen agreed, but added "All I can now hope is that, having attained this great position, he will be temperate. I accept Mr Disraeli on your guarantee." A meeting of all those to whom he was offering Cabinet posts took place at Stanley's house in St James's Square. But few had the courage to serve in a Government that recognised Protection as an open question. Gladstone said that the policy must be absolutely renounced, Lord Ellenborough and Sir Robert Inglis said the same. We have Disraeli's record of how a few others behaved: "Henry Corry had not absolutely fainted, but had turned very pale when the proposition was made to him of becoming a leading member of a Protectionist Government." J. W. Henley "sat on a chair against the dining-room wall . . . with the countenance of an ill-conditioned Poor Law Guardian censured for some act of harshness . . . no thought in the face, only ill-temper, perplexity, and perhaps astonishment." J. C. Herries "was garrulous, and foresaw only difficulties." At last Stanley gave it up and announced that he would tell the Queen he could not form a Government, upon which one of his disappointed supporters said "The best thing the Country party can do is to go into the country. There is not a woman in London who will not laugh at us."

Disraeli was deeply depressed by Stanley's failure, which was due to his insistence on Protection as a live issue, and begged him to relinquish a cause which was no longer considered practicable even by the agricultural classes. But Stanley was obdurate, and Disraeli gave up hope, writing to his sister "Yesterday our chief won the Oaks, a compensation for his other loss, or, as some think (not I), an omen of recovering it." Twice during the year '51 he toyed with the idea of retiring from the struggle; and his conviction that Protection was anathema to the country was strengthened by the enormous success of the Great Exhibition, which was opened by the Queen in Hyde Park on May 1st and was nothing less than a temple raised to the goddess Free-Trade. Even Victoria may have believed that Disraeli was becoming "temperate" when she read his description of the monstrous excrescence: "That enchanted pile which the sagacious taste and the prescient philanthropy of an accomplished and enlightened Prince have raised for the glory of England and the delight and instruction of two hemispheres." Two months after it was opened the chief apostle of Protection, Stanley, became the fourteenth Earl of Derby on the death of his father; and while Disraeli was telling his constituents that the protective system could never be brought back unless the nation as a whole desired it, the new Earl was asserting his opinion that a reimposition of duties on corn was desirable. Such conflicting views did not augur well for the Derby-Disraeli administration which was formed shortly after their utterance.

Until the last decade of his life Disraeli was always called an "adventurer" even by his own party. This was a compliment they were unconscious of paying, for it simply meant that he had been forced to fight his way to the top without birth or influence to help him, indeed with his own birth and every outside influence to hinder him. It was therefore fitting that he should owe his first office in the state to another "adventurer", whose birth however had been his only asset. Prince Louis Napoleon's *coup d'état* of December 2nd, 1851, was responsible for Lord Derby's first Government, though Disraeli had been working out a scheme whereby the colonies should be represented in the Imperial Parliament as a means of bringing the tories back to power. The secondary and direct cause of Derby's promotion was kindly supplied by Lord Palmerston, who had been up to his old tricks in showing sympathy with the Hungarian nationalist Kossuth, who had staged a revolt against Austria, and after his defeat had arrived in England. Palmerston capped this indiscretion by declaring his entire approval of Louis Napoleon's act. But now he had gone too far, public opinion being decidedly against the French President's seizure of power, and Russell dismissed him. The Whig Government were gravely weakened thereby and when a week or two later Palmerston moved an amendment to a Bill for the establishment of a local militia force, Disraeli supported him and the Government were defeated. Russell resigned, and again the Queen sent for Derby. More anxious to see a Tory Government in power than himself as leader of the House, Disraeli advised Derby to give the post of leader to Palmerston: "Don't let me be in your way . . . He would not like to serve under me, who he looks upon as a whippersnapper." It is an excellent example of Disraeli's prescience, for he felt certain that Palmerston's prestige in the country would keep them in office for years. He was also aware that he had yet to gain favour with the Court, that Palmerston's unpopularity in that circle would help to smooth his own way, and that his action would gain golden opinions from all and sundry. Derby was impressed, saying that he never would forget the generous self-sacrifice of such an offer, which "must ultimately redound to the credit and advantage of the man who makes it from public motives." This no doubt was Disraeli's view too.

An interview between Derby and Palmerston followed, and everything was going swimmingly until the latter stated flatly that he could belong to no government that contemplated the least change in the free-trade measures; whereat Derby stuck his toes in, the interview ended, and he drove straight to Disraeli's house in Park Lane. Would Disraeli be Chancellor of the Exchequer? The question had been raised before and Dizzy had pleaded ignorance of the work he would have to do. "You know as much as Mr Canning did", Derby had said. "They give you the figures." Now he accepted the post; which annoyed J. C. Herries, who coveted it and declined the Colonial Secretaryship out of pique; whereupon Disraeli offered to give it up, as he did not want it; but Derby would not let him, and asked "What am I to do for a Colonial Secretary?" Disraeli suggested Sir John Pakington for the job. Derby had already sent for Pakington to be under-secretary for Home Affairs, and he arrived at Disraeli's house while they were talking. It took Dizzy some time to convince Derby that Pakington would do for the Colonial Office; after which the latter was shown in, "elated with the impending destiny of becoming an under-secretary", reports Dizzy. But when Derby explained the situation, "Never shall I forget Pakington's countenance, as the exact state of affairs broke upon him: never did I witness such a remarkable mixture of astonishment and self-complacency." One wonders whether Disraeli remembered how his own Contarini Fleming had reacted under less inflating circumstances: "Often in reverie had I been an Alberoni, a Ripperda, a Richelieu; but never had I felt, when moulding the destinies of the wide globe, a tithe of the triumphant exaltation, which was afforded by the consciousness of the simple fact that I was an under-secretary of state." The new Chancellor of the Exchequer had every reason to feel like Contarini, but the closest onlooker would not have been aware of it.

Only three members of the new Government had held Cabinet rank before, and none of the others was even a Privy Councillor. "A dozen men, without the slightest experience of official life ... all in the act of genuflexion at the same moment ... humbled themselves before a female Sovereign, who looked serene and imperturbable before a spectacle never seen before ..." Such was Disraeli's description in *Endymion* of the swearing in of the new Privy Councillors, and he goes on to say that one of them, namely himself, "without any official experience whatever, was not only placed in the Cabinet, but was absolutely required to become the leader of the House of Commons, which had never occurred before, except in the instance of Mr Pitt in 1782." But Pitt had had the unique advantage of being the son of the great Earl of Chatham, and was half Disraeli's age when he became Chancellor of the Exchequer. It was a thrilling moment, in anticipation of which Dizzy had felt "just like a young girl going to her first ball", and the effect of which was to lay him low with "the horrors of a torpid fever", possibly accelerated by Derby's opening statement in the Lords that a duty ought to be placed on corn. Their disagreement on this subject was for a while to cause Disraeli more trouble than all the attacks of his opponents; but circumstances gradually forced Derby to drop Protection as an issue, though not his belief in it as a principle. It is well to repeat that at no time in his career had Disraeli accepted either Protection or Free-Trade as a principle, but only as an expedient, and it was no longer expedient to revive the former.

One of his jobs as leader of the House was to send summaries of the debates to the Queen, who at first read his letters with some surprise, for they were phrased in a far more personal manner than those she had received from his predecessors; but she soon got to like the free expression of his views, especially as the note of entire submission to herself was never absent. He soon made a favourable effect too on the Prince Consort, who had begun by thinking he was not a gentleman. "On Sunday I was two hours with the Prince", he informed his sister: "a very gracious and interesting audience. He has great abilities and wonderful knowledge—I think the best-educated man I ever met; most completely trained, and not over-educated for his intellect, which is energetic and lively."

The new Chancellor did not take his duties lightly. He worked so hard that he had no time for proper meals, and while preparing his budget he hardly slept. But he made up for this after the budget speech had been delivered by asking his followers to a banquet and attending those given by the other Cabinet Ministers: "in fact, never was a faction so feasted", he declared. In June '52 he said that he was up till three every morning and back in the House again at noon: "It cannot, I suppose, last very long—at least, if it do, I shall not." Parliament was dissolved on July 1st, and in the General Election that followed the tories increased their number, being the largest party in the House, though the combined Opposition of whigs, liberals, Irish and Peelites could beat them by thirty to forty votes. This year saw the opening of the new Houses of Parliament, concerning which Disraeli said in the Commons that the low standard of architecture in England was due to the fact that no architect had ever been shot, like Admiral Byng, *pour encourager les autres*, a statement that cannot have sent the Queen into fits of laughter, because it was her duty to bestow a knighthood on the architect of the new building, Charles Barry. But though he could not help breaking out like that occasionally, Dizzy was busy ingratiating himself with the Prince Consort by helping forward his scheme for a great scientific and artistic institution at South Kensington, and with the Queen by allowing in his next budget for increased expenditure on the army and navy.

This budget was his downfall, not because of its own defects but because it was his. Ten months of Disraeli as leader of the House was rather more than the chiefs of the other factions could stomach. They resented the success of genius against rank, authority and talent, and sufficient time had elapsed for their resentment to become active. Although Disraeli had not properly recovered from a severe attack of influenza, his budget speech took five hours, at the conclusion of which he was on the verge of collapse. Two leading members of the Opposition, Sir George Grey and Sir Charles Wood, presumably with the object of displaying their superior breeding, kept up a running mockery of his efforts, exchanging signs, nudges, titters, to the vast amusement of themselves and some of their high-born neighbours; and then, for a whole December week, the Chancellor was baited, taunted, ridiculed, jeered at, by the gentlemen of the Opposition, especially those who had been enraged by his attacks on Peel. But, as he said of himself in *Endymion*, "over his temper he had a complete control; if, indeed, his entire insensibility to violent language on the part of an opponent was not organic"; and he did not appear to feel, nor even to hear, what was said, sitting night after night with an expressionless face, an apathetic manner, and unseeing eyes.

When his adversaries had exhausted their vocabularies, he rose to reply, and gave them a good deal more than he had received. In the art of irony and ridicule he was their master, and a looker-on described the Opposition while he was lashing them as presenting a very strange spectacle, rigid, silent, pale in the gas-light, like the figures in the National Convention during the French Revolution. "Yes! I know what I have to face", he concluded. "I have to face a Coalition." The whigs, liberals, Irish and Peelites tried to appear indifferent. "The combination may be successful. A Coalition has before this been successful. But Coalitions, although successful, have always found this: that their triumph has been brief." He paused, hit the table of the House with his right hand, and added a familiar quotation to the anthologies of the future: "This, too, I know: that England does not love Coalitions." But the point at the moment was that this particular Coalition did not love Disraeli, and the Government were defeated by nineteen votes. Their resignation followed at once, and the Chancellor retired from his office with dignity, thanking the House for their indulgence and regretting any word he may have spoken that had hurt the feelings of individual members. He wrote to the Prince Consort that he would always remember with interest and admiration the princely mind in the princely person, and to the Queen that he humbly begged permission to lay at her feet his dutiful and grateful sense of the gracious and indulgent kindness which she had been pleased to bestow upon him. The lion of debate could become a lamb in defeat.

Chapter XVI

LOVE, WAR AND REVOLUTION

THERE are some men who have the attraction of children for women, who call forth the motherly rather than the loverly instinct in the other sex. Disraeli was one of them. An early secretary of his, David Bryce, used to tell how Mary Anne cosseted him on his return home from a sitting in the House or a political meeting. She kissed and fondled him in front of the embarrassed secretary, waited on him slavishly, fussed about him, brought him a bowl of warm water, washed his hands and dried them, curled and smoothed his raven locks, and thought of innumerable things for his greater comfort, his sultanic sense of luxury and repose. Many men would have disliked such exuberance, adulation and pampering, but Disraeli revelled in it. From youth he had been caressed and hero-worshipped by his sister to an extent that made an early companion feel he required a nurse to look after him, and in time he inspired the same solicitude in his Sovereign. But the petting was not all on one side. He treated women with a courtesy very pleasing to their vanity, a consideration very soothing to their social feelings, and a flattery most delicately adjusted to the rank and idiosyncrasy of the subject. He seemed to know exactly what to say to them, and as he really loved their company they responded naturally to his advances and were soon on easy terms with him. With men his relationship was either affectionate or formal; it was never, in the ordinary sense, familiar. With women it was affectionate as well as familiar; and his present biographer has only discovered one spiteful remark about him from a female pen, that of Lady Cardigan, who must have been vexed that he did not propose marriage to her after the death of his wife, as she had confidently expected him to do.

Like all men who are much in the public eye, he received from unknown admirers many letters which he was far too busy to acknowledge. One of these correspondents, who had formed a habit of writing about his speeches and his books, and whose admiration was largely due to his praise of Judaism, was herself a Jewess whose maiden name had been Mendez da Costa. She had married Colonel Brydges Willyams, commanding the Cornish Militia. But when Disraeli first replied to a letter of hers in 1851 she was a childless widow at least seventy years of age, and quite possibly eighty. She had asked him as a great favour to be an executor of her will, which also meant that he would be part-inheritor of her estate, and had requested him to meet her by the crystal fountain in the Crystal Palace, "an assignation . . . which I was ungallant enough not to keep, being far away when it arrived at Grosvenor Gate", he afterwards confessed. With his invariable caution he merely acknowledged her letter, stating that he would consider the question of the executorship. A month or two later he sent a conditional acceptance, adding that, as he would like to hear more about it, he would call at her home, Mount Braddon, Torquay, while he was in Devonshire that autumn. What he saw and heard was apparently of a satisfying nature, and Mrs Brydges Willyams became a close friend of the Disraelis, who took rooms in a Torquay hotel for a week or two every year and spent the afternoons and evenings with her. Though frequently asked to stay at Hughenden, it seems she never did; but she was keenly interested in everything concerning it, and Disraeli's descriptions of the house and grounds made her as conversant with the place as if she had seen it.

Throughout the twelve remaining years of Mrs Willyams's life a regular correspondence was kept up between Hughenden and Torquay. He sent her some of his books, his photograph, flowers, newspapers, venison and grouse, trout and partridges. She sent him flowers, turbots, soles, lobsters, prawns, and mutton broth. She advised him about his health, begging him to send a deputy to the funeral of the Duke of Wellington, and warning him that he sacrificed too much to fame. He advised her how to keep cool in the hot weather: "People put blocks of ice in their rooms, which produce a refreshing temperature. Try some thirty pounds of rough ice in this fashion." When he again became Chancellor in '58 he sent her a telegram, then a novelty, announcing the fact. She wanted him to take life more easily in the Upper House, but Mary Anne told her that he enjoyed his fame too much in the Lower. Her happiest moments were when she thought of his friendship, his "incomparable letters" were her greatest comfort, and she confessed herself "good for nothing except to join in a chorus of praise to the unrivalled genius of dear Dizzi." He took great interest and considerable pains for some three years over the regularisation of her coat of arms by the Heralds' College, and constantly kept her in touch with life at Hughenden. The place was so green, he wrote one May, "that I should fancy I was in the 'Emerald Isle', only my tenants do not as yet fire at me from behind my trees." The perfume of the roses she once sent was exquisite, and he felt sure they came from Cashmere. He described the changing colours of his trees, the seasonal flowers in his gardens, the beauty of his lake on which two cygnets sported, the glory of his peacocks and the hooting of his owls. In one of his letters we catch sight of him in the unaccustomed rôle of sportsman. He spent the whole of a morning trying to catch a trout for her, without success; so he made another attempt just before sunset, "and in the first twilight landed a gentleman 4¼ pounds in weight!—pretty well for our little stream, that was dry for three years. I packed him up in the flags among which he was caught last evening, and sent him off instantly from the river-side. You ought to have had him *early* this morning, so he is as fresh as day; and I told them to put a brace of grouse in the basket."

In September 1863 he reported that he and his wife had realised a romance which they had been meditating for many years: "We have restored the house to what it was before the Civil Wars, and we have made a garden of terraces, in which cavaliers might roam, and saunter, with their ladye-loves! The only thing wanting is that you should see it", but for her benefit he intended to have photographs taken of every aspect of the house, gardens and terraces. She did not live to see them. Within two months of receiving this letter she died, and at her own request was buried at Hughenden, where she lies, with her Dizzy and his Mary Anne, just outside the east end of the church. She left him rather more than £30,000.

Meanwhile the dreary empty game of politics went on. We must select only those moments which disclose the peculiar nature of our protagonist, whose mere existence relieves in retrospect the tedium of so much ado about nothing. The Coalition Government, as we have seen, was mainly inspired by jealousy and hatred of Disraeli. The new Prime Minister, Lord Aberdeen, gave the Foreign Office to Russell, the Home Office to Palmerston, the Exchequer to Gladstone, and the Cabinet of whigs and Peelites contained men who had monopolised office, under one label or another, for the past twenty years; so that it might be described as a Ministry of Mandarins, all the talents versus the solitary genius of Disraeli, who decided that the time had come to launch a weekly newspaper devoted to the tory interest. The first number of *The Press* appeared on May 7th, 1853, and Disraeli wrote leading articles for it in the early weeks of its existence, besides backing it financially. By the autumn it was costing him and a few friends £90 a week, and though the sale steadily increased it seldom made a profit, the circulation never rising above 3500. But when in '58 he sold the paper, it was running without a loss, and it lasted for another eight years.

The dislike of Dizzy by leading politicians was not shared by the younger generation, and when he received an honorary degree at Oxford in '53, though the occasion was marked by the presence of Lord Derby, who had succeeded the Duke of Wellington as Chancellor of the University, and of Macaulay, Gladstone, Grote, Bulwer Lytton and Bishop Wilberforce, it was Disraeli who received the most vociferous welcome from the undergraduates. When he had taken his seat, he inspected the ladies' gallery through his eyeglass, caught sight of his wife, and blew her a kiss. Again, after the banquet to Derby at Christ Church, the undergraduates collected in Tom quad under pelting rain to shout their enthusiasm for Dizzy, who told them that he would never forget their generous kindness.

Within a year of coming to power the Coalition Government had drifted into war with Russia. The Tsar, Nicholas, believing that the English Prime Minister was well-disposed towards him, seized the excuse of a quarrel between the Latin and Greek churches over the guardianship of the Holy Places in Palestine to extort from Turkey an admission of his right as head of the Greek Church to protect all the Christians in the Ottoman dominions; which simply meant that Turkey would come under Russian control. Through the influence of the British ambassador at Constantinople, the Tsar's demand was rejected, upon which Nicholas sent troops to occupy the principalities of Moldavia and Wallachia, later to be known as Roumania but then under the suzerainty of the Sultan. Like more recent aggressors, he proclaimed that this was not an act of war but merely a measure of security. Had Disraeli been in power, or Palmerston at the Foreign Office, the Tsar would have known what to expect and would not have acted with the easy assurance that a display of force would achieve his object. But Aberdeen had shown sympathy with Nicholas, who did not imagine that his policy would arouse popular feeling in England against him, resulting in war, for he had not been warned by the English Cabinet that they would act with France to prevent the partition of Turkey. Knowing that France and England were behind her, Turkey sent an ultimatum to Russia demanding the evacuation of the principalities. Russia rejected the ultimatum, war broke out between the two powers, the English and French fleets arrived at Constantinople, the Russian fleet destroyed the Turkish in Sinope Harbour, and the fat was in the fire.

Disraeli was of course wholly opposed to Russian aggression and supported the Government unfailingly in their war measures, but he frequently criticised the vacillation of Ministers and the lack of coordination and purpose which had encouraged the Tsar's designs. Also he believed that the Coalition could not last and tried to prepare Derby for the possibility of a Tory Government taking its place. In the autumn of '53 Mary Anne was seriously ill, and his domestic affairs were in a state of confusion. "A complete revolution in my life", he complained. "Everything seems to be anarchy." She was well enough by the middle of November to pay a round of visits with him; and alone he went to Knowsley for a few days with his chief; but Derby was translating Homer and did not wish to talk politics. Disraeli gave him no peace, and in January '54 insisted that he should invite the whole of the party to dine with him. This would mean nine dinners, and Derby did not want to give more than three; but Disraeli pointed out that three would only satisfy ninety of their followers, "and every man who is not asked is offended." He was mortified by Derby's lack of energy and ambition. In August '54 he told Lady Londonderry that they never saw their chief, whose house was always closed, and who, though wealthy, subscribed to nothing, yet expected everything to be done without him. "I have never yet been fairly backed in life", he grumbled. "All the great personages I have known, even when what is called 'ambitious' by courtesy, have been quite unequal to a grand game." And now, when everything was at stake, Derby spent his time at the Newmarket and Doncaster races or translating Homer in his country retreat. It was excessively vexing.

The situation in the Crimea, where the war was being fought out, grew steadily worse, and by the end of '54 the Ministry had become unpopular. The allies had won battles at the Alma, at Inkermann, and at Balaclava, but incompetence and mismanagement were rife, and the condition of the troops was deplorable. On a motion for a Committee of Enquiry into the War the Coalition were defeated. Their resignation followed; once more Derby was called to form a Government; and once more Disraeli offered to stand down in favour of Palmerston as leader of the House. But Derby funked the issue. He told the Queen that the whole country was clamouring for Palmerston as the only man who could carry on the war successfully, though he personally considered Palmerston totally unfit for the task. On this point Disraeli agreed with him, writing to Lady Londonderry that Palmerston was "really an impostor, utterly exhausted, and at the best only ginger-beer and not champagne, and now an old painted pantaloon, very deaf, very blind, and with false teeth, which would fall out of his mouth when speaking if he did not hesitate and halt so in his talk." Nevertheless the old painted pantaloon was more than a match for Derby, for he was cute enough to see that the latter's failure to form a Government would inevitably result in his own appointment to the chief office; and he refused the offer to collaborate. Knowing perfectly well that an efficient administration would be backed by the entire country, Disraeli implored Derby to go ahead without Palmerston; but Derby suffered from cold feet and abandoned the task. Disraeli was disgusted, and said so. By his timidity the tory leader threw away a great chance, and it took Disraeli nearly twenty years to win that victory at the polls which a successful prosecution of the Crimean War by his party would have brought about in as many months. Palmerston became Prime Minister, and, after a great expenditure of energy, Disraeli at last had leisure to look about him, one of the first people he noticed being the man who had led the famous charge of the

Light Brigade: "The great hero of London at present is Lord Cardigan, who relates with sufficient modesty, but with ample details, the particulars of his fiery charge at Balaclava, to willing audiences—as often as they like."

As Disraeli perceived, Derby's fatal refusal to seize a unique opportunity "lost us the heart and respect of all classes"; and what was a deliverance for the pusillanimous Derby was a disaster for the pertinacious Disraeli, who now had to lead a dispirited Opposition against a man who was quite as much a tory as himself, whose prestige in the country was unexampled, and who seemed to get younger as he grew older. It was a most depressing prospect, and at his age (50) no one in history except himself would have faced it with fortitude in the assurance of ultimate success. The fall of Sebastopol in September '55 should have brought the Crimean War to a close, and Disraeli did his best to persuade his chief that their object had been attained and that a statesmanlike peace was now desirable. But the country had gone war-mad, Palmerston's success had gone to his head, and, if it had not been for the fact that Napoleon III agreed with Disraeli, a new campaign would have been started to kick Russia out of the Crimea, with what calamitous consequences we can only guess. Much to the annoyance of Palmerston, Russia accepted the relatively reasonable terms offered by the allies, the war-fever subsided, and the Treaty of Paris was signed in the spring of '56.

A new recruit had strengthened the Tory party: Lord Robert Cecil, afterwards Lord Salisbury, who eventually became its leader. Disraeli formed a good opinion of him at first, but in the years ahead he was to prove very troublesome, and, not well-disposed towards Dizzy from the start, he was soon recognised as the centre of a clique in the party that was hostile to the man whom they contemptuously called "the Jew". The animosity of many among his own supporters pursued Disraeli until he was nearly seventy years of age, and most of his life was spent in provoking his declared enemies while appeasing his dubious friends. His freedom from popular prejudices was one of the things that made so many people uncomfortable. An outburst of social festivity followed the Crimean War, as it usually does after a period of bellicosity, and bands were permitted to play in the London parks on Sundays. Instantly the

Sabbatarians raised a hullabaloo, and the Government had to forbid the bands. Disraeli's comment was: "What a great man Moses must have been, to have invented a law which should agitate the 19th century, with all its boasted progress!" His attitude to American expansion was also contrary to public feeling. He told the House that when the United States "come in contact with large portions of territory scarcely populated, or at the most sparsely occupied by an indolent and unintelligent race of men, it is impossible—and you yourselves find it impossible—to resist the tendency to expansion; and expansion in that sense is not injurious to England, for it contributes to the wealth of this country." He declared that it was the business of a statesman to recognise the necessity of an increase in American power, therein displaying more foresight than was shown by his eminent contemporaries.

In August '56, suffering from "nervous debility", he went with his wife to Spa, where he was renovated by the waters and baths. In addition to his political battles, he had to fight against recurrent ill-health, which makes his achievement all the more remarkable. He thought little of doctors and their medicines. "Such are the inevitable consequences", he wrote in *Contarini Fleming*, "of consulting men who decide by precedents which have no resemblance, and never busy themselves about the idiosyncrasy of their patients." From Spa they travelled to Paris, where they were entertained at the Tuileries, Mary Anne sitting next to Napoleon III, himself by the side of the Empress Eugénie. "Our reception here has not turned our heads, but has tried the strength of our constitutions", he remarked; "once we dined out eleven days running." A further strain was put upon his constitution at the beginning of '57, when a General Election, which was nothing but a vote of confidence in the Prime Minister, brought Palmerston back to power with a personal majority of nearly a hundred over the rest of the House. The outlook for Disraeli was gloomier than ever; and the social world soon reflected his gloom, for in June '57, in the midst of the season's festivities, came the news from India of

> sword and fire,
> Red ruin, and the breaking up of laws.

In the prevailing horror aroused in England by the Indian

Mutiny, Disraeli appears to have been the only person who kept his head. The generally accepted story that the revolt was due to the abhorrence felt by native soldiers at the greasing of their cartridges with beef-fat and hog's-lard, the cow being sacred to the Hindus, the pig unclean to the Moslems, was at once rejected by the tory leader. That may have been the ostensible reason for the outbreak, but the real causes were much deeper than that, and with his oriental understanding he at once put his finger on the main factor: the recent dethronement of the King of Oudh by the East India Company, and the consequent fear among the native princes that the same thing might happen to them. Nowadays it seems almost incredible that for about a century India should have been run by an English company as a business concern, the dividends paid to shareholders being in proportion to the rate of spoliation. Yet such was the case, and Disraeli lamented the monstrous anachronism. He also saw that, apart from the resentment created by the rapacity of the East India Company, the official insensibility to Indian castes, customs and creeds, as well as the introduction of occidental forms of government, had spread alarm and discontent throughout the community and given the conspiracy of a minority sufficient material to convert the general disquietude into fanatical fury.

As usual in England, the Government did not recognise the seriousness of the situation until a great deal of harm had been done. The commander-in-chief on the spot, General George Anson, was much too old for the job, though Disraeli said that "he had seen the Great Mogul so often on the ace of spades that he would know how to deal with him"; and for a while it looked as if all the whites would be massacred. Shocking stories of atrocities reached home, and Disraeli knew that there was foundation for some of them, but the circumstantial nature of others made him doubtful. "The accounts are too graphic", he felt. "Who can have seen these things? Who heard them? . . . who that would tell these things could have escaped?" It was reported that a number of English ladies, with their noses cut off, had arrived at the house of the Governor-General. A London surgeon at once offered to supply false noses by the gross, but it was found that there was no demand.

Disraeli warned the House of the gravity of the crisis, explained how it had come about, said that the revolt must be suppressed at whatever cost, advised the Government "to temper justice with mercy—justice the most severe with mercy the most indulgent", and told them that "you can only act upon the opinion of Eastern nations through their imagination", for which reason there must be a closer relation between the people of India and their real ruler, Queen Victoria, who would respect their laws, usages, customs, and, above all, their religions. Disraeli himself was to bring this about in the second Derby-Disraeli administration, when the government of India was transferred from the Company to the Crown; and nearly twenty years later he was to establish a nearer relationship between Sovereign and people by making Victoria Empress of India. But at the moment the spirit of revenge had been let loose in the land, and in a speech to farmers at Newport Pagnell he did his utmost to create a more civilised atmosphere:

> I do without the slightest hesitation declare my humble disapprobation of persons in high authority announcing that upon the standard of England 'vengeance' and not 'justice' should be inscribed . . . I protest against meeting atrocities by atrocities. I have heard things said and seen things written of late which would make me almost suppose that the religious opinions of the people of England had undergone some sudden change, and that, instead of bowing before the name of Jesus, we were preparing to revive the worship of Moloch. I cannot believe that it is our duty to indulge in such a spirit.

The parliamentary session of 1857 was prolonged until August 28th, not because the politicians were gravely concerned over the safety of their fellow-countrymen in India, but because Gladstone, with passionate declamation, was opposing a Divorce Bill which would enable the average man and woman to obtain a remedy hitherto reserved for the rich. Nothing in their careers illustrates the disparate characters of Disraeli and Gladstone so clearly as this. While the first was concerned with the social and religious freedom of millions, the second was fighting tooth and nail against the freedom of ill-assorted couples. Yet the age thought Disraeli a worldly sceptic, Gladstone an idealistic humanitarian. In fact it was so easily taken in by claptrap in the guise of conviction that it resembles every other age.

Chapter XVII

SECOND INNINGS

FOR the second time in his career the man who had once marooned Disraeli on a mudbank in the middle of the Thames helped to rescue him from the shoal of opposition and land him on the shore of office. Palmerston's Government, which seemed so secure at the beginning of 1858, were defeated in February because he had been too considerate to Napoleon III. An Italian secret society, having manufactured bombs in England, exploded them in the neighbourhood of the French Emperor and Empress, both of whom escaped, though several bystanders were killed. Perfidious Albion was blamed for harbouring the miscreants; threats by French officers were printed in the official newspaper; a wave of anglophobia submerged France; and the Emperor's Foreign Minister angrily demanded, in effect, whether England would continue to encourage assassination. Instead of replying to the Foreign Minister's despatch in a manner that would have soothed the ruffled feelings of his own countrymen, Palmerston brought in a Bill making conspiracy to murder a felony punishable by penal servitude for life. The House of Commons gave the first reading a handsome majority; but when a private member moved an amendment censuring ministers for not replying to the French Foreign Minister's despatch, the House favoured it, the Government were defeated, and Palmerston resigned.

Derby was asked to form a Ministry; and after making an abortive attempt to detach Gladstone from his whiggish connection, did so. Disraeli was again Chancellor of the Exchequer, and his old antagonist General Peel, Sir Robert's brother, who had once challenged him to a duel, was War Secretary. The first thing they had to do was to placate Napoleon III without giving way to the French demand for harsh measures against foreign refugees who happened to disapprove of despotism. An interchange of diplomatic notes took place, and the thing was done. Their next job was the transference of India from a Company to the Crown, and this too was accomplished, Disraeli emerging so triumphantly from a series of debates on Indian affairs which threatened to unseat him that he was cheered by crowds as he passed from the Commons to Downing Street and back again. In a speech at Slough he described the collapse of the Opposition as

rather like a convulsion of nature than one of the ordinary transactions of human life. I can liken it only to one of those earthquakes in Calabria or Peru, of which we sometimes read. There was a rumbling murmur, a groan, a shriek, distant thunder; and nobody knew whether it came from the top or the bottom of the House. There was a rent, a fissure in the ground. Then a village disappeared. Then a tall tower toppled down. And then the whole of the Opposition benches became one great dissolving view of anarchy!

Immediately these excitements were over Disraeli made a personal appeal to Gladstone, who as a one-time tory might have been induced to renew his allegiance to the party, begging him to join Derby's Cabinet and assuring him of an eager welcome and a hearty support. Gladstone declined, wisely from the angle of personal ambition. He was wily enough to see that he could never hope for pre-eminence in a party that included Disraeli, whereas he might easily lead the other side when Palmerston and Russell, respectively twenty-five and seventeen years older than himself, vanished from the field. Disraeli next turned his attention to the Thames, the effluvia therefrom being particularly nauseous in the dry summer of '58, and he brought in a Bill to convert, by a system of main drainage, what had become a sewer into a river. As a statesman his motto was *Sanitas sanitatum, omnia sanitas*, and his purification of the Thames, which contributed so much to the health and amenity of the metropolis, was more important if less spectacular than many of his doings. As he once said, "a policy that diminishes the death-rate of a great nation is a feat as considerable as any of those decisive battles of the world that generally decide nothing." It was rumoured in '58 that he would be the first Viceroy of India, and there is no doubt that the splendour of the job appealed to him, also that many of his party would have been glad to see the last of him; but he had informed Lord Melbourne three years before he entered parliament that it was his intention to become Prime Minister of England, and his mind remained unchanged.

At the moment he was mainly concerned with parliamentary reform. Ever since the Bill of '32 the whigs had made a monopoly of reform; but Disraeli had always recognised that it was a matter which the tories ought to handle, especially as their great leader William Pitt would have done so had it not been for the war with France. The so-called tory opposition to reform was due to the Duke of Wellington, but that was no reason why tory sympathy with reform should not be recreated by Disraeli, who regarded the whig measure of '32 as a first, not a final, step. Russell had twice tinkered with the question in recent years, but Disraeli now determined to produce a Bill that should favour no particular class and enable every important interest to be adequately represented in the House of Commons. The latter part of '58 was a period of intensive effort for him, with Cabinet Councils galore, secret conclaves, endless conversations with all and sundry, including the Prince Consort, much trimming, deep cogitation, irregular meals, and sleepless nights. "Labour, anxiety and responsibility seem to act on me as tonics", he said. Several prominent tories were restive and had to be charmed into complaisance. One of them, Bulwer Lytton, the Colonial Secretary, did not like the look of things and asked to resign on the ground of ill-health. Disraeli talked him round, telling Derby that Lytton "expects to die before Easter, but, if so, I have promised him a public funeral." The Chancellor had a wonderful faculty of making people do what he wished, and Sir Stafford Northcote, who would one day lead the party in the Commons, reveals one of his methods: "Dizzy talked as if he had always had my interests in the very centre of his heart." But the whigs had decided that he must not be allowed to get away with it; and although Palmerston and Russell were playing against one another for the leadership of their side, they showed a united front against the Jew who had dared to challenge their engrossment of reform. Naturally they pretended that the Bill did not go far enough, and talked a lot of nonsense about votes for everybody and trusting the people, upon which Disraeli made the sage comment that "the people may have their parasites as well as monarchs and aristocracies." The insincerity of his opponents was proved during the next six years, when, after one feeble effort to pass a Bill, the whole question of reform was shelved during Palmerston's Administration, to the rage of John Bright and the radicals, who were bribed to defeat Disraeli's measure by whig promises to produce something more democratic.

While attending to the business of reform Disraeli was also going outside his department into the region of foreign policy. France and Austria were drifting into war over Italy, where there was a movement, sponsored by Cavour, against the Austrian domination in northern Italy and in favour of a united Italian kingdom, then split up into different states. Napoleon III favoured Cavour's design and agreed to help him. Disraeli, who throughout his life urged and worked for cordial relations between France and England, believed that war could be averted by British diplomacy, and sent Ralph Earle, who had once been attached to the Paris Embassy, on a confidential visit to Napoleon in order to promote Anglo-French accord. Earle's mission was successful, and if Disraeli had been at the Foreign Office there is little doubt that Austria could have been persuaded to evacuate the Roman states; but the Foreign Minister, Lord Malmesbury, who did not understand the situation so clearly as the Chancellor of the Exchequer, was represented at Vienna by a feeble ambassador, and failed to act with the necessary firmness. What helped to precipitate the conflict was the action of the whig leaders, Russell and Palmerston, in defeating Disraeli's Reform Bill at a time when the authority of the British Government on the continent was essential to the preservation of peace. Perceiving that England would shortly be distracted by a General Election, Austria attacked Piedmont; but she could not wage a successful war, even against Napoleon III, who was thus enabled to add Magenta and Solferino to the list of victories won by his family against the house of Hapsburg. Bringing the campaign quickly to a close, the Emperor entered Paris on a charger, bought from a Piccadilly horse-dealer for five hundred guineas. "A magnificent spectacle", remarked Dizzy, "which has only cost 100,000 lives and 50 millions of pounds sterling!"

The defeat of his Reform Bill was followed by an appeal to the country, and the General Election in the spring of '59 decided, as he put it, "whether we are mice or men." Though there was an increase in the tory ranks, they did not obtain an independent majority over the rest of the House, and Disraeli, desirous above all things for a continuance of tory policy, did his best to persuade Palmerston, a thorough tory at heart, to join them, promising "You would receive from me, not merely cordial co-operation, but a devoted fidelity." But Palmerston did not see why he should be Foreign Secretary under Derby when there was a prospect of becoming Prime Minister himself, and turned down the proposal. Disraeli next sounded a few independent liberals, but they could not be relied upon. He then advised Derby to make a last appeal to Gladstone; but that crafty gentleman was biding his time and would not be seduced from self-interest, unlike Disraeli who told Derby that he was prepared "to take any step and make any sacrifice, provided you remain at the head of the Administration", and at the final moment even suggested that Derby's son, Lord Stanley, should become leader of the whole party, in which event Dizzy himself would stand down, take no office, but give his whole-hearted support to a man who possessed his entire confidence and firm friendship. This magnanimous offer was inspired by a conviction that the country needed a Tory Government, and that Stanley would have the confidence, not only of their own people, but of many M.P.s who were sick of the whigs and distrusted the radicals. Incidentally his offer proves that he felt himself to be still unpopular with his party, though he was perfectly well aware that without his active collaboration with Stanley it would fall to pieces.

The whigs were equally aware that unless they presented an unbroken front, and gained the assistance of John Bright and the radicals, Disraeli would prove too much for them; so Palmerston and Russell entered into a bond of mutual loyalty, Bright was induced to support them by promises that were as solid as the breath that uttered them, a vote of censure on the Derby Administration was carried by a majority of thirteen, the Government resigned, and Palmerston became Prime Minister with Russell at the Foreign Office. Gladstone, who had voted against the whigs on this issue and who thoroughly distrusted Palmerston, illustrated his view of consistency by returning to the Exchequer, which proves conclusively that his refusal to join Derby was due to a belief that he would never become leader of a party that included Disraeli. The year 1859 had been unlucky for the latter, and it closed in grief with the death of his only sister: "My first and ever faithful friend."

Seven more years of patience-testing opposition now lay ahead of Disraeli. The period was notable for Gladstone's budgets. He has been called a great Chancellor of the Exchequer, a verdict that need not be disputed, as it is much easier to juggle with figures than with facts; but he owed a good deal to Dizzy's criticism, which he did not appreciate: "Gladstone looked like a beaten hound, and ate no ordinary quantity of dirt." There was a Statistical Congress in London during 1860, and the Prime Minister's wife received the statisticians at Cambridge House. Disraeli noted that all the men had bald heads and wore spectacles: "You associate these traits often with learning and profundity", he said, "but when one sees 100 bald heads and 100 pairs of spectacles the illusion, or the effect, is impaired." As usual, his friends gave him more trouble than his foes. His somewhat radical views with regard to reform annoyed all the reactionaries, who could scarcely be expected to agree with him that the tories should sympathise with and lead the people, not ignore and bully them. Greville noted in his diary for 1860 that "the hatred and distrust of Disraeli is greater than ever in the Conservative ranks", and a sustained attack on his leadership appeared in the chief tory organ, *The Quarterly Review*, in which his tactics were described as flexible and shameless, his behaviour reckless, and the party he had humiliated was warned of its forthcoming extinction if it continued to spend its money and labour solely for the glory and ambition of a single individual. As the party owed its very existence to Disraeli's genius, this article was considered somewhat immoderate even by those who disliked their leader. It was written by Lord Robert Cecil, whose father Lord Salisbury was Disraeli's personal friend and colleague; but there had been disagreements between father and son, and the latter had to earn money by journalism, which may have acidified his strictures on a man whom he clearly did not like personally. But Disraeli's aptitude for changing animosity to concord whenever he wished to do so was never so cleverly exhibited as in this case, for the repugnance Lord Robert Cecil felt towards Dizzy contrasts curiously with the harmony between the future Lord Salisbury and the future Lord Beaconsfield.

At the time however Disraeli resented the ingratitude among his so-called adherents made evident by this article and emphasised in another paper by the statement that his leadership was one of "chronic revolt and unceasing conspiracy." He wrote a long letter to a friend enumerating his services to the party, the members of which "chalk the walls in the market-place with my opprobrium", and stating his intention to resign a position he had unwillingly accepted, "and to which it is my opinion that fourteen years of unqualified devotion have not reconciled the party." The recipient showed the letter to a number of tory chiefs, who practically went on their knees to the writer supplicating him to take it back and assuring him of their unalterable esteem. "Tell them my fury shall abate, and I the post will keep", he might have replied in the manner of Pistol. In more parliamentary style, he allowed himself to be persuaded that the letter had not been written, and continued to lead the tory squadron, criticising the Government when it vacillated over national policy, supporting it when firm, confessing himself on one occasion "quite exhausted in listening to aide-de-camps, instructing generals of division, and writing endless despatches", and humorously complaining in the House when a number of his followers abstained from voting with him: "Tomorrow [Derby Day] I believe we shall all be engaged elsewhere. I dare say that many hon. gentlemen who take more interest than I do in that noble pastime will have their favourites. I hope they will not be so unlucky as to find their favourites bolting. If they are placed in that dilemma, they will be better able to understand and sympathise with my feelings on this occasion.'

His chief criticisms during this period were reserved for Russell's foreign policy. Life on the continent was quite exciting in the sixties, and Disraeli thought it a privilege to live at such a time. It was not a utilitarian age, he said, but an age of romance; thrones toppling, crowns going a-begging, exiles in power, adventurers in palaces, demireps setting fashions. He prophesied that Napoleon III would enjoy fifteen years of glory, and he was not far out. The crown of Greece was offered to Lord Stanley. "Had I his youth, I would not hesitate", said Dizzy. But though the romance of all these sudden changes appealed to him, he remained opposed to revolution, and when London went mad over Garibaldi during his visit in April '64 Disraeli was the only political figure of note who refused to meet him, because he was the enemy of authority as embodied in Church and State. Then there was the American Civil War, which caused strained rela-

HUGHENDEN MANOR, SOUTH FRONT

LONDON HOUSE, GROSVENOR GATE, PARK LANE

LORD PALMERSTON
Photograph in his Later Years

EDWARD STANLEY, 14TH EARL OF DERBY
By Sir Francis Grant, P.R.A.

tions between the Northern States and England, where much sympathy was expressed for the South; but Disraeli was careful not to say a word that would irritate the Federal Government: "When I consider the great difficulties which the statesmen of North America have to encounter", he told the Commons, "when I consider what I may call the awful emergency which they have been summoned suddenly to meet, and which . . . they have met manfully and courageously, I think it becomes England, in dealing with the Government of the United States, to extend to all which they say at least a generous interpretation, and to their acts a liberal construction." He protested against any move on the part of England that might create a feeling in the States that she was taking sides in the dispute, and he predicted that the America of the future would play a decisive part in world affairs.

Russell also mishandled the recurrent Polish question, complicated as usual by the so-called Polish patriots who lived luxuriously in London and Paris, from which they incited their less-fortunate countrymen to revolt. Having obtained the co-operation of France and Austria, Russell demanded of Russia that the Polish insurgents should be amnestied and a representative government established. Russia replied sarcastically that the responsibility was hers. France then counselled action; but England backed out. The result was that when Germany decided to annex Schleswig and Holstein, and English public feeling was wholly with Denmark, Russell found that he had irritated Russia and estranged France, neither of which would side with England in upholding Danish rule in those provinces. The Whig Cabinet had reduced Great Britain to a state of isolation, and had to confess their inability to cope with the situation alone. Disraeli criticised their action over Poland, and made a prophecy which was fulfilled about eighty years later: that a war to maintain the independence of Poland would be a general and protracted war which would change the map of Europe, where the name of Poland would not be found. On the Schleswig-Holstein matter he attacked the Government at length, and in announcing the policy of his party he again looked ahead and foretold an event that we have lived to see:

We will not threaten and then refuse to act. We will not lure on our allies with expectations we do not fulfil. And, sir, if ever it be the lot of myself, or any public men with whom I have the honour to act, to carry on important negotiations on behalf of this country, as the noble lord and his colleagues have done, I trust that we at least shall not carry them on in such a manner that it will be our duty to come to Parliament to announce to the country that we have no allies, and then declare that England can never act alone. Sir, those are words which ought never to have escaped the lips of a British Minister. They are sentiments which ought never to have occurred even to his heart. I repudiate them, I reject them. I remember there was a time when England, with not a tithe of her present resources, inspired by a patriotic cause, triumphantly encountered a world in arms. And, sir, I believe now, if the occasion were fitting, if her independence or her honour were assailed, or her empire endangered—I believe that England would rise in the magnificence of her might, and struggle triumphantly for those objects for which men live and nations flourish.

Throughout these years of tory opposition the power and prestige of the Established Church were being lessened by the hostility of dissenters, the lack of conviction among its own members, the nullifying effects of what used to be known as the Higher Criticism, and the growing agnosticism of the age. The Church of England made a strong appeal to Disraeli, not only because it was a symbol of the spiritual life, but because it was rooted in the race, conserving what was best in the traditions of the people. It was, he said, "part of our history, part of our life, part of England itself", and he described it as "the only Jewish institution that remains." He therefore resisted every encroachment on its influence and its rights, and inspired the churchmen in the Commons as well as those outside to repel all attempts to weaken its position. People were saying that the age of faith had passed, to which he replied that "the characteristic of the present age is a craving credulity", but that, without the guidance of a Church, "sustained by the tradition of sacred ages and by the conviction of countless generations", human beings would create altars and idols in their own hearts and imaginations. Thus he upheld the distinctive creed of the Church; and when Dean Stanley said to him that the Athanasian Creed should be omitted from the prayer-book, he remarked: "Mr Dean: no dogmas, no deans." He constantly spoke at meetings of churchmen, and at one of them he expressed a sentiment that shook the country with laughter and was repeated for the next half-century as the drollest thing ever uttered by a statesman. Bishop Wilberforce asked him to speak in the Sheldonian Theatre, Oxford, on November 25th, 1864, on behalf of a society for the endowment of small livings. Darwin's *The Origin of Species* had appeared in 1859, and people were beginning to believe that man had evolved from simian ancestors. But Disraeli preferred the statement in the Book of Genesis that God had created man in His own image, in other words that man was a fallen angel, and in the course of his speech to the learned and learning assembly he said that he was not prepared to accept the teachings of the lecture-room as more scientific than those of the Church. "What is the question now placed before society with a glib assurance the most astounding? The question is this: Is man an ape or an angel? My Lord, I am on the side of the angels . . . It is between these two contending interpretations of the nature of man, and their consequences, that society will have to decide. Their rivalry is at the bottom of all human affairs . . ." The idea of a man who was not naturally a solemn bore and prig claiming to be on the side of the angels was too funny for words and was mostly ridiculed in cartoons. It did not occur to anyone that Disraeli was merely stating his conviction that the spirit of man, not the animal in man, was his essential quality, distinguishing him from the rest of creation and justifying his predominance.

While in opposition Disraeli was careful to improve his relations with the lady he would one day have to advise. In January '61 he and his wife were asked to stay at Windsor Castle, and their visit irritated the wives of Cabinet Ministers who had not received a similar invitation. December of that year saw the death of the Prince Consort, and Disraeli remarked to the Saxon Minister that "we have buried our Sovereign. This German Prince has governed England for 21 years with a wisdom and energy such as none of our kings have ever shown." From their first meeting Disraeli had formed an extremely high opinion of the Consort, his tribute to whom in the Commons earned the Queen's thanks. She sent him engravings of pictures of the Prince and herself, and he acknowledged them as "a hallowed gift." Moreover it was repeated to him that the Queen had said more than once that he was the only person who had appreciated the Prince. Her gratitude was signified in a manner that caused much heart-burning in aristocratic circles. In 1863 the Prince of Wales was married to Princess Alexandra of Denmark. There was scarcely room for the number of royal guests, ambassadors, Cabinet Ministers, etc., who had to be asked to the ceremony in St George's Chapel, and when the list was finally drawn up it was found that only four seats were left for disposal. The Queen allotted two of them to Disraeli and his wife. The rage, mortification and indignation of various dukes and duchesses were extreme, and their temperatures were not lowered when it became known that Her Majesty had favoured Disraeli with a long private audience.

His speech on the resolution to grant a sum for the erection of a public monument to the late Consort procured him another present from the Queen—her own copy of the Prince's speeches with an inscription—and another letter expressing "her deep gratification at the tribute he paid to her adored, beloved, and great husband." She had shed many tears over it, but her broken heart had been soothed by "such true appreciation of that spotless and unequalled character." In reply he said that, "in venturing to touch upon a sacred theme", he had spoken from his heart, and in estimating the Consort's character he declared that "The Prince is the only person, whom Mr Disraeli has ever known, who realised the Ideal." Such agreeable interchanges show that Disraeli had already mastered the art of pleasing sovereigns, and his correspondence with the King of the Belgians at about this period displays an adroitness in flattery and diplomacy that should be studied by aspirants for power and place.

His growing reputation was recognised in 1863 by his election as a Trustee of the British Museum following the death of Lord Lansdowne; and two years later his social presentability was acknowledged by Grillion's dining club, an exclusive group which had steadily barred him from membership on account of his origin and public behaviour but which now felt that he was too important to be ignored and asked him to join them. He did so, though he knew that he would be bored to death if he attended their meetings. Evidently he dined with them once, and found their company excessively dull, "a dozen prigs and bores (generally) whispering to their next-door neighbours over a bad dinner in a dingy room." In fact it was his settled opinion that a men's dinner-party, in middle life, was horrible.

At the General Election of '65 Palmerston's popularity in the country brought his party back to power, and seeing no chance of returning to office himself Disraeli again offered to vacate the post of Opposition leader, which would enable Derby to form an anti-revolutionary government with the whigs. Derby flatly refused to do anything of the kind, and said that no one would have supported him with Disraeli's ability, faithfulness and perseverance. Indeed Dizzy made a business of his pleasures for the sake of the cause, or rather did things in his spare time that he would rather not have done, and in the late summer of '65 his wife accompanied him on a tour of country-houses, spending several days at Raby, at Lowther, at Ashridge and at Woburn. He regarded these visitations as a duty, because he met people of every political complexion and could "feel the pulse of the ablest on all the questions of the day." It was a duty he felt less willing to perform as the years went by, because it was an effort to mix with people who cared for him about as little as he cared for them. "I detest society really, for I never entered it without my feelings being hurt", he once said; and country-houses were particularly obnoxious, for he had no sympathy with the tastes or pursuits of those who dwelt or stayed in them. He always hoped to find someone who would interest him, but he scarcely ever did, and at length abandoned the search. The day-to-day happenings were of a conventional and distasteful kind, consisting mostly of eating, dressing, the slaughter of pheasants, and conversation thereanent. Once, at Crichel, about 1200 birds were killed, and Dizzy said "the sky was darkened with their uprushing, and the whir of their wings was like the roar of the sea." Mary Anne told a friend that "Whenever we go to a country-house the same thing happens: Dizzy is not only bored, and has constant ennui, but he takes to eating as a resource; he eats at breakfast, luncheon and dinner; the result is, by the end of the third day he becomes dreadfully bilious, and we have to come away." But in the process of boredom his power of observation was not numbed, and when staying at Woburn Abbey he noted that the main feature and organic deficiency of the Russell family was shyness, his host doing his best to cover it up with an air of uneasy gaiety. During his visit to Raby he also spotted a young man named Monty Corry, who, desirous to impress him, assumed a manner of undue gravity. But one wet afternoon the girls of the party forced the youngster to dance and sing a comic song, in the course of which Disraeli, who was supposed to be busy writing letters in his room, appeared at the door and stood for some time sombrely surveying the frolic. The young man was in despair; but he need not have worried, because Disraeli had enjoyed his performance, summed him up favourably, and after dinner that evening said to him "I think you must be my impresario." Monty Corry became his private secretary, factotum, and most intimate friend.

Before parliament met again Palmerston had passed away; rather surprisingly because, though eighty years of age, he had shown no signs of departure. Following a recent division in the House of Commons, he had climbed a long staircase to the ladies' gallery in order to embrace his wife; within a month or so of his death he had eaten a dinner which began with two plates of turtle soup, a large helping of cod and oyster sauce, a pâté, two greasy-looking entrées, a plate of roast mutton, a huge slab of ham, and a considerable portion of pheasant; and when someone expressed a hope that, with the bitter north-east wind then prevailing, he was taking more care of himself than usual, he replied "Oh! I do indeed. I very often take a cab at night, and if you have both windows open it is almost as good as walking home." Disraeli was really sorry when he heard of the death of his old opponent, whose geniality, energy and sagacity had brightened up the debates, and who had always treated him with kindness and courtesy.

The new Prime Minister, Russell, was in the Upper House, having taken an earldom some years before; and the new leader of the Commons was Gladstone, whose only resemblance to Palmerston was that they were both born of woman. With their old reactionary leader safely dead and buried, Russell and Gladstone turned their attention to reform, and introduced a moderate Bill, which would have been passed if Gladstone had not attempted to frighten the House with universal suffrage and class-warfare. Before the debate on the second reading he made what Disraeli called one of his "pilgrimages of passion" in Lancashire, where he viciously attacked his opponents as aristocrats who were hostile to the interests of the people. This was the beginning of a policy from which the nation has increasingly suffered; but the end is not yet. Disraeli regarded the electoral franchise as a privilege, not a right, and said that the best among all classes should be granted the privilege, the effect of universal suffrage being "the tyranny of one class, and that one the least enlightened." After many heated debates, and considerable mismanagement by the Government owing to Gladstone's bad temper, an Opposition amendment was carried, and the Russell Ministry resigned in June '66. But for a while it had looked as if Gladstone would carry the Bill, and Disraeli had written to Mary Anne: "I think of you, which always sustains me, and I know we shall find many sources of happiness without politics, if it comes to that."

It had not come to that.

Chapter XVIII

THE GREASY POLE

FOR the third time Lord Derby went to Downing Street with Disraeli as his Chancellor of the Exchequer, whose private secretary from now to the end of his life was Montagu Corry. Reform riots broke out within a few weeks, and the mob burst through the railings of Hyde Park to hold unauthorised meetings, trampling on the flower-beds to mark their contempt of law and order, but at the close of the parliamentary session Disraeli informed the Queen that the pulse of the House was very low, adding that "extreme unction will not be administered, I believe, until Friday." During the recess he meditated on reform, an agitation for which was being conducted in the country by John Bright, and at length decided to bring in a Bill. It was not an easy undertaking, for, being in a minority, he had not only to please his adherents but to placate his opponents. This meant much modification of his own policy, and the perpetual exercise of his patience, tact and skill. At the very last moment, just before he rose in the House to outline his scheme, a leading tory ratted. This was the man who had attacked him so mercilessly in *The Quarterly Review*, then Lord Robert Cecil, now Lord Cranborne, soon to be Lord Salisbury. He was Indian Secretary in Derby's third Cabinet, and had agreed the reform proposals at a recent meeting thereof, but now stated that they would ruin the Conservative party and that he could not support them. "This is stabbing in the back!" said Disraeli. Cranborne remained adamant and violently attacked the Bill during its passage through the Commons. Two other tories left the Cabinet with him, and the three vacancies were filled by three dukes, which calls to mind a passage in one of Dizzy's novels, wherein the heir to the richest dukedom in the kingdom is described as a republican of the deepest dye, "opposed to all privilege, and indeed to all orders of men except dukes, who were a necessity." Disraeli characteristically repaid Cranborne's "treachery" by praising him in the House for his commanding talents, clear intelligence, capacity for labour and power of expression; and it is curious to reflect that when Cranborne became Lord Salisbury he benefited from the new Reform Bill as a conservative Prime Minister far more than did the man whom he had abused for bringing it in.

As might have been expected, the real opposition to the Bill came from Gladstone, who could not conceal his mortification over the prospect of reform being engineered by the tories, above all by his detested rival. The fact that Disraeli had always wished to improve upon the whig Bill of '32, and had compelled his party to realise that they and not the whigs were the true protectors of the people, was in Gladstone's view merely an instance of Dizzy's machiavellian villainy, and the liberal leader foamed at the mouth. "The right hon. gentleman gets up and addresses me in a tone which, I must say, is very unusual in this House", drily commented Disraeli. "Not that I at all care for the heat he displays, although really his manner is sometimes so very excited and so alarming that one might almost feel thankful that gentlemen in this House, who sit on opposite sides of this table, are divided by a good broad piece of furniture."

The Bill extended the franchise to borough householders and doubled the electorate. For Disraeli it realised the dream of his life by establishing Toryism on a national foundation, but he had to make many concessions of which he disapproved. Gladstone's factious hostility to the Bill was simply due to his annoyance that it was not his and a keen desire to take Disraeli's place. His envy was too obvious and spoilt his chance of wrecking the measure. Lord Houghton met him at breakfast in May '67 and noted that he was "quite awed with the diabolical cleverness of Dizzy, who, he says, is gradually driving all ideas of political honour out of the House, and accustoming it to the most revolting cynicism", or, put in another way, he had been made to look ridiculous by a far abler man and felt his inferiority so keenly that, as a sop to his vanity, he assumed that evil had triumphed over good. Certainly Disraeli would not have pretended that the political arena was a breeding-ground of virtue. "Look at it as you will, ours is a beastly profession", he said to a fellow-member. But it provided excellent opportunities for power and glory, which were not without solace.

We have the evidence of G. W. E. Russell, a fervent Gladstonian, who had been brought up in the whig tradition of mocking and distrusting Disraeli, and was a nephew of the Russell whose Reform Bill was now being superseded, that one figure towered above all the others in the parliament of 1867, that even Gladstone played a secondary and ambiguous part. "The ridiculed and preposterous Dizzy", says Russell, was absolute master of both sides of the House, a giant among pigmies. In fact Disraeli was at the top of his genius during the passage of his Bill; and when the Government got a majority at the first division on April 12th '67 he was cheered vociferously. On his way home he dropped in at the Carlton Club and received a welcome unique in the annals of that institution. The members mobbed him, shouted themselves hoarse, drank his health, and wrung his hand numb. They implored him to stay and sup with them, but his wife was expecting him and he refused. "Dizzy came home to me", she related. "I had got him a raised pie from Fortnum and Mason's, and a bottle of champagne, and he ate half the pie and drank all the champagne, and then he said: 'Why, my dear, you are more like a mistress than a wife'." She thought this a very high compliment, as indeed he had meant her to think.

When the 1867 Reform Bill passed its third reading in the Commons without a division, everyone recognised that the achievement was a purely personal one. Disraeli had done it entirely off his own bat. He never consulted his colleagues in the House; they spoke at a word from him, or were silent when he did not wish them to speak; his power seemed to be despotic and mesmeric; and his own restraint, his ability to hold his tongue, was as remarkable as his readiness to deal with any objection, any detail, any fact or argument. Every quality of a great leader was his at command; he could ridicule, conciliate, exasperate, soothe. He spoke more than three hundred times, was always in his place, conscious of every word and move of his opponents, prepared for all emergencies, never once caught out. It was an astounding performance, and Gladstone was not the only awestruck person in the House. Derby was elated. "Don't you see how we have dished the whigs?" he exclaimed when someone criticised their revolutionary measures. At the Mansion House banquet to Ministers, Disraeli could proudly claim to have terminated the monopoly of reform by the so-called progressive parties. "The

Tory party has resumed its natural functions in the government of the country", he affirmed. "For what is the Tory party unless it represents national feeling? . . . The Tory party is nothing unless it represent and uphold the institutions of the country." The whitebait dinner at Greenwich at the close of the session was a hilarious affair, and Disraeli was actually seen to laugh when the Lord Advocate, a naturally solemn and formal person, sang a jocular Scottish song. Soon after that Dizzy and Mary Anne went to Edinburgh, where the freedom of the City was conferred on him by the Corporation and the honorary degree of LL.D. by the University. They were entertained at a banquet, and he spoke on the Reform Bill: "I had to prepare the mind of the country, and to educate—if it be not arrogant to use such a phrase—to educate our party. It is a large party, and requires its attention to be called to questions of this kind with some pressure." In dealing with the attacks on him and his policy that had recently appeared in the whig *Edinburgh Review* and the tory *Quarterly Review*, he said that no man admired those periodicals more than himself:

> But I admire them as I do first-rate, first-class post-houses, which in old days, for half a century or so—to use a Manchester phrase—carried on a roaring trade. Then there comes some revolution or progress which no person can ever have contemplated. They find things are altered. They do not understand them, and, instead of that intense competition and mutual vindictiveness which before distinguished them, they suddenly quite agree. The boots of the 'Blue Boar' and the chambermaid of the 'Red Lion' embrace, and are quite in accord in this—in denouncing the infamy of railroads.

Disraeli also addressed an evening meeting of working men in the Music Hall, and to everyone's amazement enchanted his audience: those who went to jeer remained to cheer. Sir John Skelton met him the next day at Lord Advocate Gordon's house, and was so much impressed by his olive complexion, coal-black eyes, imposing forehead and mask-like face, that "I would as soon have thought of sitting down at table with Hamlet, or Lear, or the Wandering Jew." But Disraeli proved more companionable than any of those characters, for in speaking of his reception by the working men he said "I fancied, indeed, till last night, that north of the border I was not loved; but last night made amends for much. We were so delighted with our reception,

Mrs Disraeli and I, that after we got home we actually danced a jig (or was it a hornpipe?) in our bedroom."

In September '67 Lord Derby had a particularly bad attack of gout, a disablement to which he was increasingly prone, and hinted in a letter to his chief lieutenant that he might have to retire from public life. Dizzy replied that he selfishly hoped Derby would not retire, "as my career will terminate with yours." Two months later Mary Anne was seriously ill, and when Gladstone made a sympathetic reference to her in the House it was noticed that her husband had tears in his eyes. Public and private anxiety together were too much for him, and he was laid up, writing little pencilled notes to his wife because he could not leave his room, nor she hers. One of them ran: "You have sent me the most amusing and charming letter I ever had. It beats Horace Walpole and Mme de Sévigné." Another told her that "Grosvenor Gate has become a hospital, but a hospital with you is worth a palace with anybody else." He was scarcely well again before he had to deal with the Irish Fenians, who murdered a policeman at Manchester and blew up Clerkenwell prison in London. Disraeli took immediate steps to subdue the criminals, while Gladstone took advantage of the crimes to demand reforms in Ireland.

Early in '68 the gout held Derby in its grip and he decided to resign his office, writing to thank Disraeli for twenty years of cordial and loyal co-operation and for "the courage, skill, and judgment, with which you triumphantly carried the Government through all the difficulties and dangers of the last year." Derby advised the Queen to appoint Disraeli in his place, advice which Her Majesty was extremely anxious to follow. In reply to Disraeli's assurance that he would always consider himself the deputy of his old chief, Derby wrote that he could not permit it: "You have fairly and most honourably won your way to the highest round of the political ladder, and long may you continue to retain your position." Nevertheless, Disraeli continued to seek Derby's advice on matters of moment and kept him in touch with governmental doings. In his first letter to the Queen after accepting office, Disraeli offered his devotion and said that it would be his delight and duty to make things easy for her, begging at the same time for the guidance of one whose judgment "few living persons, and probably no living prince, can rival."

On February 27th, 1868, he went down to Osborne for his first audience as Prime Minister. The Queen received him with a radiant face, saying "You must kiss hands", which, falling on his knee, he did "in faith and loving loyalty."

There were the usual jokes of opponents when his promotion became known. Some said that his elevation would make him *dizzy*. Others thought it the funniest thing that had ever happened: "What! Old Diz! Prime Minister! Well, the last Government was the Derby; this is the Hoax!" (Oaks.) Disraeli himself was naturally excited and happy at the fulfilment of his ambition, though he well knew that the situation was precarious. He replied to someone's congratulations, "Yes, I have climbed to the top of the greasy pole." But there was one regret. "If only your sister had been alive now to witness your triumph, what happiness it would have given her!" said a friend. "Ah, poor Sa, poor Sa! We've lost our audience, we've lost our audience", he murmured sorrowfully. On a different note, and one that might have jarred on his Sovereign, he acknowledged the felicitations of a lady who stopped her brougham in St James's Street to observe "You are at last in your right place, where you ought to be." "What is the good of it all so long as your husband is alive?" he rejoined. Mary Anne, now 75 years of age, was in raptures, and held a grand reception in the new Foreign Office. "Dizzy in his glory, leading about the Princess of Wales; the Prince of Wales, Mrs Dizzy—she looking very ill and haggard. The impenetrable man low." Thus Bishop Wilberforce in his diary. But very soon the impenetrable man made the Bishop more fluent.

The whigs, liberals, radicals and Irish together had a majority of sixty odd over the new Government, and Gladstone had now become leader of the Opposition party in succession to Russell. These two figures, Disraeli and Gladstone, were to dominate the political scene for the next thirteen years; and it would be difficult to find two men in all history who had so little in common, whose natures were so diametrically opposed. It has already been said that the only noticeable similarity between Palmerston and Gladstone was that they were both born of woman. In the case of Disraeli and Gladstone, they might have sprung from different species. A famous socialist who was also a close if not acute observer of men and events, Henry Mayers Hyndham, wrote:

"Why Mr Gladstone, who changed his opinions whenever it suited his convenience, after turning from the extremest Toryism to advanced Liberalism, should have been credited with the highest political morality, while Disraeli, who, having once chosen his party, stuck to it all his life without the slightest shadow of turning, was regarded as a man of few scruples, I am at a loss to understand." The explanation is simple. Apart from the fact that Englishmen instinctively distrust anyone and anything alien to themselves, Gladstone was the mouthpiece of his race and period. Everything that is impulsive, irrational, incoherent, and hysterical in the English people found expression in that Englishman, who also contained within himself the peculiar qualities of an age that exhibited self-righteousness, moral indignation, democratic enthusiasm and religious emotionalism; everything in short that Disraeli could not endure. Though he was the outstanding figure of the late Victorian epoch, his fame penetrating to places where no other Englishman's name was even known, we can now see that Gladstone was neither a great man nor a great character; for he lacked the imagination, honesty, wisdom and tolerance of the first, the humour, charity and consistence of the second. He was a creature of fantasy, the victim of hallucination, a phenomenon, whose fanatical driving-power and remarkable command of imposing if somewhat obscure phraseology captivated the large and newly enfranchised lower and middle classes, making them feel that he was an inspired political prophet and a godlike personality; since people are easily impressed by one who possesses common qualities on a vast scale, and invariably suspect one who possesses uncommon qualities which they do not share. He was more of a portent than a person, a fiery force, a compulsive element, at the mercy of his own rhetoric and completely losing sight of material things when under the influence of his frenzied outpourings; for the power of oratory can sway the orator as much as the power of office can sway the officer. Politics with him was a matter of morals, with Disraeli a question of expedients. In his eyes Disraeli was a devil; in Disraeli's eyes he was a madman. But Gladstone was as crafty as he was impulsive, as malevolent as he was self-righteous. He played the political game with uncanny ability, and Disraeli needed all his wits to outmanœuvre so wily and unscrupulous an antagonist.

What disabled Gladstone as a human being, but contributed greatly to his personal majesty and public achievement, was a total lack of humour. He could shout with glee over riddles that would amuse boys of twelve, but his own jokes, said Lord Derby, were no laughing matter. He loved disputation and would argue about anything: he once discussed, earnestly and lengthily, the grave question of whether there was more to eat in a boiled or a poached egg. But like all men of his type he was a complete egotist, took no part in any conversation that did not interest him, and had no small talk whatever. When not holding forth on his own subjects, he withdrew into himself; when not haranguing he was mute. Queen Victoria could chat away gaily about her paintings and her distant German cousins with the sympathetic and courteous Disraeli; but she had to listen while Gladstone lectured her on the Hittites or Homer or the Athanasian Creed.

Their dissimilarity of attitude in social life is best conveyed by an anecdote. One year at the Royal Academy banquet Disraeli (who had just become Lord Beaconsfield) criticised the pictures to Robert Browning: "What a terrible display! How entirely destitute is our English School of all spirituality, all ideality, in painting!" But in his speech after the dinner he said that the feature which most forcibly struck him in the surrounding exhibition was the high tone of spirituality and ideality. Browning thought this very funny and related it to Gladstone, who glared at him and said "Do you call that story amusing, Browning? I call it devilish." Yet if guests were to say what they truly thought on such occasions, there would be no public banquets; and as it was the Prime Minister's duty to make a speech, he clearly felt that he had better say the exact opposite of what he considered quite obvious, in the hope that intelligent people would appreciate the irony. Gladstone would have pumped up some spurious emotion for the occasion, and before sitting down would have persuaded himself that he was the apostle of integrity. A good deal of his fury with the tory leader was due to a secret conviction that Disraeli despised his fiery oratory and derided his ardent opinions. It was perhaps his only conviction that was firmly based on truth. His speeches and writings made Dizzy's head ache.

A journalist of the time wrote of "the ambidextrous constitution" of Gladstone's mind, which prevented him from making a candid statement. Undoubtedly his mind was tortuous, and a maze of conflict while communing with himself, but when he had reached a decision he was forthright enough, because, having hypnotised himself into believing that his was the voice of justice and truth, his assertions were vatic in authority and histrionic in intensity: he boiled over, his words rushing forth in a cataract of burning eloquence. One of his greatest admirers, Henry Labouchere, said "I don't object to Gladstone always having the ace of trumps up his sleeve, but merely to his belief that God Almighty put it there." The point is that he really did believe himself to be the instrument of God, and so the sentiments and moral platitudes and theatrical attitudes which in another would be rightly dismissed as cant and humbug were in his case the fermentations of his inmost being.

With such a man it is hopeless to look for consistency and impossible to harmonise the guile of his policy with the sincerity of his emotions. His jealousy and hatred of Disraeli no doubt caused his change of front over the question of the Irish Church. He wanted to break the new Prime Minister, to banish Satan from the Treasury bench, and he saw a chance of doing so by whipping up the feeling in the country in favour of church reform. Hitherto he had refused to support the whigs in their attacks on the Protestant Church in Ireland, and right up to the year 1866 had resisted every attempt to interfere with it. But within three weeks of Disraeli's promotion, Gladstone announced the Liberal party's new policy: the disestablishment and disendowment of the Irish Church. He contrived to get the support of Archbishop Manning, who had previously been in friendly correspondence with Disraeli and who had probably been induced by Gladstone to believe that the Roman Church might benefit from the revenues of the disendowed Protestant Church. It did not take Gladstone long to convince himself that his was a righteous cause; though when it became clear that his move had united Roman Catholics, Dissenters, Secularists, Radicals, spoliators generally, and even Anglican ritualists, it was permissible to wonder whether political trickery was not a more suitable description of the party cry for 'justice to Ireland' and 'religious equality.' In the Commons debate Disraeli was gently ironic. Curious, he said, that Gladstone and his friends should have suddenly recog-

" CRITICS "

Mr. Gladstone : " Hm !—Flippant ! " *Mr. Disraeli* : " Ha !—Prosy ! "

" *Punch* " *cartoon by Sir John Tenniel*

" THE JUNIOR AMBASSADOR "

By Ape

GEORGE SMYTHE, 7TH VISCOUNT STRANGFORD

By R. Buckner

nised the vital importance of a question towards which they had been completely indifferent when in power. Curious, too, that a controversy which had lasted seven hundred years should have become so urgent the moment he had taken office. "It has come on us like a thief in the night", he told a colleague. The Bishop of Winchester had just suffered a paralytic stroke, and Disraeli attributed Gladstone's violent course partly to that. "Strange that a desire to make Bishops should lead a man to destroy Churches", he remarked to Lord Derby. Announcing his own decision to stand firm against the spoliators, he said: "I view with great jealousy the plunder of a Church, because, so far as history can guide me, I have never found that Churches are plundered except to establish or enrich oligarchies", and he believed that the State, disjoined from the Church, was merely an affair "of the police office, of the tax-gatherer, of the guard-room."

While this question hung like a thunder-cloud over Disraeli's Administration throughout his nine months of office, other matters demanded and received his attention. By passing the Corrupt Practices Bill, he ensured the principle that bribery and such-like misdemeanours at political elections should henceforth be dealt with by judges instead of politicians. A war in Abyssinia, caused by the refusal of King Theodore to release the British consul and envoy whom he had capriciously imprisoned, was brought to a successful conclusion by Sir Robert Napier; and though it cost double the sum voted for it, which, said Disraeli, was "likely to be the case in all wars for which I may be responsible", it was finished in one campaign, and raised British prestige in the East. "Money is not to be considered in such matters", he wisely said: "success alone is to be thought of." He also took over the electric telegraph system for the Postmaster-General's department, and passed a law which put an end to the popular spectacle of public executions.

His relationship with the Queen during his short tenure of office became more personal than had been the case with any Prime Minister since her first, Lord Melbourne, and was later to become even warmer than his. The letters which Disraeli sent her were of such a nature that she responded with flowers. Never before had she been told everything that went on behind the scenes, and never before had she experienced such considerate and humanly respectful treatment, which unconsciously influenced her to dislike his political opponents. "Really there never was such conduct as that of the Opposition", she wrote to him, and again "The Queen is really shocked at the way in which the House of Commons go on", meaning the way in which Gladstone and company were not being kind to Disraeli. He presented her with his novels, and she reciprocated with her *Leaves from the Journal of our Life in the Highlands*, in which he discerned "a freshness and fragrance . . . like the heather amid which it was written." After that, in talking of literature with her, he would sometimes refer to "We authors, ma'am", and once he was heard to say "Your Majesty is the head of the literary profession." In September '68 he went to spend ten days at Balmoral Castle as Minister in attendance. At Carlisle a crowd collected on the station platform and cheered him. "It was an ordeal of ten minutes", he reported to his wife: "I bowed to them and went on reading, but was glad when the train moved." Separation from Mary Anne distressed him; it was, he said, a great trial "which no one can understand except those who live on the terms of entire affection and companionship like ourselves: and I believe they are very few." The Queen made his stay as pleasant as possible, but nothing could reconcile him to the separation from his wife: "I am sustained by the speedy prospect of our being again together, and talking over 1000 things." And on the eve of his departure from Balmoral he wrote: "The joy of our soon meeting again is inexpressible."

Not the least of a Prime Minister's worries is the appointment of suitable people to particular posts, but Disraeli managed to get some amusement out of it. Having promoted Lord Abercorn to a dukedom, he noticed that it made him "very happy, and six inches taller." Lord Mayo became Viceroy of India, and it was one of Disraeli's happiest appointments, though Gladstone threatened to cancel it if he came to power and would no doubt have done so had the Queen not put her foot down. The relations between England and America were greatly improved by Disraeli's Government, as a result of which a notable Senator, Reverdy Johnson, was appointed Minister in London. Disraeli at once asked him down to Hughenden to meet the hero of the Abyssinian war, who had just been created Lord Napier of Magdala. It seems that Johnson's visit was a success. "The ladies like him", wrote Disraeli. "He has eleven children, and 33 grandchildren, so they call him Grandpapa . . . His manners, tho', at first, rather abrupt and harsh, are good; he is self-possessed, and turns out genial." Disraeli himself was always genial with people he liked, and never went out of his way to be the opposite with those he disliked. "I have given him the mercy of my silence", he said to someone who asked why he had not replied to a vicious attack by a man he despised. A particularly pleasing feature of his character was his habit of returning good for evil. John Leech had cruelly ridiculed him in *Punch* from the beginning of his career, satirising him as a spiteful ringleted viper, a Jew dealer in cast-off notions, etc, etc. Leech's widow died in '68, and Disraeli, hearing that her two children needed help, continued to them the pension that had ceased with her.

The cleverness of Gladstone's campaign for the disestablishment and disendowment of the Irish Church lay in the fact that it appealed to everyone's cupidity, and Disraeli tried to counter it by making ecclesiastical appointments that would unite the greater part of the Church of England and win its support for the Tory party. This could only be done, he thought, by appealing to its evangelicals, not to its ritualists, for he had already seen the country's reaction to "papal aggression" and knew that the High Church party was thoroughly distrusted by the majority of protestants on account of its Romish tendencies and practices. His job therefore was to fight what he called the "Rits and Rats" (ritualists and rationalists) and though the bent of his own mind was towards the High Church he started to make Low Church appointments. Unfortunately he knew very little about the clergy and not much about the Establishment, for though a regular churchgoer he had not mixed with prominent churchmen, nor had he heard the famous preachers of the day. Some years later than the period we have reached Dean Stanley met him in the street one Sunday and asked him to enter Westminster Abbey, where he would hear a sermon by a canon of his own appointment, F. W. Farrar. Dizzy was fascinated by the windows, the effects of light and shade, the devotion of the crowd. "I would not have missed the sight for anything!" he exclaimed; but it was clearly a novel experience for him, a sort of Arabian Nights entertainment. Now, in 1868, ignorant of the names and descriptions of the people he was recommending for promotion, he began to study Crockford's clerical directory, and to spend hours talking and writing and receiving private reports about vicars, canons, archdeacons, deans and bishops. One important personality he knew well, Samuel Wilberforce, Bishop of Oxford, the diocese in which he resided; and Wilberforce did his utmost to induce Disraeli to make High Church appointments. But Disraeli discovered by cautious enquiry that Wilberforce was "more odious than Laud" in the country: he was believed to have strong Romish inclinations; three of his brothers and two brothers-in-law, Manning being one of them, had joined the Roman Church, and even his daughter and her husband had followed them into the papal fold. Moreover Wilberforce had been the close friend and counsellor of Gladstone. His advice was therefore received by Disraeli with one ear and dismissed through the other.

The Prime Minister commenced his plan to rally the protestants and rout the Gladstonians by appointing a strong evangelical to the Deanery of Ripon. At once he encountered opposition from the Queen, who had been trained by the Consort in Broad Church principles and was against the fanaticism of both High and Low. She told Disraeli that she wanted "moderate, sensible, clever men", neither evangelical nor ritualistic, to be given the chief offices. "Where are they to be found?" he enquired. She mentioned one: Dr Magee, Dean of Cork. But the objection to Magee, from a political point of view, was that he had no influence in the Church. However, the Queen carried her point, and Magee was made Bishop of Peterborough, justifying his description as a moderate, sensible, clever man some years later, when he was mobbed by rioters while consecrating a cemetery. "I inflicted on them the ignominy of the episcopal blessing, and dismissed them from my mind", he informed the House of Lords. Magee had written to Disraeli asking for a minor appointment and perhaps daring to hope for a canonry. He received a comedian's reply. On the first page the Prime Minister regretfully refused his application for a minor appointment, but on turning it over Magee found that he had been given a bishopric instead.

The next vacancy that occurred was the highest in the Church. The Archbishop of Canterbury died, and the Queen insisted that the only person fit for the position was the then Bishop of

London, A. C. Tait, a liberal in politics and a broad churchman, neither of which persuasions appealed to Disraeli, who must have had an almost heated argument with the Queen, because he emerged from the royal closet in an irritable frame of mind, saying to Lord Malmesbury "Don't bring any more bothers before me; I have enough already to drive a man mad." Tait became Archbishop, and it was generally expected that the see of London would be offered to Wilberforce, who shared the expectation. But Disraeli was convinced of his universal unpopularity, and did not mention him to the Queen, who would have approved the choice. When Wilberforce heard that he had been passed over he felt the affront keenly, resumed his intimacy with Gladstone, whom he called great and earnest and honest, and became a bitter critic of Disraeli, whom he called tricky and cunning and unprincipled. His attitude was certainly human if not markedly Christian; and it did not become more christlike when, Gladstone having made him Bishop of Winchester, he found himself portrayed as a somewhat worldly prelate in Dizzy's next novel. "My wrath against D. has burnt before this so fiercely that it seems to have burnt up all the materials for burning . . ." he wrote. The roasting of others having formerly been a pastime of holy men, it was a step in the right direction for a bishop to cremate himself.

All Disraeli's carefully considered moves on the clerical chessboard came to naught; Gladstone checkmated him with the effective slogans of justice and equality, and the new working class voters were easily gulled into believing that their enfranchisement was due to the whigs and liberals, not to the tories. Gladstone's "pilgrimages of passion" had already become a feature of electoral campaigns, surpassing in popularity the tours of religious revivalists, and proving even more attractive than a circus. His eloquence was described by Lord Derby as "balderdash and braggadocio", but it went down with the mob, and doubled the liberal majority in the House of Commons. Disraeli immediately resigned without waiting to be defeated by a vote in parliament.

On leaving office in December '68 he was sixty-four years of age, his wife seventy-six, and having attained the object of his ambition it seemed a dreary prospect once more to lead and again to reanimate a depressed Opposition. But on private and public grounds the Queen was against his retirement, and said that he could render her most useful service out of office. Derby, too, declared that his presence in the House was indispensable; and the probability is that, even among the groves of Hughenden, he would have pined for the benches of Westminster. There was another alternative: he could withdraw to the House of Lords. But both he and his Sovereign knew that his peculiar gifts would be of far greater value to the country in the Commons, for there was no one else who could match Gladstone in debate and check his dangerous enthusiasms. Disraeli, however, wished his wife to enjoy what expediency prevented himself from taking, and asked the Queen to bestow a title on Mary Anne. He suggested that she should be created Viscountess Beaconsfield in her own right, a place with which he had long been connected, and the nearest town to Hughenden which had not yet been ennobled. In granting his request, the Queen expressed "her deep sense of Mr Disraeli's kindness and consideration towards her, not only in what concerned her personally, but in listening to her wishes. . . ." His grateful acknowledgment of her favour began: "Mr Disraeli at your Majesty's feet . . ."

Chapter XIX

THE IMPENETRABLE MAN

WITHIN a week or two of his resignation Disraeli's brother James died suddenly, leaving him £5000 and something less pleasant, the cares of an executor. His private circumstances were now satisfactory. A tory admirer had bought his debts from the moneylenders in 1863, charging him three per cent instead of the ten per cent he had previously been paying, which meant a gain of some £5000 a year. In '66 his gross annual income was in the region of £9000, but by that time he was benefiting from the legacy of Mrs Brydges Willyams. It was therefore easy for him to advise a friend "Do not let your mind dwell upon what you want and what you have not got: always fix your mind upon what you have got." He had got Hughenden with its trees, which he preferred even to pictures, a wife he adored, and a comfortable income. But one can only be carefree and indolent if one is mentally and physically healthy, and his bodily health gave him as much trouble as the mental disease caused by recurring spasms of ambition.

To many of his supporters he appeared to have lost the zest for political conflict when faced by Gladstone's huge majority. Of course he opposed the Irish Church Bill, but not with his old energy. He adopted an almost fatalistic attitude, though he warned the House that the liberal policy would eventuate in civil war and the severance of the union between England and Ireland, as indeed it did. The Government having deprived the bishops and rectors of their property, the Irish people naturally expected that the landlords would be deprived of theirs; and he described what happened as an immediate result of Church disendowment and the release of Fenian criminals: "Landlords were shot down like game; respectable farmers were beaten to death with sticks by masked men; bailiffs were shot in the back; policemen were stabbed; the High Sheriff of a county going to swear in the grand jury was fired at in his carriage and dangerously wounded; households were blown up, and firearms surreptitiously obtained." Gladstone's Land Act followed, but it did not satisfy the Irish; and as it again became necessary to suppress crime, the Government asked for a secret committee to enquire into the lawlessness rampant in Westmeath. Disraeli had a few more observations to make about Gladstone: "Under his influence and at his instance we have legalised confiscation, consecrated sacrilege, condoned high treason; we have destroyed churches, we have shaken property to its foundation, and we have emptied gaols; and now he cannot govern a county without coming to a Parliamentary Committee! The right hon. gentleman . . . is making government ridiculous."

Lord Derby died in October '69 and his son Lord Stanley, who had been Disraeli's intimate friend for many years and Foreign Secretary in his recent Cabinet, became the fifteenth Earl. The party wanted him to take his father's place as leader in the Lords, but he refused. Then it was suggested that Lord Salisbury, who succeeded his father in April '68, and who, as Lord Robert Cecil and Lord Cranborne, had virulently attacked Disraeli, should lead the party in the Upper House; but that was ruled out on account of his continued hostility to Dizzy. Indeed, in the autumn of '69, he again felt it necessary to fling mud at the tory chief in *The Quarterly Review*, calling him, though not by name, a base and dishonest leader, whose conduct merited the utmost contempt. In the end the Duke of Richmond became head of the party in the House of Peers.

Apart from his Irish legislation Gladstone's main achievement during the 1869–70 sessions was the Education Act, which in effect made elementary education compulsory throughout the country. Disraeli's Government had also done something along these lines, and he did not oppose Gladstone's Bill except to criticise the undenominational nature of religious teaching in the schools, the dogmas of the schoolmaster being substituted for those of the priest. Nearly all the famous Victorians cherished an innocent belief in the mental and spiritual advantages of general education; but after eighty years of enforced instruction we are beginning to wonder whether a level of intelligence that enables the majority to enjoy the products of Hollywood, while a minority discovers how to blow the world to bits, exactly realises the dreams of those hopeful pioneers. The solution of the problem seems to be that children should be taught how to read and write as well as simple arithmetic, after which they should be at liberty to cease their education or continue it along congenial lines: they have a right to the key of knowledge, but must unlock and open the door for themselves.

Disraeli's apparent lack of vigour in these years of Gladstone's first Government was due to four things. First of all, he believed that if he waited patiently Gladstone would sooner or later enrage the country with the feebleness of his foreign policy, and that attacks on the Government over home affairs would merely strengthen it. Secondly, his health was poor, as always after periods of intense activity, and he was compelled to take things easily. Thirdly, he was quietly building up a large Tory party organisation. And, fourthly, he spent some months during 1869–70 in writing a novel. He told a friend that his illness had made him think too much of himself, a habit that made a man selfish and disgusted his friends. Yet in spite of his preoccupation with his health and his novel, he managed not only to perform most of his parliamentary duties but to establish the Tory party on a popular basis it had never before enjoyed. He was in fact the first person to create a party machine, for he perceived that the new electorate which his Reform Bill had brought into being must be systematised in an efficient and up-to-date manner. He appointed an excellent manager, John Eldon Gorst, who acted throughout under his close supervision. A Central Conservative Office was instituted in Whitehall; local associations were formed; each constituency was encouraged to choose its own candidate and keep him prepared for emergencies, but candidates were to be supplied by the Central Office when required and then approved by the local committees; the conditions in every borough were carefully studied at headquarters; constant communication was kept up with the local managers, expert advice given, and by 1872 the whole organisation was in good running order. It was a remarkable achievement, the result of which became apparent at the next General Election; but we may question whether Disraeli would have approved of its consequences; for the Liberal party soon bettered his instruction, the Labour party followed suit; independent politicians have practically disappeared from the House of Commons; Ministers are no longer subject to parliamentary control; and men are at the mercy of their machines.

It is strange to think that in the preliminary stages of this nation-wide plan Disraeli was calmly composing a work of fiction, his first since *Tancred* twenty-two years earlier. No one except his wife knew that he was writing it, not even Monty Corry, who opened all his letters, dealt with all his papers, and possessed his entire confidence in political affairs. He had refused an offer of £10,000 for a novel, made to him by a publisher on his resignation from office; and *Lothair* was brought out by Longmans in May 1870. As with all his novels, this one is interesting to us now solely for the light it throws on the author. Though none of his novels is a work of genius, nearly all of them are the works of a genius, but one whose function in life is not that of a creative artist. Great literature results from the complete harmony of feeling and thought. Their disharmony in first-class writers produces such work as the story of Little Nell in *The Old Curiosity Shop*, where the emotion is unchecked by thought, or Gulliver's *Voyage to the Houyhnhnms*, where the intelligence is unsoftened by feeling. In Shakespeare their harmony is seen in the marvellous balance of *Lear*, their disharmony in the monstrous aberration of *Timon*. Disraeli suffered from a permanent disjunction of thought and feeling, due to the fundamental conflict in his nature: he longed to be an artist and he longed to be a statesman, the two desires being irreconcilable and opposite. His natural genius was for action, his success in which would have been thwarted by his artistic sense had he not possessed the patience and perseverance of his race. His talent as a writer was marred by his desire for conquest in another sphere, for he failed to attain the equipoise of thought and feeling, the detachment, of the pure artist.

We need not therefore consider his novels as works of art, only as signs of his progress as a politician; and the interesting thing to remark about *Lothair* is that the hero, instead of searching for a political, religious or sociological faith, as in the earlier novels, has become the object of the search. In other words, Disraeli has achieved his ambition, has been Prime Minister, and therefore embodies the prize for which other men fight. The Church of Rome, the Church of England, and the revolutionary forces of Nationalism, contend for his soul. Rome, chiefly in the person of a Cardinal (modelled on Manning), has a good innings, and is matched against a Bishop of the Established Church (Wilberforce). Then Revolution appears in the person of Theodora, a saintlike woman to whom Lothair is passionately attached, and whose low voice sounds "like the breathing of some divine shrine." The hero is beguiled into fighting for it (Revolution) on account of her (Theodora). The scene moves to Italy. We hear of a fabulous female whose influence among the revolutionists in France is as great as Garibaldi's in Italy, and whose name is Mary-Anne; but we do not know whether the author's wife appreciated the compliment. Of Garibaldi we are told that "when he stamps his foot men rise from the earth", though not apparently in sufficient numbers, for he is defeated at Mentana, Theodora being killed and Lothair badly wounded. Our hero is nursed back to health by Roman Catholics, who use his miraculous recovery as propaganda for their faith, which disgusts him; and Lothair would not have been Disraeli if he had not set sail for the Holy Land, where a Syrian consoles him with philosophy: "As for Pantheism, it is Atheism in domino. The belief in a Creator who is unconscious of creating is more monstrous than any dogma of any of the churches." After all the pother about his soul, he eventually subsides into the Church of England; at least that is the religion of the lady he marries.

It seemed to the Victorians a miracle that a famous statesman should be capable of writing novels, and Disraeli played up to them by making his tales as miraculous as possible: the plots are preposterous, the incidents ridiculous, the backgrounds luxurious, and the characters nebulous. Princes, princesses, dukes, duchesses, lords and ladies, flit through the pages, and are described as lovely, gracious, distinguished, exquisite, charming, and so on. It is perhaps to Disraeli that we can trace a malign influence on the writers of reminiscences, whose adjectives of praise become more luscious as their objects rise in the social scale. He ridicules a painter or pressman, but he would not dream of ridiculing a peer. The most entertaining person in the book is 'Mr Phoebus', an artist, who is a sincere admirer of the English aristocracy: "On the whole they most resemble the old Hellenic race; excelling in athletic sports, speaking no other language than their own, and never reading." So he gives practical advice to Lothair: "That imperfect secretion of the brain which is called thought has not yet bowed your frame. You have not had time to read much. Give it up altogether. . . . We may know a great deal about our bodies, we can know very little about our minds." And again: "Man is born to observe, but if he falls into psychology he observes nothing, and then he is astonished that life has no charms for him, or that, never seizing the occasion, his career is a failure." Mr Phoebus has no illusions about his fellow-painters: "If you want to know what envy is you should live among artists. You should hear me lecture at the Academy. I have sometimes suddenly turned round and caught countenances like that of the man who was waiting at the corner of the street for Benvenuto Cellini, in order to assassinate the great Florentine." But not being envious himself, he wishes others to delight in his glory: "I should like to get over to the Academy dinner . . . and dine with the R.A.s in my ribbon and the star of the Alexander Newsky in brilliants. I think every Academician would feel elevated."

In this novel Disraeli again warns the world against the secret societies which would one day successfully subvert both church and state and seize power. They denounce "all the great truths and laws on which the family reposes . . . Their religion is the religion of science." The fight of the future would be between the Church and the secret societies: "They are the only two strong things in Europe, and will survive kings, emperors, or parliaments." Along with these grave matters we can enjoy the scintillations to which the earlier novels have accustomed us:

"'I believe that nothing in the newspapers is ever true', said Madame Phoebus. 'And that is why they are so popular', added Euphrosyne; 'the taste of the age being so decidedly for fiction'."

"'My idea of an agreeable person', said Hugo Bohun, 'is a person who agrees with me'."

"I am not fond of Irish affairs: whatever may be said, and however plausible things may look, in an Irish business there is always a priest at the bottom of it."

"The pursuit of science leads only to the insoluble."

"I have always thought that every woman should marry, and no man."

"The great majority of men exist but do not live."

"A Protestant, if he wants aid or advice on any matter, can only go to his solicitor."

"If every man were straightforward in his opinions, there would be no conversation. The fun of talk is to find out what a man really thinks, and then contrast it with the enormous lies he has been telling all dinner, and, perhaps, all his life."

"Nothing in life is more remarkable than the unnecessary anxiety which we endure, and generally occasion ourselves."

"You know who the critics are? The men who have failed in literature and art."

None of Disraeli's works had been warmly received by the critics, and when, later, he wrote a preface to *Lothair*, he gave them further cause for coolness: "There are critics, who, abstractedly, do not approve of successful books, particularly if they have failed in the same style." Disparaging reviews, tinged by political prejudice, were written by the pundits of *Blackwood's*, the *Athenaeum*, the *Edinburgh*, and the *Quarterly*, the last-named calling the novel an outrage, a sin against taste, a mass of un-English verbiage, and as dull as ditchwater; so in the preface to which allusion has been made Disraeli referred to those critics who "flatter themselves that, by systematically libelling some eminent personage of their time, they have a chance of descending to posterity."

The one fascinating aspect of the publication is not in the novel but in the novelist. That a man who had just been Prime Minister of England, at its most spiritually costive and moral-bound period, should have turned aside to write a book of gossamer satire and gaudy romance, was enough to unite against him all the tories, liberals, churchmen and dissenters in the land. How could such a man be serious? they asked. Tory heads wagged disapprovingly, Liberal faces expressed something between complacence and reproach, the godly folk frowned. It was, in fact, a prime example of the independence and incalculability of genius, the sort of thing that makes Disraeli the most attractive figure in the history of English politics. No one knew what he would be up to next. Nor did he. But the general public felt no misgivings, and the novel was amazingly successful. Streets, horses, ships, songs, dances and perfumes, were named after the leading characters. Edition followed edition, and in America 80,000 copies were sold within six months. A few people disliked the sketches of themselves which appeared in the story, particularly Professor Goldwin Smith, who objected to being called a social parasite and published a letter which, referring to the author's expressions as "the stingless insults of a coward", helped to send up the sales.

While the English people were busy buying and discussing *Lothair* the Franco-German war broke out, and Disraeli, the soundest prophet in English political life, at once perceived its true significance, explaining to the House of Commons that it was quite unlike any recent war, for it represented "the German revolution, a greater political event than the French revolution of last century . . . Not a single principle in the management of our foreign affairs, accepted by all statesmen for guidance up to six months ago, any longer exists. There is not a diplomatic tradition which has not been swept away. You have a new world, new influences at work, new and unknown objects and dangers with which to cope, at present involved in that obscurity incident to novelty in such affairs . . . The balance of power has been entirely destroyed, and the country which suffers most, and feels the effects of this great change most, is England." A man who could look so far ahead, and accurately foretell the effects of a new national feeling in the centre of Europe, would also have foreseen a more recent development of power-mania in the east of Europe and taken early measures to make it ineffective. He could judge character as well as events, and put his finger on the main weakness of Napoleon III, whom he called good-natured, good-hearted, good-tempered, but "not a man of honour. In fact, that character is rather rare out of England. At least I have found it so in life, and I have seen not a little of Sovereigns and Ministers."

Seeing that France and Germany were otherwise engaged, and that England was too weak to act alone, Russia decided that the time had come to tear up the treaty, making the Black Sea neutral, which she had signed after the Crimean War. Gladstone's Government stupidly threatened a war, and then climbed down, agreeing to a Conference which met on the understanding that the treaty would be modified. Disraeli proceeded to make Gladstone sit up. Indeed an observer of the scene said that the Prime Minister could scarcely keep his seat while his antagonist cut him up with the utmost sang-froid, and when at last he lept from it to reply "he was in a white passion, and almost choked with words." But these rages were partly theatrical, and if his rival were being useful he could be gentle. When, for instance, several public men in America, including the President, publicly abused Great Britain for not settling the claims against her arising from the Civil War, Gladstone assured the House that Disraeli's prudence and forbearance during the conflict entitled him to criticise the U.S. without offence. "Though I should look upon it as the darkest hour of my life", said Disraeli, "if I were to counsel or even support a war with the United States, still the United States should know that they are not an exception to the other countries of the world; that we do not permit ourselves to be insulted by any other country in the world, and that they cannot be an exception." Times have changed, and Great Britain now permits herself to be insulted by every country in the world without exception.

As usual Disraeli suffered more from his soi-disant friends than from the pinpricks of his declared enemies during these trying years of opposition. The tories had now evolved into conservatives, just as the whigs had evolved into liberals, in both cases because the old names had narrowed their appeal to the electorate; and the author of *Lothair* was scarcely a person to create confidence among those who wished to conserve their prejudices along with their property. To them it was a most suspicious circumstance that a Prime Minister should write novels in his spare time. A tract on religion? Yes. A political study? Of course. A treatise on economics? Certainly. A philosophical thesis? Quite in order. An essay on literature? Well . . . But a love-story: definitely NO. And so they hoped that the new Lord Derby would become their leader, the subject being seriously canvassed in clubs, at public meetings, and in the press. Even Disraeli's strongest supporters toyed with the idea of displacing him in favour of his late chief's son. It is curious that such a feeling should have gained ground at a moment when his own unadvertised efforts to bring about a great party triumph were on the eve of success. Somehow he got to hear of what almost amounted to a conspiracy, and instantly offered to resign his position to Derby if the party wished him to do so; though he added that in that event he would no longer lead them in the Commons but sit below the gangway. The malcontents were terrified by such a prospect, and ceased to conspire. This lack of loyalty having once more manifested itself, he became a little terse with the tory chief in the Upper House, writing to the Duke of Richmond to express his regret "at the habitual want of communication which now subsists between the leaders of our party in the two Houses." The Duke gave a satisfactory explanation and said that he was "most anxious that you should be satisfied that I have not been guilty of any want of courtesy towards you." After that harmony reigned, but Disraeli would stand no nonsense from any peer of the realm. "Talk not to me of dukes!" he once exclaimed: "Dukes can be made."

No more inclined to butter up the people than the peers, he never indulged in stump-oratory about the country after the fashion of Gladstone and Bright, rarely speaking outside his own constituency and the Commons. Matthew Arnold met him at Latimer in January '72 and found him very pleasant and amiable. Explaining why he had not made a public speech during the recess, he said "The Ministers are so busy going about apologising for their failures, that I think it a pity to distract public attention from the proceeding." His own popularity was not gained by such means, and must have been founded on a sure instinct among his countrymen for character, for someone they could depend on when the spouters and demagogues failed them. The first sign of this feeling was shown in the autumn of '71 when the youthful politicians of Scotland made him, instead of Ruskin, Lord Rector of Glasgow University. A prophet is not without honour, he may have thought, save in his own country and in his own House, where they know too much about him. But he would have been wrong, for a surprising demonstration of popular favour took place on February 27th, 1872, when the Prince of Wales drove to St Paul's Cathedral in order to offer up thanks for his restoration to health after an attack of typhoid fever. All the leading public figures followed him in their carriages, and it was noticed that Gladstone's reception by the crowd was either cool or unfriendly. But returning from the Cathedral a tremendous ovation was accorded to Disraeli, accompanying him all the way from the City, up Regent Street, along Oxford Street, down Park Lane to Grosvenor Gate, where he left Mary Anne, and continuing until he reached the Carlton Club. A member saw him in the Club talking county business to another member; but he had a strange far-away look in his eyes and appeared statuesque in his immobility; it was as if he knew for certain that he would again be Prime Minister.

This seemingly sudden access of popularity was also made evident at Manchester, which he visited with his wife that Easter, and where he was given a tumultuous reception. Their carriage was drawn through the town by admirers; in pelting rain the deputations from Conservative Associations paraded before him with their banners; and he spoke for three and a quarter hours to a packed meeting in the Free Trade Hall, with the assistance of two bottles of white brandy, which looked like water and was finished by him in large doses diluted with the liquid it resembled. He entertained his audience with a short account of the Gladstone Government, which had behaved "like a body of men under the influence of some deleterious drug. Not satiated with the spoliation and anarchy of Ireland, they began to attack every institution and every interest, every class and calling in the country":

> As time advanced it was not difficult to perceive that extravagance was being substituted for energy by the Government. The unnatural stimulus was subsiding. Their paroxysms ended in prostration. Some took refuge in melancholy, and their eminent chief alternated between a menace and a sigh. As I sat opposite the Treasury Bench the Ministers reminded me of one of those marine landscapes not very unusual on the coasts of South America. You behold a range of exhausted volcanoes. Not a flame flickers on a single pallid crest. But the situation is still dangerous. There are occasional earthquakes, and ever and anon the dark rumbling of the sea.

He spoke once more in June at a Crystal Palace banquet, declaring that the whole energy and ability of the Liberal party had been devoted to the disintegration of the British Empire: "And, gentlemen, of all its efforts, this is the one which has been the nearest to success." As for their claim to be the people's party, Disraeli saw it in this light: "The tone and tendency of Liberalism cannot be concealed. It is to attack the institutions of the country under the name of Reform and to make war on the manners and customs of the people under the pretext of progress." He seldom made a speech without coining a phrase that became familiar in men's mouths as household words. A few may be quoted:

"Justice is truth in action."

"The English nation is never so great as in adversity."

"I have learnt again what I have often learnt before, that you should never take anything for granted."

"A university should be a place of light, of liberty, and of learning."

"There can be no economy where there is no efficiency."

"How much easier it is to be critical than to be correct."

"Increased means and increased leisure are the two civilisers of man."

"An author who speaks about his own books is almost as bad as a mother who talks about her own children."

"The new philosophy" (i.e. a belief in physical and material equality) "strikes further than at the existence of patriotism. It strikes at the home; it strikes at the individuality of man. It would reduce civilised society to human flocks and herds."

Were the speaker alive today, he would have less to retract than any other politician of the past.

Chapter XX

THE INEVITABLE HOUR

THE excitements of Manchester had been too much for Mary Anne, now eighty years of age, and she became seriously ill; but the vigour of her spirit was such that she rallied and kept a number of social engagements. The older she grew the odder she got, saying the most unexpected things and dressing in the strangest fashion. "I could not help occasionally pitying her husband for the startling effect her natural speeches must have upon the ears of his great friends", wrote Sir Stafford Northcote to his wife. But his pity was wasted, for Dizzy wholly enjoyed her impromptus, relating them to his friends, as in this instance to Corry: "She delighted Fortescue by telling him that she had heard him very much praised. He pressed her very much when and where. She replied, 'It was in bed'." Everyone who knew her recognised her warm-heartedness and generosity. She declared that her happiness and buoyancy were due to her husband's constant care and affection: he never troubled, never contradicted her. And she returned his affectionate care. Once, in driving with him to Westminster where he had to take part in an important debate, her finger caught in the door of the carriage. The pain was great, but she went on chatting and laughing as if nothing had happened, lest his concern for her should prevent him from doing his best. "We have been married thirty-three years, and she has never given me a dull moment", he said. Separation, even for a few days, was unpleasant to both of them; each was necessary to the other's contentment. Asked by a fellow-Jew, Bernal Osborne, what feeling he could possibly have for that curious old lady, Disraeli replied "A feeling to your nature perfectly unknown: gratitude." Superficial people have inferred from this remark that he was grateful merely for her financial assistance at an important moment in his career. But gratitude is the corollary of love. The person who has once known love is always grateful for life, because the experience illuminates the whole of existence; and resentment with life is due to the lack of it.

At Hughenden, in May '72, it became clear that she was dying slowly of cancer. She could not eat and was in constant pain. "To see her every day weaker and weaker is heartrending", he wrote to Corry, "... to witness this gradual death of one who has shared so long, and so completely, my life, entirely unmans me." They were never apart now, and when he had to attend the House she accompanied him to London, making a few efforts to appear at social functions; until, one evening in July, she collapsed at a party and had to be taken home, after which she accepted no more invitations. Disraeli wrote little notes to her from his place in the Commons, and she to him from Grosvenor Gate. "I have nothing to tell you, except that I love you", one of his began. "I miss you sadly. I feel so grateful for your constant tender love and kindness", was her reply. He would dine with no one but her, and whenever possible he took her for drives. It was the first summer they had ever spent together in London, and they explored the suburbs as well as the nearby country of Essex, Surrey and Middlesex, being amazed at the miles of villas that were springing up in every direction, the gin-palaces which he called "gorgeous palaces of Geneva", and the "feudal castles", one being the new City prison in Camden Road, which, he said, "deserves a visit, I mean ex ernally." In August and September they covered some 220 miles by carriage, and Mary Anne's health seemed to have improved, so they went to Hughenden in October. She was even well enough to entertain a few friends there towards the close of November, including Lord John Manners, Lord Rosebery, Sir William Harcourt and Lord Ronald Gower, from the last of whom we learn that Dizzy left the conversation at dinner to his wife, and that he seemed far more distressed than she over her illness; his face, usually so impassive, being filled with suffering and woe. She died on December the 15th.

Though he must have been glad that her agony was not prolonged, he was overwhelmed by her death, and he could not deal with the messages of condolence that poured in by every post. The Queen, the Prince and Princess of Wales, foreign monarchs, statesmen, ambassadors, were as sympathetic as the farmers in his neighbourhood. Gladstone's letter inevitably included a pompously pious platitude: "I do not presume to offer you the consolation which you will seek from another and higher quarter." Disraeli's reply was heartfelt: "Marriage is the greatest earthly happiness, when founded on complete sympathy." At the end of the year he was at the house in Park Lane where he had spent half his life "in unbroken happiness" and at which he was staying for the last time. He came across a letter which had been written to him seventeen years earlier by his wife in the belief that she would die before him, asking that they should be buried in the same grave, saying that he had been a perfect husband to her, and advising him not to live alone: "Some one I earnestly hope you may find as attached to you as your own devoted Mary Anne."

For a while he resided at Edwards's Hotel, George Street, Hanover Square, but he could not bear the strangeness and solitude of his new existence and said tearfully to Lord Malmesbury "I hope some of my friends will take notice of me now in my great misfortune, for I have no home, and when I tell my coachman to drive home I feel it is a mockery." At once his friends asked him to quiet dinners; and, fortunately, a political crisis helped to relieve the heaviness and misery of his life. The Government's Irish University Bill was defeated in the Commons by the small majority of three, and Gladstone resigned. Disraeli was asked by the Queen to take over, but he assured her that he could not do so with a minority in the House and said that Gladstone ought to remain. When he heard this Gladstone, a political trickster himself, naturally suspected his rival of a trick, and Disraeli had to give the reasons for his refusal in a formal statement to the Queen. He knew that if he tried to govern with a minority he would court political disaster and destroy his chances at the next election. Gladstone knew it too, and explained to the Queen that, according to precedent, the Opposition should make every attempt to form a Ministry. But Disraeli was too wily for him; and after several days spent in verbal and written communications between the Sovereign and her recalcitrant counsellors, Gladstone resumed office.

Disraeli returned to Hughenden in July '73 and for several weeks was occupied in going through his wife's papers and putting them in order. He discovered that she had kept every word he had ever written to her, and every hair that she had cut from his head, a service she had performed at intervals of two or three weeks throughout their thirty-three years of married life. On August 10th he was able to tell Corry that he had finished his painful duty: "She has died for me 100 times in the heartrending, but absolutely inevitable, process." He stayed on at Hughenden in solitude and silence. On September 11th he said that he had not exchanged a word with another human being for a month, and that he had realised the feelings of "the fellow in the Iron Masque." He found solace in his parks and gardens, his pictures and books, never leaving his own grounds. "It is a dreary life, but I find society drearier." At the end of the month he visited London, but finding it intolerable he went down to Brighton, where he put up at the Bedford Hotel. Early in October he was staying with Lord and Lady Bradford at Weston in Shropshire, and one day he was persuaded to go cub-hunting at Chillington, some five miles away. He had only been on horseback twice in the last twenty-five years, but he faced the ordeal at the age of sixty-nine with equanimity. A friend met him at Chillington and noticed that he was wearing low shoes and white cotton socks and that his trousers were rucked up almost to the knees. In the course of the day they passed near the house of an old squire named Giffard, whom Disraeli had known well and who was now too ill to leave his armchair. Someone told Dizzy that it would be a kindly act if he called to see the squire. "No!" he said firmly. Pressed to do so, as Giffard would be distressed if he passed by without stopping for a chat, Disraeli still refused. On returning to Weston he was so exhausted that, having dismounted, he reeled and almost fell against the stable wall. He then explained why he had not called on Giffard: "It is necessary that I should give you my reason for not dismounting: it was founded upon my experience of this morning. I should have been glad to shake hands with my old friend, but I was convinced that, did I get off my horse, it would be a physical impossibility for me again to place myself in the saddle."

In November '73 he had to be installed as Lord Rector of Glasgow University, and when he received a list of the engagements arranged for his visit he complained to a friend: "My plans assume that I shall return to England alive; when I see the programme of the Glasgow week, it seems doubtful. Nothing can be more inhuman; and if there were a society to protect public men, as there is to protect donkeys, some interference would undoubtedly take place." However he survived, and his address to the students pleased them so much that they re-elected him in '74. In December he stayed at Sandringham, Blenheim, Ashridge, and other palatial places, and spent Christmas at Trentham. He had never much cared for "merrie Xmas" even as a boy: "I always hated factitious merriment, in the form of unnecessary guzzlement, and those awful inventions, round games, worse even than forfeits, if that be possible!" But apparently he managed to escape from Trentham without having suffered from boredom or biliousness, and continued his visits to country residences, Crichel, Heron Court, Bretby Park, until the end of January '74, when he returned to Edwards's Hotel, moving in a few weeks to a house he had taken at 2 Whitehall Gardens, within a short walk of Westminster.

Meanwhile a number of by-elections had shown that the country was getting tired of Gladstone's unsteady foreign policy, and in January '74 he advised the Queen to dissolve Parliament, in the hope that he would remain in power for another six years by making an appeal to the pockets of the citizenry and promising the abolition of the income tax. This sudden decision took Disraeli by surprise; but he was not unprepared, and in his speeches to the electorate he was able to show that the economies of the Liberal Government had gravely impaired England's position abroad, and would result in unnecessary expenditure whenever she was called upon to uphold it. The result of the General Election in February made Gladstone realise that his countrymen were not much attracted to what his rival called plundering and blundering. Disraeli's party obtained 350 seats, Gladstone's 245, the Irish Home Rulers 57; which meant a Conservative majority of about 50 over the rest of the House and 100 over the Liberal party alone. On February 18th Disraeli went to see the Queen, and assured her that, whatever the difficulties, her wishes would be carried out, perhaps with the mental reservation that he would be able to change her wishes when politically desirable. His difficulty in forming a Cabinet was mainly concerned with one man: Lord Salisbury, whose gifts made it necessary that he should be a leading member of the Government, instead of a hostile tory critic outside it. With characteristic finesse Disraeli approached him through two women, his sister and step-mother, and at length he was prevailed upon to meet the Prime Minister, though it is reported that he went through a severe internal struggle before doing so. Personal ambition coupled with the size of the Conservative majority doubtless helped to mitigate the misgivings of his conscience and to accelerate his mental process, for within a day or two of their meeting the Queen approved his appointment as Secretary of State for India. The Earl of Derby was again Foreign Secretary, and Sir Stafford Northcote became Chancellor of the Exchequer.

The business of Ministry-making for a man in his seventieth year, who for the first time had complete control of affairs, was thrilling but tiring. The interviews and correspondence kept him in the same room for days on end, and at the beginning of March, worn out, he went down to the Bedford Hotel at Brighton to recoup his strength. The "soft breezes and azure waters" did him good, and he was able to meditate on the long journey he had travelled between 1837 and 1874, and the many difficulties he had overcome: his origin, his foppishness, his debts, his novels, his ill-health, the disaster of his maiden speech, the rage of the Peelites, the antipathy of his party, the lethargy of his leader, his alien peculiarities, the liberalism of the age, the national distrust of genius and wit.

He once told the Duke and Duchess of Richmond that the last words of his first speech in parliament, drowned in a roar of ridicule, had been: "When I rise in this assembly hereafter, a dropped pin shall be heard." No man was ever more sure of himself. "Everything comes if a man will only wait", he wrote in *Tancred*, amplifying the maxim in *Endymion*: "I have brought myself by long meditation to the conviction that a human being with a settled purpose must accomplish it, and that nothing can resist a will that will stake even existence for its fulfilment." And again in the same novel: "There is nothing like will; everybody can do exactly what they like in this world, provided they really like it. Sometimes they think they do, but in general it is a mistake."

This is true; but, as he well knew, the sacrifice of everything else to the one desire is essential, and the question imposed itself upon him: was the victory worth the sacrifice? When congratulated on his final triumph, he remarked, "Yes, but it has come too late", and four years later, at the summit of his glory, he was heard to murmur: "Power! It has come to me too late. There were days when, on waking, I felt I could move dynasties and governments; but that has passed away." His wife, too, had passed away, and that was the saddest thought of all.

Chapter XXI

GLORY AND THE GOUT

THE success of the Conservative party at the election was of course seen by Gladstone as the triumph of Beelzebub, and his conduct would have attracted the attention of psycho-analysts if they had been invented by that time. First of all he behaved like a spoilt child, saying that he would only attend the parliamentary session occasionally. Then he made sudden incursions for the purpose of opposing whatever the Government proposed in a manner that must be described as neurotic. A year later he retired from the leadership of the Opposition, which was taken by Lord Hartington. This act of self-immolation produced symptoms of hysteria in the ex-leader, his ravings over the "Bulgarian atrocities" in '76, which might easily have resulted in a European war, making the Queen believe him to be mad. But, like Hamlet, he was only mad north-north-west: he knew how to catch votes.

There was much to agitate him in the calm progress of Disraeli's invention: Tory Democracy. The first two Labour members to appear on the political scene were returned for this parliament, Thomas Burt and Alexander Macdonald, the last of whom told his constituents in '79 that the Conservative party had done more for the working classes in five years than the Liberals had done in fifty, and at a Labour Congress thanked the Government for passing two Acts which constituted, according to a Trade Union Manual of Labour Laws, the charter of the social and industrial freedom of the working classes. In brief, Disraeli's Government tackled the problem of slum-clearance, erected new houses for artisans, formed Friendly Societies, secured the people's savings, gave workmen legal equality with their employers, lessened the working hours in factories, protected merchant seamen from the dangers of unseaworthy ships, prevented further enclosures of common lands, improved sanitation, cleansed the rivers of impurities and, in general, established the principles of Tory Democracy: that all government exists solely for the good of the governed, that all institutions are to be maintained only so far as they promote the happiness and welfare of the people, and that public functionaries are trustees, not for their own class, but for the nation as a whole.

Very reluctantly Disraeli also dealt with Ritualism in the Church of England. In private he described the practices of the ritualists as "high jinks", and he would have left them to their mummeries if his hand had not been forced by the Archbishop of Canterbury and the Queen, who insisted that the Government should support the Archbishop's Bill to check the prevalence of Ritualism. His Cabinet consisted of both High and Low churchmen, all of them prejudiced one way or the other, and he had to steer with an eye on every point of the political compass. A very awkward moment occurred when Salisbury advised his fellow-peers to ignore the blustering majority in the Lower House, which had passed an amendment to the Bill. This irritated the Commons, and Disraeli had the unwelcome job of appeasing his followers without provoking an important colleague, whom he described as "a great master of gibes and flouts and jeers." It was deftly done, and he succeeded in getting the Bill passed without the amendment that had annoyed Salisbury. He also managed not to annoy Salisbury, and a year later asked him to suggest "a good High Church Dean who is not a damned fool", as a result of which J. W. Burgon, remembered today solely for his line on Petra, "A rose-red city, half as old as time", was made Dean of Chichester. While suppressing "high jinks" Disraeli extended the influence of the Church by creating new dioceses, St Albans and Truro, in '75–6, and establishing four more sees by a Bill in '78: Liverpool, Newcastle, Wakefield, and Southwell. Archbishop Tait described what Disraeli had done for the Church as the greatest ecclesiastical reform since the Reformation.

In attending to such matters he did not neglect a necessary function of the State: the acknowledgment of its artists and scientists. He was consistently kind to men of letters and generous to their dependants when left poorly off. He wished there were some such order as the Legion of Honour for remarkable men, and when it was proposed that the well-known physicist, Professor Stokes, should receive recognition he said "I am sorry that society persists in cheapening a simple knighthood. It satisfied Sir Isaac Newton and Sir Walter Raleigh. Would it satisfy Stokes?" It was also suggested to Dizzy that Tennyson and Carlyle should be honoured, and he wrote to the Queen saying that the first could be made a baronet, and the second, who was childless and poor, might be offered the Grand Cross of the Order of the Bath, plus a pension. The Queen agreed, and Disraeli wrote to them personally. In his letter to Carlyle he said that the names of only two living authors would be remembered: "One is that of a poet; if not a great poet, a real one; and the other is your own." In his letter to Tennyson he did not think it necessary to distinguish between a great poet and a real one, but said that "by an hereditary honour, there may always be a living memorial of the appreciation of your genius by your countrymen." Tennyson declined the baronetcy but asked that it might be conferred, after his death, on his son. Nine years later he accepted a peerage on the recommendation of Gladstone. Carlyle also declined the G.C.B. and the pension. "Titles of honour, of all degrees, are out of keeping with the tenor of my poor life", he wrote. As for money, "after years of rigorous and frugal, but, thank God, never degrading poverty", it had become "amply abundant, even super-abundant in this later time." But he described the offer as "magnanimous and noble, without example in the history of governing persons with men of letters." This was no exaggeration in view of the fact that he had never written or spoken of Disraeli except in terms of contempt, referring to him as a juggler, a Hebrew conjurer, an absurd monkey, a mountebank, a self-seeking impostor, and all the other phrases with which writers who would themselves like to be rulers plaster politicians; and although he mentioned Disraeli's action to Lady Derby with gratitude and high appreciation, it did not hinder him, a few years later, from speaking of "the cursed old Jew, not worth his weight in cold bacon . . . the worst man who ever lived." Another writer to whom Disraeli was especially courteous, Matthew Arnold, used the same sort of language. "I don't want to talk about my things, I want to talk about *you*", said Dizzy when they met, adding that Arnold was the only living Englishman who had become a classic in his own lifetime. Yet Arnold called him a charlatan; so we must assume that these eminent men understood the exact meaning of their opprobrious terms from internal evidence. Their attitude merely goes to show that if a man wants to be universally liked he must never do anybody a good turn.

Perhaps the famous authors whom he wished to honour, and the lesser-known ones whom he actually helped, were jealous of his rivalry in their own department. His reputation as a novelist and a wit was certainly as high as his political reputation, until he became Lord Beaconsfield and the success of his foreign policy eclipsed his other achievements. His remarks were repeated so often in society that other phrase-makers may have felt envious. It was said that he never let off his fireworks unless a woman was present, which may explain why so many gained currency:

"Great men never want experience."

"Nobody is forgotten when it is convenient to remember him."

"No man is regular in his attendance at the House of Commons until he is married."

(Of Charles Greville, whose diaries were published in '74) "He was the most conceited person with whom I have ever been brought into contact, although I have read Cicero and known Bulwer Lytton."

(To someone who had said the weather was horrible) "Never quarrel with Nature!"

"You should treat a cigar like a mistress; put it away before you are sick of it."

"In these days neither wealth nor pedigree prevail: for the former the world is too rich; for the latter, too knowing."

(Coming away from a wedding) "This is a dismal business: it always depresses me. After a funeral I am cheerful. I feel that one has got rid of someone."

"Popularity is the Echo of Folly and the Shadow of Renown."

(To a friend who hoped he was very well) "Is *anybody ever very* well?"

(To a north-countryman who said that his daughters read Dizzy's novels with avidity) "This is fame!"

The following could only have depended on male testimony:

(To a colleague on the front bench, about another M.P. who was speaking) "For twelve years this man was a bore: he has suddenly become an institution."

THE COUNTESS OF BRADFORD
By Edward Clifford

" NEW CROWNS FOR OLD ONES ! "

(Aladdin adapted)

" *Punch* " *cartoon by Sir John Tenniel*

(To someone who said that a member was getting out of his depth while treating of a subject in the House) "Out of his depth! He's three miles from the shore."

(When Lord Robert Cecil, in his maiden speech, paused to yawn) "He'll do", said Dizzy.

At a dinner-party Delane, the editor of *The Times*, had to leave early to return to work, and after he had gone a young man asked Disraeli for his honest opinion of Delane. Dizzy looked at the clock and said: "News can be brought here from Serjeant's Inn in about half-an-hour. Delane has been gone a quarter. Should the news be brought to us that Delane has been found dead in his cab before we part this evening, I will tell you what I think of him."

Once, when feeling very ill, he rose from his seat in the Treasury office, saying to a secretary "Don't bother me with the routine work. Please attend to all of it yourself." He walked slowly to the door and opened it. "But of course if there is any really important decision to be made . . ." he paused, and a second before closing the door behind him added, "make it."

A member of parliament who had been offered a knighthood did not feel easy in his mind about it, asked Dizzy's advice, and was told to accept it but to tell everyone that he had refused it. "Why?" "Because you'll get all the credit of having rejected it until you receive it." "And then?" "You'll get all the glory of receiving it after having rejected it."

Talking with friends at Hughenden, he said that he could not remember a public house called the King's Arms at Berkhamstead. "But you must remember the house, sir", insisted one of his guests: "there was a very handsome barmaid there—monstrous fine gal. You must have been in the King's Arms, sir." "Perhaps if I had been in *her* arms, I might have remembered it", answered Dizzy.

Many of the lighter touches in his House of Commons speeches were also retailed in clubs and drawing-rooms all over the country. A good example occurred during the debate on the Irish Peace Preservation Bill, after several opponents had pooh-poohed his belief in the persistence of Ribbonism, a secret movement in Ireland, so named from the green badge worn by its members, its object being to prevent landlords from evicting tenants whatever the circumstances and to prevent tenants on pain of death from taking land wherefrom others had been evicted. Said Disraeli:

> There was once a member of this House, one of its greatest ornaments, who sat opposite this box,. or an identical one, and indeed occupied the place which I unworthily fill. That was Mr Canning. In his time, besides the discovery of a new world, dry champagne was invented. Hearing everybody talking of dry champagne, Mr Canning had a great desire to taste it, and Charles Ellis, afterwards Lord Seaford, got up a little dinner for him, care of course being taken that there should be some dry champagne. Mr Canning took a glass, and after drinking it and thinking for a moment, exclaimed "The man who says he likes dry champagne will say anything." Now I do not want to enter into rude controversy with any of my hon. friends opposite who doubt the existence of Ribbonism; but this I will say, that the man who maintains that Ribbonism does not exist is a man who—ought to drink dry champagne.

As usual with men who gain a great reputation for wit, the time came when he had only to open his mouth at a dinner-table for people to look expectantly mirthful, and, like Talleyrand, merely to say "Ah!" to get a laugh. But he disliked dining out in the last twenty years of his life, especially with males, and must have suffered tortures when entertaining all the members of his party in the spring of '75. "I have now dined 242 members of the House of Commons and sixty peers", he wrote in April of that year, ". . . there are 112 members of the Commons to be invited, and they are not contented unless they meet a certain portion of swells." In addition to the boredom, he was suffering from gout, which made its first serious appearance shortly after the tory victory in February '74, beginning in his left hand, and soon reaching his feet. So severe was the attack in May that he could not attend the House. The Queen was greatly concerned and advised him not to sit in hot rooms, as the sudden change of atmosphere when he went out would be hurtful. He promised to obey her commands. Throughout the year he was seldom free from the complaint, and at last the Queen and his physicians recommended him to stay at Bournemouth during the most severe winter weeks, the "salubrious air" at that spot having recently been discovered by the medical profession. When it became known that he was expected there, the local conservatives wanted to meet him at the station with a brass band and were with difficulty dissuaded from such a course. Should it occur to them to give him a send-off, he said that he would leave in a balloon. The weather at Bournemouth was intensely cold and included snowstorms. He was bored: "If I had the charm of composition, it would be more bearable; but business does not absorb; it is despatched and then everything is flat." The Dowager Duchess of Exeter was staying in the place, and seemed anxious about the state of his soul, recalling that when at Burghley he had been a reader of the Bible. "I hope I have searched the scriptures", he said. "But what have you found? Have you found the truth?" she asked. "I have found many things; but if I were to attempt now to detail them to you, you would lose your drive, and I observed your carriage at the door."

The gout accompanied him back to Hughenden, where, like Crusoe, he took infinite delight in his silent companions, his books and trees. He loved his library, and liked to watch the sunbeams on the bindings of the books. But he had little time for reverie, for he was called at seven in the morning with the post and the Government bag, started work at nine, and remained at it most of the day. The second post came at eleven, together with the newspapers, which he had to read or glance through. At one o'clock the daily messenger appeared with the despatch boxes, and concentrated effort was necessary to get the replies done in time for the London post. In addition to all this, telegrams in cypher frequently arrived and had to be dealt with. His only proper meal in the day was lunch, for which he allowed half-an-hour and on which he lived. In spite of his illness he found the conduct of affairs extremely interesting. "It is worth living in such times!" he declared; and though he sometimes complained of the nuisance of power and patronage, he honestly confessed that it was affectation to speak of them as boring: "The sense of power is delightful. It is amusing to receive the letters I do, especially since Deaneries were in the market. I had no idea that I was an object of so much esteem, confidence, public and private, and respectful attention—and as nobody in the world, were I to die tomorrow, would give up even a dinner-party, one is sensible of the fun of life." On the other hand fame had its drawbacks. Train-journeys, for example, could be a penance. Once he had to wait an hour, first at Salisbury and then at Southampton; on each occasion he was recognised, a group collected, and he knew how it felt to be a lion in a zoo. When strolling on the platform he would suddenly hear the cry "Here he is!", followed by the steps of little boys running after him, hip-hip-hurrahs from scattered knots of passengers, and, if his luck were out, "For he's a jolly good fellow." At Salisbury he went into the refreshment-room, where the girl who supplied him with tea asked him to autograph her favourite book, *Henrietta Temple*. He had not the courage to refuse.

We must try to see him more clearly than his fellow-passengers were able to do, and the place in which to see him at his best was the House of Commons, where now, whenever he was on his feet, his auditors were so quiet that the rustle of a paper sounded like an interruption. As with all institutions that had stood the test of time, he venerated the Commons. "Let us remember we are a senate, not a vestry", he would say, and he was jealous of the traditions of the House, while allowing the latitude implied by his remark: "The rules were made for gentlemen." He always entered the chamber some five or ten minutes before the commencement of public business, and it was noticed that he combined a reverential bearing with a manner of easy confidence. He walked slowly up the whole length of the floor, and when he reached the corner of the table he made obeisance to the Chair with lowly dignity. Most M.P.s felt self-conscious over this ceremony: some tried to evade bowing at all, hoping to escape notice in the crowd; others made an ungracious nod; others hurriedly and blushingly accomplished an awkward bend of the backbone; Gladstone got out of the difficulty by always entering from behind the Speaker; but Disraeli regarded it as a necessary duty, a courtly recognition of the supremacy of the Chair.

His complete control of the entire House, while in opposition and in power, a control that no one else of his day equalled, no one since his time has approached, and possibly only Chatham before him possessed, was due in part to the fact that he was always present, by which means he was able to keep abreast of the temper of the assembly, feel its pulse, know how it would react. Even when it was sitting through the dinner-hour he only left his place for a brief period to snatch a hasty meal within the precincts or to join his wife in one of the courts at St Stephen's for a pleasanter but equally rapid meal in her brougham. Then, too, he was always prepared; he knew everything about the subjects of debate, had an amazing memory for facts, for what others had said, and never depended on notes. Once he made great play with a piece of paper, which he scrutinised with care from time to time in order to make Gladstone feel uncomfortable, and finally tore up; but another member had the curiosity to gather the bits together, only to find that not a word was written on them. Disraeli's physical appearance and immobility added much to his personal authority. He sat with rigid head and body, gazing vacantly into space, his arms folded across his breast, his hat tilted slightly over his brows, one knee crossing the other. He never took his ease, never lolled, never relaxed, hardly even moved except on rare occasions during an opponent's diatribe at his expense, when the foot of the pendent knee might be seen to curve upwards slightly; or, if the attack were exceptionally vehement, he might shift his body round very slightly in a westerly direction, place his forefinger over his eyeglass, glance for perhaps three seconds at the clock over the entrance door, put away the eyeglass, and relapse into an attitude of coma. His oriental impassivity enraged Gladstone, whose furious speeches and angry glances at the facinorous buddha opposite had the effect of making the graven image, if possible, more indifferent, less lifelike; an image, however, whose lack-lustre eyes noticed everything, and whose somnolent pose covered an awareness of the slightest change in the emotional atmosphere. No one in the House ever heard him laugh or saw him smile; his usual expression when speaking was one of patient and melancholy endurance. The semi-circular wrinkles on either side of the mouth, noticeable in Dickens and many humorous actors, were in his case not formed by the facial distortion of mirth. In the fifties and sixties he scarcely ever took part in the social chit-chat of other M.P.s, holding himself aloof, apparently unconscious of those around him, encouraging no confidences in the lobbies or committee-rooms, and gliding noiselessly from place to place like a phantom. But from the moment he became Prime Minister in '74 he kept in touch with the more promising young men of the party, talking to them in the lobby, encouraging them to gossip, doing his best to make them speak, showing great interest in their affairs, and giving them all the advice they needed.

Another quality that contributed to his absolute supremacy in the House was once described as "a sublime sort of tact." He was fair and polite to opponents, discouraging interruptions from his own side when they were speaking, whereas his predecessors in office had been tricky and brusque. No one could administer a snub with greater effect than he, but even that was done in a manner that delighted everyone except the man who had called it forth. To give an example. John Bright had been absent from parliament for about two years. In the past he had done his best to annoy Disraeli by leaving his place ostentatiously while the tory leader was addressing the House. Now, on his return, one of the first things he did, after cracking himself up, was to advise the Prime Minister in an insolent manner to pay close attention to the speech of an authority on turnpikes. After listening to what was said, Disraeli got up, dealt with the subject of turnpikes, and then remarked "I now come to the member for Birmingham." Bright was a very vain man, and at these words preened himself, waiting expectantly for the conventional sequence: "whom we are all glad to see back again." Instead, Disraeli placed his glass in his right eye, gazed for several seconds at Bright, and then calmly remarked in a tone of depreciation: "of whom we have not seen much of late." Bright was livid with rage, and after members had enjoyed a good laugh Disraeli continued: "The hon. gentleman has indulged us once more this evening with that self-complacent catalogue of his own achievements with which in former years the House was familiar. I fail to find anything novel in his remarks, and I pass on at once to the member for——", etc.

But Disraeli's pre-eminence in the parliament of his time was mainly due to his genius as a speaker; and here we are at once faced with the perplexing fact that he was no orator as Gladstone was, as Burke and Chatham had been. He had none of the tricks of that trade; he could not touch the hearts of men nor bring tears to their eyes; there was no emotion in his voice; he could be dismal, but not pathetic; he never suffered from a rush of words to the tongue, never spoke as one inspired, never lost command of himself, never attempted the flights of eloquence, the pseudo-poetry, of the born demagogue; always he spoke as a man of the world, never in the style of a prophet. Yet from the moment that the sallow-cheeked, expressionless, and apparently moribund figure came to life, unfolded his arms, raised his head, shook himself together, drew up his shoulders, and rose from his seat, an electric wave passed through the House, the members of which seemed to become as motionless as he had been, the thrilling silence being that of a playhouse, not a senate. At first the words came slowly, with the utmost deliberation, and every syllable could be heard in all parts of the chamber. His voice was beautiful, the articulation perfect, the phrasing sure. He pronounced 'parliament' in four syllables, "business' in three, and no word was slurred. The peculiarity of his delivery was that the tone of his voice became more musical as it increased in volume. He indulged little in gestures, depending entirely on vocal accomplishment, on minute rhetorical inflections, on pauses, on grace of manner, polish of phraseology and disciplined restraint. Somehow his self-command gave him command over others; and such was his passionless power that every sentence seemed significant, every movement expressive, every change of key momentous. It was a triumph of the art that conceals art, his utterly untheatrical method producing an effect that was in the highest degree dramatic. As he went on his voice became fuller, more resonant, and sometimes almost clamorous, but in a second it would drop to an easy familiarity, each change carefully calculated to make the desired impression.

As was noted in an earlier chapter, he never surpassed his speeches on the repeal of the Corn Laws, and seldom again reached their level; for as he consolidated his position in parliament, his eloquence became burdened with the heavier matter and more imposing manner expected of a statesman; but he could not change his nature, and even his most elaborate orations were lit up here and there with flashes of sarcasm and gleams of ridicule. He had a quaint habit, when about to score a humorous point, of producing a handkerchief from his pocket, passing it from his left hand to his right, and giving a cursory cough as he passed it back, just beneath his nose, from right to left. As a rule, when speaking, his elbows were pressed closely against his sides, the hands open and slightly turned inwards towards each other; but at moments of apparent intensity he threw out his hands, palms upwards, jerkily, as if he were splashing the House with water that reached up to his own waist. Although at intervals during his last years in the Commons he was a martyr to gout and asthma, he was able to shake off his ailments when addressing the House, and sometimes he astonished members by rising with difficulty in obvious pain and speaking with the logic and lucidity of one whose mind was as free from care as his body was untroubled by suffering.

It was fortunate that his complaints did not disable him, for throughout the entire period of his Ministry he had to keep a watchful eye on Russia and Germany. While Gladstone had been restricting his interest to home affairs, Russia had been adding province after province to her dominions, and Bismarck was beginning to consider England a back-number as a continental influence. When Russia reached the borders of Afghanistan, the Amir asked the British Government to promise military assistance if he were attacked. Gladstone refused, and Russia at once became the dominant influence in Afghanistan. Shortly after Disraeli returned to Downing Street the Tsar of Russia visited London, and with such a ticklish situation on the Indian frontier the Prime Minister was most anxious to preserve friendly relations with him. But it happened that the visit was extended for two days beyond the time when Queen Victoria had arranged to travel north to Balmoral, and she refused to alter her plans. This provoked a crisis. Disraeli knew that the Tsar would regard her departure from London before his as an insult; and so, when the appeals of Derby, Salisbury and the Prince of Wales failed to shake her purpose, he begged her as a personal favour to postpone her journey. "My head is still on my shoulders", he reported after the interview. "It is for Mr Disraeli's sake and as a return for his great kindness that she will stop till the 20th", she wrote. Salisbury congratulated him on having averted an Afghan war. But he had no faith in a real understanding with Russia, and knew that he had only gained a breathing space in which to prepare for future trouble. For a man afflicted by the gout the Tsar's visit was onerous. After attending a great banquet at Windsor one day, he arrived in London at noon the next, had an audience with the Tsar at Buckingham Palace at three, attended the House of Commons at four-thirty, dined at Marlborough House to meet the Russian Emperor that same evening, and finished up with a ball at Stafford House. "It is difficult to get through such a day", he wrote, "and I have to change my dress as often as an actor!"

His next undertaking was to convince Bismarck, the dominant personality on the continent, that England was again to be reckoned with now that Gladstone was no longer in a position to weaken her foreign policy. Bismarck was the only statesman of that age worthy of Disraeli's steel; but though the one had absolute power while the other was accountable to parliament, it was "the old Jew", as Bismarck called him, who won the first and last bouts. They had met in 1862, when Bismarck had frankly confessed that, after reorganising the Prussian army, he intended to declare war on Austria, dissolve the German Diet, subdue the minor States, and unite Germany under Prussian leadership. "Take care of that man! He means what he says", remarked Dizzy to the Saxon Minister. Bismarck's meaning had become quite clear by 1874, with Austria humbled, France crippled, Russia friendly, and Germany united under a Prussian monarch. Now it was the Pope's turn. But Bismarck's subjection of the churches to the State annoyed the Catholics in Belgium, and he issued a warning to that country which convinced Disraeli that Germany would make life impossible for the smaller nations unless her course were checked. "We shall have no more quiet times in diplomacy", said he with his usual prescience, "but shall be kept in a state of unrest for a long time: probably till the beginning of the next thirty years' war." He saw Bismarck as "another old Bonaparte", who must be bridled. France was showing signs of recovery from the *débâcle* of 1870, and it looked as if Bismarck would manufacture a case against her preparatory to crushing her finally. Disraeli acted promptly. He got into touch with the Russian Ambassador and said that England would support a movement for peace by the Tsar, who was on the point of meeting the German Emperor. At his instigation the Queen also wrote to both Emperors. The moment Bismarck realised that Russia and England were acting together to arrest his bellicose designs, and that England was no longer to be a cypher on the continent, he climbed down and pretended to be pleased at the amicable agreement between Tsar and Kaiser.

With Russia ostensibly in friendly vein, with Bismarck momentarily restrained and trying to look happy about it, Disraeli increased the expenditure on the army and navy and turned his attention to India, on which Russia had been casting a wistful eye. He believed that the only way to unite the various princes and peoples of that country was to strengthen their feeling for the throne, and in 1875 he arranged for a tour of India by the Prince of Wales. In addition to the cost of the journey, he got the Commons to vote £60,000 for the Prince's personal expenditure, a sum that was considered insufficient by H.R.H.'s private friends. But Albert Edward, though a thoroughly spoilt child according to Dizzy, was also the most amiable of mortals, and treated the matter light-heartedly. "What a shabby concern this vote is!" said the Duke of Sutherland to him. "If I were you, sir, I would not take it. I would borrow the money of some friends at five per cent." "Well, will you lend it me?" enquired the Prince. The Duke said no more. By that time there had not been a place or a living in Disraeli's power to bestow that the Prince had not asked for one of his friends, always the most unqualified candidates. But Dizzy had decided that he must not be silly merely because the Prince was good-natured.

During the royal visit, which took place in the winter of '75–6, a new Viceroy of India was appointed: the second Lord Lytton, son of Bulwer. Dizzy had first seen him as a boy at school and had 'tipped' him. "It was the first tip he ever had; and now I have tipped him again, and put a crown on his head!" He was also determined to fix an imperial crown on the head of his royal mistress. Oddly enough he had made an oriental personage in *Tancred* say that the Queen of England should transfer the seat of her Empire from London to Delhi, which shows that long before India was transferred to the Crown he had pictured Victoria as Empress of India. The time had now come to make her so, but his duties as Prime Minister were of such an arduous nature that he would willingly have postponed the business had the Queen not urged him to settle it. So he went down to discuss the question with the Indian Secretary, Lord Salisbury, at Hatfield, his first visit there since the death of his old friend, the second Marquis. Afterwards he wrote to his host that he remembered his visit with great pleasure, though he told Lord Derby that it had been extremely dull, another example of that combined politeness and honesty which in his case was so often called insincerity. But everyone behaves in the same way more or less, and he was only more polite and more honest than other people.

In '76 he managed to persuade the Queen to open parliament in person, which she had rarely done since the Consort's death, and the rush of M.P.s to see her in the Lords was so tumultuous that Dizzy himself was nearly knocked down and trampled on. His speech introducing the Royal Titles Bill displayed his usual cleverness in sensing the feeling of the House. He started by saying that a number of titles had been suggested by various persons. Then, speaking very slowly and watching the effect of every word, he went on: "I have heard a title mentioned, the title of 'Empress of India'." He paused for about four seconds, before adding: "I have no reason to suppose that this may have the preference over any other. I have heard others suggested." Had the House shown the slightest disapproval when he mentioned the title, he could have continued without in any way committing himself, but in this way he discovered the general disposition of the members. Later there was some opposition from his enemies, which the Queen thought extraordinary and incomprehensible. Gladstone suffered from a succession of "white rages" and made speeches "of vituperative casuistry, imagining every combination which could never happen." Several nonconformists associated the word 'Empress' with debauchery. *The Times* and *Daily Telegraph* (which Disraeli called the *Delirium Tremens*) were pompously absurd. And Robert Lowe, whose animus against Disraeli was pathological, disgraced himself. He had been Chancellor of the Exchequer in Gladstone's Government, and had never missed an opportunity to gird at Dizzy, whose pallid face and dyed black hair contrasted strangely with the rubicund complexion and white hair of the other, a contrast which suggested to a witty M.P. that Lowe should address his *bête-noire* thus:

> My hair will be white as long as I live
> While yours will be black as long as you dye.

In a speech to his constituents Lowe stated his belief that, whereas the Queen had long wished to assume the title of Empress, at least two previous Prime Ministers had resisted her pressure, but that at length she had found a more pliant person. This was a grave accusation for a Privy Councillor and one-time Minister to bring; the question was raised in the House; and Disraeli proceeded to make mincemeat of Lowe, reading a message from the Queen in which she declared that there was not the slightest foundation for the calumny. Lowe apologised abjectly. "He is in the mud, and there I leave him", said Disraeli. A few years later Gladstone picked him out of it and made him a peer.

All this factious opposition, added to his physical sufferings, wearied Disraeli, who had to steer the Bill through parliament. But, as he said, "If you want to govern the world you must know how to say 'Bo' to a goose", and he had to say 'Bo' to a great many geese before the session was over. Everything was at last satisfactorily settled, and on January 1st, 1877, the new Viceroy, Lord Lytton, before a resplendent gathering of potentates at Delhi, proclaimed Queen Victoria as Kaisar-i-Hind, Empress of India, while the Indian princes saluted her as Shah-in-Shah Padshah, Monarch of Monarchs. On the same evening the Prime Minister dined with his Sovereign at Windsor. Instead of her usual simple dress she was adorned with masses of oriental jewellery, and against all etiquette he rose to the occasion by proposing her health in a florid speech that would not have been out of place in his novel *Alroy*. To the amazement of her courtiers, she got up when he sat down and half-bowed, half-curtseyed to him, smiling prettily.

But he had already done a service to his country of far greater value than this service to his Queen: he had secured the new trade route between England and the East. In 1869 the Suez Canal was opened; and instead of travelling to India via the Cape of Good Hope or enduring the acute discomfort of the overland journey from Alexandria to Suez, passengers could now do the trip quickly and easily. The Canal was made by a Frenchman, Ferdinand de Lesseps, with French money, and about half the shares were held by a French company, the other half by the Khedive of Egypt, through whose country the Canal passed. Very soon over three-quarters of the trade going through the Canal to and from the East was British, and its ownership and control in the event of war became a matter of moment to England. Naturally Gladstone made no attempt to secure British interests in it, though he had several offers from de Lesseps to do so when it failed to make money in the first years of its existence. It was still being worked at a loss in '74, and de Lesseps increased the tonnage duties, an increase that infringed the terms of the concession and was considered excessive by an International Commission. De Lesseps scorned the Commission, dared the British Admiralty, refused to let ships through unless they paid the higher rates, and would not listen to reason until the Khedive mobilised an army to expel the French company. Disraeli then communicated with his friend Baron Lionel de Rothschild, who sent his son to Paris in order to tell de Lesseps that the British Government were willing to buy the Canal if terms could be arranged. But de Lesseps, still smarting from Gladstone's refusals to treat with him and from the British attitude to the increased duties, would not make a reasonable deal. Suddenly the interest was shifted from the Frenchman to the Egyptian.

On Monday, November 15th, 1875, Frederick Greenwood, editor of *The Pall Mall Gazette*, called at the Foreign Office and told Derby that the Khedive was about to sell his shares in the Canal to a French syndicate. Greenwood had heard this from Henry Oppenheim, a financier with interests in Egypt, and he urged the British Government to buy the shares. It is more than probable that Disraeli heard the same thing at Lionel de Rothschild's house the night before Greenwood called. Though Derby was not enthusiastic, Disraeli jumped at the chance. At first it appeared that the Khedive had already consented to sell his shares to the French syndicate; but the British representative in Egypt insisted that the negotiations should be delayed until his Government made an offer. The Khedive agreed, and the matter was at once discussed by the British Cabinet. Disraeli was determined to obtain the support of all his colleagues, and had to overcome the opposition of, among others, the Foreign Secretary and the Chancellor of the Exchequer. On November 18th he informed Queen Victoria that the Khedive, who was on the verge of bankruptcy, wanted from three to four millions sterling by the 30th of that month. "Scarcely breathing time!" he added. "But the thing must be done." So anxious was the Khedive to obtain money that, while negotiating with the British Government, he signed an agreement to mortgage his shares with the French syndicate, and de Lesseps did his utmost to get the support of the French Government in raising the necessary sum. But the French Foreign Minister did not wish to offend the British Government, which had already done his country a good turn at Berlin early that year, and sent an emissary to Derby, who replied that as about four-fifths of the shipping that used the Canal was British, his Government did not wish the Khedive's shares to be owned by another French company. Without the sanction and help of the French Government de Lesseps failed to procure the sum that was needed; and on November 25th, ten days after Disraeli's first move in the complicated business, the contract was signed in Cairo whereby England purchased the Khedive's interest in the Suez Canal.

But now came the question of how to lay hands on four million pounds within a few hours. The consent of parliament was necessary, and parliament was not sitting. Disraeli was equal to the emergency. He told his secretary, Corry, to remain just outside the Cabinet room; and when the decision to obtain a loan had been reached, he would put his head out of the door and say one word, "Yes", upon which Corry was to go straight to Rothschild. The head emerged, the word was uttered, and Corry hurried off to New Court, where he told Rothschild that the Prime Minister wanted £4,000,000 the following day. The Baron selected a muscatel grape, ate it, disposed of the skin, and asked: "What is your security?" Corry replied: "The British Government." Rothschild said: "You shall have it." Had Disraeli applied to the Bank of England, there would have been discussions, board meetings, questionings, lack of secrecy, disturbance of the money market, and other nuisances. As it was, after a fortnight of unceasing labour and anxiety, the job was done in a trice, and Disraeli was justified in claiming "Alone I did it!" All the gamblers, plunderers and financiers in the world had been arrayed against him, he declared, and he had baffled them all.

There was little opposition when parliament met, though it goes without saying that Gladstone was indignant and censorious: the Vicar of Satan on earth had stolen another march on him. England was pleased; France was displeased; the Crown Prince of Germany (afterwards Wilhelm II) said "How jolly!"; Russia said nothing. But the Queen was in ecstasies when she received her Prime Minister's letter: "It is just settled: you have it, Madam."

Chapter XXII

THREE LADIES

MEN who desire power are seldom of a warm and humanly affectionate disposition, the longing for fame and the longing for love, the two chief motives which govern mankind, being competitive and usually irreconcilable, the first signifying a will to conquer, the second a wish to capitulate. Disraeli was one of the rare exceptions in history of a man who hungered for fame and won it, yet could not exist without love. "I live for Power and the affections", he said. Unfortunately for his peace of mind, the older he grew the more tender-hearted he became, the keener his desire for feminine fondness. "I am certain there is no greater misfortune than to have a heart that will not grow old", he complained; and so we find him at the age of seventy falling in love with another man's wife and exhibiting the same rashness, the same abandon, the same irrational symptoms, as a youngster in his first transports.

Soon after the death of his wife two women, whom he had first met in London society when they were famous beauties, showed him much sympathy in his sorrow. They were sisters, one being Lady Chesterfield, a widow two years his senior, the other Lady Bradford, a married woman fifteen years his junior; and both of them were now grandmothers. The daughters of Lord Forester, the elder had been married to the sixth Earl of Chesterfield, and the younger's husband, the third Earl of Bradford, was Disraeli's colleague as Lord Chamberlain from '66 to '68, as Master of the Horse from '74 to '80. "There is nothing like female friendship—the only thing worth having", Dizzy once wrote to Lady Londonderry; and if he had been content with that his relations with his new friends would have been entirely harmonious; but he fell in love with the younger one at an unfashionable speed, and as she was a married woman with a family, while he was about to be Prime Minister of England, the relationship was bound to bring a good deal of unhappiness with it.

Within a few weeks of his intimacy with the sisters he was addressing them as 'Dearest' and telling them that the only happy hours he had spent that year were in their company. He went to stay at Bretby with Lady Chesterfield, at Weston with the Bradfords, and all of them visited him at Hughenden. Lady Chesterfield had more strength of character than Lady Bradford, whose intelligence, gaiety and sympathy won him completely. Though he loved the first, he was in love with the second; and in order to acquire Lady Bradford as a sister-in-law he proposed marriage to Lady Chesterfield, who refused him not only because the idea of marrying when past seventy struck her as rather silly but because she knew why he had made the proposal. And indeed there is little doubt that, fond though he was of Lady Chesterfield, the constant attention he paid to her was due chiefly to his love of Lady Bradford. On two or three occasions he admitted that he kept up a continual correspondence with the elder sister and visited her so frequently solely because he knew it pleased the younger. "When I am calling on her I am always thinking of you", he informed Lady Bradford; and it was the recollection of their sisterhood that made staying at Bretby tolerable to him, for the gossip he heard only differed from that of the servants' hall in the superior pronunciation of the gossipers.

Lady Bradford's name was Selina (Greek for the moon) and he told her that "It is not a slice of the moon I want; I want all." He wrote her over a thousand letters at all sorts of times and places, during debates in the Commons, while busy with despatches, when ambassadors or Ministers were waiting to interview him, on train-journeys, just before or just after seeing the Queen, and sometimes he wrote twice or thrice a day, keeping her informed of all his doings and imparting secret political information, the disclosure of which would have shocked the members of his Cabinet. In almost every letter he recorded his feelings for her, saying that she was never for an instant absent from his consciousness, that to see or hear from her every day was absolutely necessary to his existence, that he could recall every word she had said every time they had met, that great affairs were no specific for the anxieties of his heart, that letters from her were read before all the urgent despatches sent to him

QUEEN VICTORIA, 1875
After von Angeli

GROUP AT HUGHENDEN, 1874

Left to right, seated : Lady Bradford, Lady Wharncliffe and Benjamin Disraeli.
Standing : Montagu Corry, Lord Bradford and Lord Wharncliffe. *In front :* Lord Pembroke.

by special messengers, that his life was passed in trying to govern the country and thinking of her, that when she was away from London he rose every day to a sunless sky, that he only went into society or stayed at country-houses on the chance of meeting her, that she was dearer to him than life, and that, while fortune, fashion, fame, power, might increase happiness, they could not create it, for it sprang from the affections.

At first, it seems, she responded in a manner that encouraged him to believe that his love was returned. A passage from one of her letters ran: "Have confidence in me, believe in me, believe that I am true—oh! how true!" And on the day before her visit to Hughenden in May '74 he could scarcely contain himself: "It is quite a dream, and I am as restless as if I were as young as the Spring." Clearly it flattered her vanity that the most famous man in England was at her beck; his daily letters, his regular calls, his slavish admiration, his delicate attentions, were both soothing and inspiriting, and for a while she played up to him. But then something happened. Perhaps her husband raised objections, or her friends hinted that the Prime Minister's behaviour was placing her in a false position, or her lover was too exigent, or she became conscious of a situation which the social and political world might think faintly ridiculous. Whatever the reason, her manner when they met at Montagu House at the end of June '74 was chilling, and she appeared to avoid him. He wrote to ask why, admitting that his society in public might embarrass her and so be disagreeable. Unfortunately, he said, his imagination had not deserted him with youth: "It would have involved me in calamities, had not nature bestowed on me, and in a large degree, another quality—the sense of the ridiculous." That sense had at last convinced him that his conduct during the past year had been absurd: "But I linger round the tie on which I had staked my happiness." She replied in a kindly manner, and he was happy again.

But not for long. Her warming sympathy was too often followed by a chilling demeanour, her interest by indifference. She started to read his novels, and he welcomed another tie between them. "My works are my life", he said. "They are all written from my own feelings and experience"; and he assured her that, if he were to write them again, he would still be able to recreate the amatory emotions which he had felt and expressed in youth. But more than a year passed without her mentioning a single person or opinion in them, and he concluded that she had not read them through, or that, having done so, they had not impressed her, which was still more mortifying. He used to call every day at her house, 43 Belgrave Square, but she put a stop to this, saying that three times a week was quite enough. She also told him not to write so often. He replied that he could not endure such restrictions, and begged her to let him call regularly if only for a minute and write daily if only a word. His brain was tolerably strong, he said, but his heart was too soft, and he tried to console himself with the reflection that "I have had at least my dream . . . reached the pinnacle of power and gauged the sweetest and deepest affections of ye heart." When the doctors sent him to Bournemouth, he wrote that "there is something in my case which physicians know nothing about and could not comprehend. My heart yearns for the presence of those I love." He was very unhappy, could not bear solitude, yet found the company of others wearisome: "I want to see only one person, whom I never see, and I want to see her always. Otherwise I would rather be alone." He did not care to lament that he was wretched or miserable, knowing that she would only think such terms fantastic, but of course he could not help telling her about it. He lived on the bare hope of seeing her: "This may be a slight affair to you; to me it still is everything."

Early in '75 he had to admit that he was subject to jealousy, and some years later his feelings found expression in his last novel: "When a man is really in love, he is disposed to believe that, like himself, everyone is thinking of the person who engrosses his brain and heart." It was absolutely true, and he felt a pang whenever she praised another man's qualities. She continued to ration his visits, and he likened himself to King Lear, whose retinue was restricted by his daughters. There was no reason why 'three times a week' should not become 'once a week', till at last the inevitable question came 'why once?' With the world at his feet he nevertheless felt dreary, lonely, unhappy, and tried to overcome his depression with work. Outwardly all was going well; but, like Hamlet, all was ill about his heart. Without love one did not live; one just existed in a grey world. It was joy to see her in public, rapture to see her alone. He thought of her during Cabinet meetings, slept badly when she did not bid him good-night at a party, was deeply hurt when she made an excuse for not accompanying her husband to Hughenden. If there were a likelihood of seeing her for a few minutes when she was passing through London, he said that he would alter the hour of a Cabinet meeting. Sometimes, to amuse her, he repeated jokes that he had heard: for example, he asked her what were the three great objects of a lawyer? and supplied the answer: (1) to get on, (2) to get onner, (3) to get onest. Away from home he once wrote to her on paper without mourning edges, and she expressed pleasure; but he replied that he had sometimes been on the point of "terminating this emblem of my bereavement" when the thought that he was no longer the object of someone's entire affection overcame him and he retained the sign of sorrow. "Once—perhaps twice—during the last two years, I have indulged in a wild thought it might be otherwise—and then something has always occurred which has dashed me to the earth." He knew that the great affairs with which he had to deal should have satisfied him; but they did not; and he sighed for her whole-hearted sympathy.

He begged both the sisters to send him their portraits for his gallery at Hughenden. Lady Chesterfield sent hers, and he told her that he would hang it near Lady Blessington's. "Perhaps you will say she ought not to be in such society. Pardon her, she was kind to me!" And he added: "The portrait of the cold-hearted Selina is not here." But early in '76 he received Selina's and assured her that "I would sooner have it than stars and garters." He could not bear to leave it behind when he went to London, where Lord Bradford saw it, apparently without annoyance or surprise. Though her acquaintance had "lent sweetness and solace to the sunset of my life", he continued to grieve that he saw her so seldom and said that he would never regain his health unless she relented. In April '76 he wished everything at the bottom of the Red Sea along with the Suez Canal shares. "I really am too old for ambition, and, except that I shall rarely see you again when my reign is over, the loss of my sceptre would not break my heart, I can assure you." It seemed to him that she was kind to everybody except himself, and he came to a sorrowful conclusion: "I fear our Romance is over, if indeed it ever existed except in my imagination—but still I sometimes dreamed that the dream might last until I slumbered for ever."

It is to his correspondence with Lady Chesterfield and Lady Bradford that we owe so many fascinating glimpses of his relationship with Queen Victoria, though one fears that he would not have considered such gossip as the marrow of biography and history. He objected to a passage in J. A. Symonds's book on the Renaissance in which two statesmen are described as "playing a game of diplomatic écarté." There was something offensive, he remarked, in a grave historian illustrating his narrative by reference to a transient game. The only possible comment is that the most memorable passage in his own Life of Bentinck refers to a horse-race, and that Drake's game of bowls is better remembered than any single incident of the Spanish Armada. So, too, a few passages in his private letters to the sisters bring himself and his Sovereign back to life with a vividness unattainable by a grave historian like, say, John Morley, whose Life of Gladstone in three volumes of speeches, letters and sober commentary, is more deadly than death.

With that strange premonition of coming events which was a feature of Disraeli's political instinct, he wrote in a short story, *The Infernal Marriage* (1834): "Without doubt there are few cards better than her royal consort, or, still more, the imperial ace. Nevertheless, I must confess, I am perfectly satisfied that I have the Queen on my side." The time came when he was to hold the royal Consort, to play the imperial ace, and to have the Queen in his hand as long as he remained Prime Minister. Forty years after that story was published he told Lady Bradford: "I must say that I feel fortunate in having a female Sovereign. I owe everything to woman; and if in the sunset of life I have still a young heart, it is due to that influence." It was fortunate for Queen Victoria, too, that she should have a Prime Minister who could take her out of herself, emancipate her from the heavy sorrow that lay like lead upon her, and transform her from a brooding and secluded figurehead into a vivacious and sociable female. Perhaps this was his most notable achievement as a statesman, for it popularised the monarchy in Great Britain and gave the English throne a prestige throughout the world which it has never lost. When in 1868 he informed the House of Commons that he was Prime Minister "by favour of the Queen", he was violently assailed by the whigs, liberals and radicals, most of whom regarded the Sovereign as a puppet who reigned by their favour. But England was the Israel of Disraeli's imagination, her monarch the unifying influence of the race, and he was determined to assert the prerogative of the Crown on every suitable occasion. There may even have been moments when he fancied himself as King Solomon, Victoria as the Queen of Sheba.

His attitude to her was determined by four factors, each deriving from something fundamental in his own nature: he was her servant, her adviser, her friend, and her jester. As her servant he recognised that she knew more about State business than anyone in the country, and he admired the woman as much as he reverenced the Sovereign. "She opened all her heart and mind to me, and rose immensely in my intellectual estimation", he reported from Balmoral. "Free from all shyness, she spoke with great animation and happy expression; showed not only perception, but discrimination of character, and was most interesting and amusing." For this reason he often consulted her on questions before bringing them to the notice of the Cabinet, and his Foreign Secretary, Derby, once asked whether he was not "encouraging her in too large ideas of her personal power." He probably was, but he had two good reasons for doing so: a high opinion of her political wisdom, and a desire to make her participate more actively in State occasions. As her adviser, he knew that the more she opened her mind to him the better he would be able to foresee events, the better prepared to deal with them; and the more he was able to take her advice the greater likelihood that, when they disagreed, she would follow his. As we have noticed earlier in this narrative, he had the rare ability of making others believe that the ideas he had put into their heads were their own. So with the Queen, who was delighted by the success of the Suez Canal purchase, which he attributed to her clear-sightedness, her sympathy with his action, and her support of it. As an immediate result of this praise, she granted him a veritable catalogue of requests, making no objections to any of them, "nothing but smiles and infinite *agaceries*." He was however quite capable, in reverential mood, of fancying that she had done the things for which he had really been responsible. "We are never so pleased as when we please others", he once remarked, "and, in our gratified generosity, attribute to them the very results we have ourselves accomplished."

But the peculiar quality of their relationship lay in the fact that, as her friend, he treated her as a woman to be wooed quite as much as a Sovereign to be worshipped. This was second-nature with him, for his attitude to most women was of a semi-platonic, semi-amorous, half-courtly, half-familiar nature. At the end of his life he said to Matthew Arnold: "You have heard me accused of being a flatterer. It is true. I am a flatterer. I have found it useful. Every one likes flattery; and when you come to Royalty, you should lay it on with a trowel." If anyone but Disraeli had said this, we could accept it without demur as a plain statement of fact, but where he is concerned the qualification is necessary that his flattery was instinctive; it was part of his desire for harmony, his love of pleasing women, of placating men. Useful it certainly was, but he did not exercise it solely for use. In his case there was not a little kindliness in it. "I never deny; I never contradict: I sometimes forget", was the rule he kept when conversing with the Queen. It was prompted by the feeling of a gentleman no less than by the policy of a statesman.

The proof that his behaviour to her was largely spontaneous is that she, an extremely shrewd, candid and open-hearted person, never suspected him of insincerity. Nor indeed could he have won her respect and affection if he had been the Hebrew conjurer of Carlyle's fancy, the charlatan of Arnold's. "Some one always knows everything", he said of her when a lady of the Court tried to keep a marriage-engagement secret. And it was true. Victoria had an extremely sharp eye for character, missed nothing that was going on around her, and founded her likes and dislikes on a sure instinct for what was admirable and despicable in human nature. She knew that Disraeli's flattery expressed something poetic in his temperament, and what in another man would have been artificial in him was simply oriental. Unless this is understood their relationship is mystifying, for it was more like that of a Queen with her favourite courtier than of a Sovereign with her Prime Minister: it was intimate but respectful, devotional but stately, affable but ceremonious. He seemed to know by instinct when to treat her as an equal and when to behave like a vassal. In the rôle of fellow-creature he would break through the stiff formality surrounding her by asking across the dinner-table such a question as: "Madam, did Lord Melbourne ever tell your Majesty that you were not to do this or that?" In the rôle of subject he would say, with a low bow in her direction: "We are in the presence of probably the only Person in Europe who could tell us that or this."

Above all he amused her. His lack of shyness, his surprisingly unconventional conversation, his complete self-assurance, his insinuating manner, his reckless disregard of Court etiquette; such qualities, which in another would have enraged her, fascinated her in him, because they were an essential part of his humorous personality; and Victoria, though brought up in a rigidly proper manner and disciplined almost beyond endurance to duty and the gravity of her position, was naturally disposed to laughter. It was noticed that she smiled continually while talking with Dizzy, whereas her face was nearly always set in solemnity when conversing with any other of her Ministers. The amusement was not all on one side. He extracted every ounce of comedy from the situation in which he found himself; and as he could simultaneously admire, love and laugh at a person, just as he could see something funny in a thing he revered, Victoria soon became for him "the Faery", perhaps because the contrast between her and Spenser's Faerie Queene or Shakespeare's Titania appealed to his sense of the ridiculous.

As a counsellor he made life easy for her, as a companion he made it delightful, her gratitude being expressed in a constant solicitude for his health, her pleasure in the cordiality of her behaviour. "I can only describe my reception by telling you that I really thought she was going to embrace me. She was wreathed with smiles, and, as she talked, glided about the room like a bird." That was in August '74, when he was suffering from gout, and she actually asked him to sit down. He remembered how, ten years before, she had received Lord Derby, who, though recovering from a severe attack of the same complaint, had been compelled to stand throughout the interview, the Queen saying that she feared he would suffer, but offering no seat, so severe was the etiquette. Yet now she could not endure the thought of a gouty Premier in pain. Although he refused on this occasion to take advantage of her offer, the time soon came when he sat through all their private talks, and he replaced the chair against the wall after each audience so that the breach of etiquette should not be observed. She mothered him, as his wife and sister had done, visiting him in his bedroom when he was ill at Balmoral, placing her yacht at his disposal for passages to and from the Isle of

Wight, insisting that he should not change his clothes in case he might feel the cold, refusing to let him travel in an open boat, allowing his private secretary to accompany him to Osborne, begging him to consult Sir William Jenner about his asthma, excusing him from regular attendance at Balmoral, and sending him letters almost every day and presents almost every week. In February '75 two bouquets of primroses and one of snowdrops arrived from Osborne. In acknowledging them he said that at a banquet that evening he would wear the snowdrops on his heart to show, among the stars and ribbons of the guests, that he also was decorated by a gracious Sovereign. Then he told her that in the middle of the night it had occurred to him that it must be all a dream, and that this was the Faery gift of another monarch: "Queen Titania, gathering flowers, with her Court, in a soft and sea-girt isle, and sending magic blossoms, which, they say, turn the heads of those who receive them." His own head would assuredly have been turned, he declared, if his sense of duty to her Majesty had not exceeded his conceit. There was a good deal of feeling as well as fun in all this, for he loved to romanticise his life; and, all the circumstances considered, nothing more romantic could have been imagined than his favoured position with the most powerful monarch on earth. Thanking her for some pink may which she had sent from Windsor, he said: "It was a gift worthy of Queen Elizabeth, and of an age when great affairs and romance were not incompatible."

Though permitted a freedom of speech which in any other Minister would have been rebuked, Disraeli never forgot the value of humility. "He himself, if he may venture to mention such a subject, is fairly well", he once wrote to her. But the prevailing note in his correspondence and conversation was one of affectionate flattery. "He cannot have a happy Xmas when your Majesty is in grief", he wrote shortly after the death of Princess Alice, going on to tell the Queen that she had been his guardian Angel, that what he had done and said aright had been due to her. "He often thinks how he can repay your Majesty, but he has nothing more to give, having given to your Majesty his duty and his heart." He was careful to show great courtesy to all those in her confidence, and even sent his respects to her favourite Scottish gillie, John Brown. In their different way, her letters to him were quite as unusual as his to her: they expressed her sense of gratitude for his extreme kindness, his devotion, his consideration for her feelings. She never forgot his birthday; she gave him her views on friendship; she revealed her private opinions on politics and public life in a manner, as he put it, "very remarkable and such as, I think, were never addressed before to a Minister of State." She sent him flowers, books, and other presents frequently, and ordered a copy of a picture of herself painted by von Angeli to be specially done for him "by an excellent artist." When the copy was finished, she showed it to him. "I think I may claim, Madam, the privilege of gratitude," he said, dropping on his knee. She extended her hand, which he kissed rapidly three times, and she gave him a squeeze. Later she asked as a favour that his portrait should be painted for her by von Angeli, and later still he endured torturing hours sitting for a bust which she wanted. The friendly nature of their intercourse was shown when he had to break off an interview by getting up and saying that a special train was waiting to take him from Windsor to London. "Run away, run away directly", said Victoria, smiling very good-naturedly, and Dizzy reflected that "instead of being dismissed, I dismissed my Sovereign."

There were drawbacks to this friendship between Monarch and Minister, the main one being that she began to believe he would do anything she wished him to do. Up to a point this was true. When she wrote to say that he must stop vivisection, he introduced a Bill to control what he called "this horrible practice." When she displayed concern over the slaughter of young seals, he made the Board of Trade bring in a Bill to establish a close-season for the seal fishery. When she demanded that the theft of ladies' jewels should cease, he instructed Scotland Yard to do its best. But when she insisted that England should go to war with Russia, he had to restrain her. In fact she came more and more to rely on his advice, and her frequent public appearances in the later years of her reign were due to the influence he had brought to bear on her during the six years of his Ministry. He showed infinite patience with her, as he did in all important affairs of State. His equanimity seems only to have been disturbed by little things, which are indeed the really irritating things. Staying at Osborne or at Sandringham or at Bretby, he often complained of the stationery: the ink was muddy or like asphalt, the paper was spongy or like greasy tin, the pens were made from the geese on a common, and so on. He told his correspondents that, as his ideas and expressions depended on his pens, ink and paper, when they were of inferior quality his style and genius were annihilated. "I cannot understand people giving you bad stationery", he grumbled. "It costs so little more to give good." He should have known that, to the average owner of a large English country-house in those days, the notion that anyone would want to write letters was too bizarre to be considered. Sometimes, no doubt, Dizzy wished the Queen had the same stationery that was supplied to her guests. It might have curbed the flow of her correspondence.

Chapter XXIII

ELYSIAN FIELDS

IN 1875, as in 1950, imperialist Russia would very much have liked to occupy Constantinople, and for the same purpose: a vast increase of power in Europe via the Mediterranean Sea. Disraeli never faltered in his conviction that Russia was a menace to civilisation, and he supported the feeble, bankrupt and thoroughly debased Ottoman Empire solely because he recognised that the futility and corruption of the Turks were less dangerous to Europe than the slavery and barbarism of the Tartars; and the hardest task of his career was to keep England from siding with Russia against Turkey in 1876, while Gladstone was doing his utmost to whip up the humanitarian sympathies of the English people into the condition of frenzied indignation necessary to precipitate a war which would have left Russia in command of the Bosphorus and Dardanelles.

Several of the Balkan States were in the hands of the Turks, and the Christian populations were subjected to Mahommedan domination. For some years Russia had been encouraging the conspiracies of secret societies, nationalist in origin, with the object of creating a general revolution against Turkish control, ostensibly in the cause of independence and Christianity, actually to achieve Russian supremacy by uniting the Slav peoples. Gladstone saw in all this the glorious aspirations of a downtrodden race; Disraeli discerned the cunning of the Kremlin; and we can now see more clearly than any of their contemporaries which of the two was right. The Tsar of Russia cared as much for the Christians as a cuckoo for a thrush, and "he and all his court would don the turban tomorrow, if he could only build a Kremlin on the Bosphorus", said Disraeli. Russia's brutal treatment of the Poles, to say nothing of her own people, should have been sufficient to warn the English humanitarians that, in the matter of atrocities, the Christians had nothing to learn from the Mahommedans.

The first revolt took place in Herzegovina in July '75, and the supineness of the Turkish administration was such that by the autumn the insurrection had spread to Bosnia. If the Turks had possessed common energy, or even pocket-money, remarked Disraeli, the thing would have been settled in a week. As it was, Servia and Montenegro supported their fellow-Slavs and an international situation was created. Russia, Austria and Germany combined, and, not realising that they now had to deal with Disraeli instead of Gladstone, sent a memorandum to Turkey proposing an armistice of two months, during which certain demands must be met, otherwise "efficacious" methods would be applied. A copy of this memorandum, drawn up in Berlin, reached Disraeli, who at once spotted the hand of Russia, perceived the danger, and resented the fact that England's advice had not been asked. He called a meeting of the Cabinet, put forward his views, secured the agreement of his colleagues that England should not support the Berlin proposals, and despatched a fleet to the Dardanelles. As his action was followed by a palace revolution in Constantinople, the deposition of the Sultan, and the promise of reform by his successor, the three powers responsible for the memorandum were able to climb down with dignity, and Great Britain was again recognised as an authority to be considered and consulted in matters affecting Turkey. Bismarck was much impressed by Disraeli's attitude, and intimated his willingness to follow England's lead in future negotiations; but the Russian Chancellor, Gortchakoff, was excessively annoyed; and though he agreed to withdraw the demands on Turkey, his pacific intentions were not convincing. "I am as anxious as anyone to keep well with the Russians", said Disraeli, "but there is no acting with people when you cannot feel sure that they are telling truth." For that matter, he found it impossible to rely on the word of anyone outside England.

His lack of confidence was justified. Incited by Russia, Servia and Montenegro declared war on Turkey in the middle of '76. But before that happened there had been an insurrection in Bulgaria, brought about by the secret societies against which Disraeli had so frequently warned his countrymen. It began with a massacre of Turkish officials, and the Sultan's troops exacted vengeance on such a scale, mostly on unarmed and harmless people, that a howl of horror and indignation went up from the humanitarians of Europe, who had previously confined their criticisms to Siberia and the knout, and the Russian Government must have refrained with difficulty from sending a letter of grateful thanks to the Sultan. A lurid account of the Turkish atrocities appeared in *The Daily News*, and Disraeli, not having been informed of what had occurred by the British Ambassador at Constantinople, was inclined to discount the reports. Questioned in the Commons, he admitted that "proceedings of an atrocious character" had undoubtedly taken place in Bulgaria, as always happened in wars of insurrection, but he could not believe all the stories that filled the papers, of girls being sold as slaves, of more than ten thousand people being imprisoned, of indescribable tortures being inflicted, and so forth. "I doubt whether there is prison accommodation for so many", he said, "or that torture has been practised on a great scale among an Oriental people who seldom, I believe, resort to torture, but generally terminate their connection with culprits in a more expeditious manner." As jokes were expected of him, this remark produced a laugh, and he was heard to mutter "What is there to laugh at?" But in the controversy which followed he was accused by his opponents of making fun of the subject, and one of the most humane and gentle men was execrated as a callous cynic. He was angry with the Foreign Office and the Ambassador for not keeping him posted with the necessary information, but he was proved right about the exaggerations in the newspapers; and though he described the affair as "a horrible event which no one can think of without emotion", he did not see why the British Empire should denounce its treaties, change its traditional policy, and expel the Turks from Europe, as demanded by the Opposition, solely because the Sultan's troops had behaved with ferocity. In short he knew that the expulsion of the Turks would mean the arrival of the Russians on the shores of the Mediterranean Sea. "What our duty is at this critical moment is to maintain the Empire of England. Nor will we agree to any step, though it may obtain for a moment comparative quiet and a false prosperity, that hazards the existence of that Empire."

With these words, uttered on August 11th, 1876, Disraeli bade farewell to the House of Commons. He gave no hint of his departure, and a fellow-member said that it was the only occasion on which he had ever seen Disraeli really asleep in the House during part of a debate, though another member declared that he had observed tears in the Prime Minister's eyes when making his last speech. At the conclusion of the sitting, he walked slowly down the floor of the House to the bar, turned, surveyed the scene of his many triumphs, and then walked slowly back again, disappearing behind the Speaker's chair. Later he was seen, wearing a long white overcoat and lavender kid gloves, leaning on Corry's arm as he left the precincts; and the following morning, to the amazement of nearly everyone, *The Times* announced that he had been created Earl of Beaconsfield and Viscount Hughenden.

His peerage had been necessitated by his illness. From January '76 onwards he was in frequent pain and compelled to take severe remedies in order to keep at work. Bronchial asthma followed the gout, and attendance at Cabinet meetings was dangerous, but, as he said, "One must run risks in life, or else it would be as dull as death." In the Commons he noted that, from the expression and general demeanour of his colleagues, "they thought the Burials Bill, which we were discussing, was rather a fitting subject for their chief." The Queen was insistent that he should go to the Upper House, where he would be less fatigued, as she felt "the immense *importance* he is to the Throne and country." He asked permission to make enquiries of the party chiefs in the Lords. The Duke of Richmond at once said he would be delighted to abandon the leadership of the House and serve under Disraeli. Lord Derby approved the move, and Lord Salisbury said "You would be very heartily welcomed by the House of Lords: and you would give life to the dullest assembly in the world." Disraeli himself wished to resign the Premiership in favour of Derby, who however emphatically declined the post, adding that he would not serve under anyone but his present chief. The doctors went on tinkering with their distinguished patient, and one of them, Sir William Gull, ordered him to drink port wine, which very nearly finished him off. At last he decided that he could no longer carry on in the Commons, and, having arranged for Sir Stafford Northcote to lead the party there, he reported that "the Faery insists upon my changing my name at once." She also expressed her willingness to settle any part of his titles on his nephew, but Dizzy said "He must fight his way." The new Earl was very definite on the subject of his name, which some people mispronounced with a short vowel for the first syllable. Beaconsfield, he asserted, was the field of the beacon, not a beckoning field.

Everyone noticed that the temperature of the Commons went down when he went up to the Lords. On the morning of the announcement members collected in small groups and talked in hushed voices as if there were a coffin in the place. "All the real chivalry and delight of party politics, seem to have departed; nothing remains but routine", wrote the Whip, Sir William Hart Dyke. Many others felt the same; they had lost all personal interest in the strife; duty had taken the place of pleasure. "The days of the giants are over", said one; and a prominent opponent, Sir William Harcourt, remarked that "Henceforth the game will be like a chessboard when the queen is gone—a petty struggle of pawns." Apart from the fascination of his personality, Disraeli's kindness to the smaller people had been as unusual as his courage in fighting the greater; and he had widened the horizon of youth by showing what genius could do with every outside circumstance hostile to its operation.

On February 8th, 1877, Parliament was opened by the Queen, at whose left hand stood Lord Beaconsfield, clothed in scarlet and ermine, holding aloft the Sword of State, motionless, mysterious, mythical. Though scarcely recovered from an attack of illness, he insisted on going through with the ceremony, which for him was "a chapter in life!" The House of Lords was generally regarded as the grave of eloquence, but he instantly controlled it as easily as he had subdued the other House. He spoke in the same manner, and each word was audible everywhere; he even aroused laughter and cheers in that decorous assembly. His semi-ironical, semi-complimentary style pleased the peers. When, for example, Lord Granville criticised the Government's policy, the Prime Minister made the necessary explanation, and closed with the words: "So your lordships will see that there is not one word of truth in the statement which the noble Earl as Leader of the Opposition in your lordships' House has very properly made." It is clear that he was not quite so moribund as he confessed when replying to someone who thought he would find the Lords tame after the Commons: "I am dead; dead, but in the Elysian fields."

With Dizzy safely out of the way, Gladstone started his

'atrocities' campaign. He had not participated in the debates that had occurred in the Commons; but finding that he could make political capital out of the situation, or, put less bluntly in his own words, finding "that the question was alive", he wrote a pamphlet on *The Bulgarian Horrors*; and, with a lack of tact equalled by his load of malice, sent a copy to the Prime Minister. His one aim in life was to smash his great opponent, and here was a heaven-sent opportunity, the politics of heaven being always Gladstonian. It is debatable whether a man who humbugs himself can be called a humbug, but Dizzy may be excused for thinking Gladstone a Tartuffe, since the basis of this agitation, which would have been disastrous for England if her Prime Minister had not kept his head, was not Gladstone's desire to expel the Turks from Europe but his passion to expel Beaconsfield from Downing Street. He was able to convince himself that the worst stories of the atrocities were true because they were more favourable to his purpose; and his campaign irresistibly reminds one of similar crusades by recent dictators whose sense of truth was at best sketchy and whose foaming oratory swept nations off their feet. He could even delude himself that Russia was fighting for Christianity, and a man who could do that was, in the words of Polonius, "far gone." Dizzy called Gladstone's pamphlet the worst of the Bulgarian horrors, which enraged the liberals who did not appreciate the fact that the policy it advocated would have plunged Europe into war. If Gladstone had proposed to the House of Commons and the Speaker that they should all go to the top of Greenwich Hill (where his speech was made) and then roll down to the bottom, it would not have been more absurdly incongruous, said Dizzy, than his declaration that the Turks should be kicked out of Europe.

All through the autumn of '76 the Prime Minister stood firm against the agitation which convulsed the country and even made the Queen urge him to denounce the Turkish criminals in more definite terms. But he alone knew the appalling danger of the agitation, and in private letters called Gladstone's conduct treasonable, describing the man himself as an unprincipled maniac, an envious and vindictive hypocrite, with one commanding characteristic: "whether preaching, praying, speechifying, or scribbling—never a gentleman!" Russia was of course encouraged by the ferment and expected the support of the

British Government in her designs against Turkey. At the beginning of October '76 Beaconsfield called a Cabinet meeting, as a result of which Turkey, which had been waging a successful war against Servia, was told that she must agree to an armistice, and that if she refused she would be left to her fate. At the same time Russia was informed that she must not occupy Turkey. "Affairs had come to such a pass, through the conduct of Gladstone and Co, that it was necessary to try this last card", said Dizzy, who summarised the situation thus: "It will be long before the mischief the 'atrocity agitation' has done us on the Continent will be remedied. In June last we dictated to Europe, and now every Power looks askance." He was taking a big risk in playing the last card. "If we succeed I shall be a hero, and if we fail they will call me a quack", he had once said, and it was especially true at this moment with England in one of her periodical fits of moral indignation. He succeeded up to a point. Turkey agreed to an armistice but wanted one of six months. This being rejected, she continued operations against Servia, with so much success that Russia stepped in and, under threat of war, compelled her to submit to an armistice of six weeks. The Tsar's autocratic action did not help the atrocity-mongers in England, but failed to surprise Dizzy, who made the wise remark: "It should be noticed we gain nothing with Russia by conciliation or concession." Lord Salisbury went to Constantinople as Britain's representative at the Conference of powers during the armistice; and while he was away the Prime Minister made preparations for war in case Russia should march into Turkey and occupy the capital. The Intelligence Department did not serve him well, and he said it should be called the department of Ignorance; but in time he discovered what naval and military forces would be necessary to seize the Bosphorus and the Dardanelles and to hold Gallipoli in case of emergency. The Conference broke up without reaching any decision, because Russia and Turkey failed to achieve a compromise, and in January '77 Beaconsfield wished "they were all—Russians and Turks—at the bottom of the Black Sea." The only good effect of the Conference was the signing of a peace treaty between Turkey and Servia.

In April, encouraged by the language of Gladstone and others to believe that English sympathies were with him, the Tsar declared war against Turkey, and the one leading statesman of Europe who was wholly opposed to Russia's intentions was crippled with gout. The situation was complicated by the attitude of his Sovereign, whose indignation with the Tsar found expression in letter after letter, and a private communication to her chief Minister that "if England is to kiss Russia's feet, she will not be a party to the humiliation of England and would lay down her crown." It was not a question of upholding Turkey, she proclaimed, but of Russian or British supremacy in the world. Beaconsfield, as the real guardian of his country's welfare, could not act on her downright view of the case; moreover the country had not yet recovered from the deluge of Gladstone's pro-Christian and anti-Turkish platitudes; and he had to walk warily. He decided on a policy of temporary neutrality, but warned Russia that if British interests in the near East were imperilled his Government would be forced to protect them. Meanwhile Gladstone continued his attacks in the Commons, with no one of his rival's stature to answer him, and in effect advocated a policy of helping Russia in her noble endeavours on behalf of the Balkan Christians. What with the Queen spurring him to fight the Tsar, the Gladstone gang goading him to fight the Sultan, and the gout hindering him from doing anything, Beaconsfield was not in the best of spirits during the spring of '77. "Ah!" he repined, "when one has got everything in the world one ever wished for and is prostrate with pain or debility, one knows the value of health, which one never could comprehend in the days of youth and love." The doctors could do nothing. First they attributed his complaint to the weather; then they suggested a change of scene; Sir William Jenner had sent him to Bournemouth; Sir William Gull had told him to go to Ems. "I should like to send them both to Jericho", he said. In August he was so ill with asthma that he had to spend the whole of one night sitting in an armchair and leaning over the back of another. He was still further depressed by Lady Bradford's pro-Russian sentiments. "I often ask myself what single point of sympathy there is between us", he complained, and at the end of July he mourned over the wreck of his hopes: "Four years ago! It makes one very sad. I gave you feelings you could not return. It was not your fault; my fate and my misfortune."

His main public concern that year was to be ready for trouble without seeking it; and he told the English Ambassador at Constantinople that if the Porte were to invite the presence of the British fleet in the Bosphorus and a military occupation of Gallipoli, he would advise the Cabinet to agree, but that the proposal must come from the Turkish Government. He was also worried over two of his leading colleagues. Salisbury, as a strong churchman, seemed inclined to favour a Russian occupation of Constantinople; and Derby was showing signs of weakness in his handling of foreign affairs: "Such a Foreign Minister the Queen really never remembers!" exclaimed Victoria, threatening once again to abdicate if the Russians reached Constantinople. "Be bold!" she admonished Beaconsfield, counselling him to call his followers together and tell them "that it is not for the Christians (and they are quite as cruel as the Turks) but for conquest that this cruel, wicked war is waged, that Russia is as barbarous and tyrannical as the Turks!" He did not need her advice, and had to reply that there were not three men in the Cabinet who would support a declaration of war against Russia; but that if Turkey would ask England to occupy the Dardanelles, all would be well. The statement that Christians were as cruel as Turks was quickly proved true when the Russians advanced through the Balkans; and while the Queen expostulated in hourly telegrams, Gladstone gradually became less articulate on the subject of atrocities.

The Russian advance was held up at Plevna towards the end of July '77, but Beaconsfield did not relax his efforts to make the Cabinet recognise the gravity of the situation. Salisbury soon adopted his view, but Derby remained opposed to intervention even if the Tsar's troops were to occupy Constantinople. In the autumn Beaconsfield went to Brighton to see what the air at that "treeless Capua" would do for his bronchial asthma. But he was so ill that he said he would resign his office if he had the courage to face the inevitable scene with the Queen. He tried a new physician, Dr Kidd, who diagnosed Bright's disease and managed to get him well enough to attend the Lord Mayor's banquet, at which, in referring to his protection of British interests, he used a phrase which thereafter went into general circulation: "Cosmopolitan critics, men who are the friends of every country save their own, have denounced this policy as a selfish policy. My Lord Mayor, it is as selfish as patriotism."

Plevna fell to the Russians in December, and Beaconsfield determined to act without the co-operation of his Foreign Secretary. To manifest her whole-hearted sympathy with her chief Minister, the Queen visited him at Hughenden, and stayed to lunch, the only time in her reign that she ever accepted the hospitality of a Premier in office, except that of Melbourne in 1841. Beaconsfield had a deal of trouble with his Cabinet, and at one point threatened to resign if his policy were not endorsed, which brought them to their senses. Victoria's anxieties added to his own, and his labours were not lightened by such messages as this: "Oh, if the Queen were a man, she would like to go and give those Russians, whose word one cannot believe, such a beating!" Derby continued to oppose everything and to propose nothing, and when it became necessary to send a British fleet through the Dardanelles he talked of resigning. The Queen was delighted to hear of this, and to mark her confidence in Beaconsfield said she would like to confer on him the Order of the Garter. But he did not wish to bribe himself and declined it, telling the Queen "There is no honour and no reward that with him can ever equal the possession of your Majesty's kind thoughts." The fleet was ordered to proceed to Constantinople, where the Russians were daily expected; a Vote of Credit for an increase in the armed forces was agreed by the Cabinet; and Derby tendered his resignation, though as a consequence of the peculiar situation which then developed he remained in office for another two months. What happened was that the British Ambassador to the Porte, Henry Layard, sent a telegram saying that the Turks and Russians had reached an agreement as to peace terms, and that the question of the Straits would be settled between the Tsar and a Peace Congress. This necessitated the recall of the British fleet, which returned to the entrance of the Dardanelles. But next day Layard sent another telegram to say that the question of the Straits was to be settled, not between the Tsar and Congress, but between the Tsar and Sultan. Neither could be trusted; but as it would have been humiliating to send a third order to the fleet within twenty-four hours, the matter rested there for a while. At this extremely critical moment, when the prestige of Great Britain was vital to the peace of the world and the maintenance of western civilisation, Gladstone informed an audience at Oxford on January 30th, '78, that his object had been "to the best of my power, for the last eighteen months, day and night, week by week, month by month, to counterwork as well as I could what I believe to be the purpose of Lord Beaconsfield." Dizzy's comment to Lady Bradford was apt: "What an exposure! The mask has fallen, and instead of a pious Christian, we find a vindictive fiend, who confesses he has, for a year and a half, been dodging and manœuvring against an individual—because he was a successful rival!"

The British Government decided that the Russian demands on Turkey were excessive, for they practically amounted to the future domination of the Balkans by Russia, and, vastly more important for Great Britain, to the creation of a strong Russian influence in the Straits. The country rallied to the Government, and a patriotic song was bawled in every music-hall and whistled by every errand-boy. Taking a word from Goldsmith's *The Vicar of Wakefield*, a rhymster named G. W. Hunt gave it a new meaning and sent it roaring round the Empire:

We don't want to fight, but by jingo if we do,
We've got the ships, we've got the men, we've got the money too.
We've fought the Bear before, and while Britons shall be true,
The Russians shall not have Constantinople.

Beaconsfield was the man in whom the country trusted at this time, and he alone dictated the policy of the Cabinet. On the last day of the debate dealing with the Vote of Credit, the opposition to which collapsed, a vast crowd collected at Downing Street and escorted the Prime Minister to the Lords, cheering themselves hoarse.

Meanwhile, despite peace-parleys, the Russian armies continued to advance, and early in February were threatening Constantinople. Victoria was deeply agitated and one day wrote three letters to Beaconsfield, owning that her first impulse was "to lay down the thorny crown"; but he reassured her with the news that a British fleet was on its way to the Turkish capital, and that all the neutral powers had been invited to make a similar gesture. He told her that if she were displeased with the actions of her Government, she had the constitutional right to dismiss them, and he thanked her for the camellias and primroses which she had sent him: "Truly he can say they are 'more precious than rubies'; coming, as they do, and at such a moment, from a

Sovereign whom he adores." Though still Foreign Secretary, Derby took a back seat in the conduct of affairs, often criticising the warlike moves of the Prime Minister, who now began to consult Lord Salisbury on such matters. Secret negotiations with Austria resulted in an agreement between the two countries; an Austrian army took the field; and Russia was told either to leave Constantinople or to let Gallipoli and the Straits be occupied by British or neutral powers: further that the peace terms with Turkey must be submitted to a Congress for concurrence or rejection. Meanwhile Beaconsfield was preparing for the possibility of a military expedition, and in the docks and arsenals

sweaty haste
Did make the night joint-labourer with the day.

For a while Russia bluffed, and everyone except Beaconsfield expected war; but after the departure of Derby from the Foreign Office, and the arrival of seven thousand native Indian troops at Malta, their first appearance in Europe, Russia gave in, and agreed to submit all her proposals for discussion and agreement by a Congress of the other nations. "If we are bold and determined we shall secure peace, and dictate its conditions to Europe . . . We have to maintain the Empire and secure peace; I think we can do both", wrote Beaconsfield at a crucial stage of the proceedings; and his courageous policy was justified. Salisbury became Foreign Secretary, and Beaconsfield offered Derby the Garter, an unexampled act of generosity if we consider that Derby had deserted him at a moment when he needed the unstinted support of his chief lieutenants.

Throughout all the trials of those testing months Beaconsfield was writing long reports to the Queen which contained phrases unlike any she had yet read, or was ever to read, in the letters of her other Prime Ministers: "He feels there is no devotion that your Majesty does not deserve, and he only wishes he had youth and energy to be the fitting champion of such an inspiring Mistress as your Majesty." "If your Majesty is ill, he is sure he will himself break down." "The violets and primroses came to him when he was in a somewhat exhausted and desponding mood, and he felt their magic influence." "He lives only for Her, and works only for Her, and without Her all is lost." She scolded him for visiting her in March '78 when he had a bad cold, though Victoria herself was in a similar plight, and he told Lady Bradford that "The Kingdom was never governed with such an amount of catarrh and sneezing." When he hinted that he would like to represent Great Britain at the European Congress, which was to be held at Berlin, the Queen informed the Prince of Wales that she did not think her Prime Minister strong enough to take so long a journey, as he was "my great support and comfort, for you cannot think how kind he is to me, how attached! His health and life are of immense value to me and the country, and should on no account be risked."

As Russia had assented to all England's material demands concerning the Straits and the Balkans, England had to allow Russia the footing she had won in Asia Minor. But Beaconsfield safeguarded England's interests by secretly entering into a defensive alliance with Turkey, and arranging that Great Britain should occupy the island of Cyprus in order to check any further Russian progress in those regions. With this pact in his pocket, Beaconsfield left for the Berlin Congress on June 8th, 1878, Salisbury having preceded him. The simultaneous absence of the two chief tories from the Lords was deplored by the leader of the Opposition in that House, Lord Granville, but Beaconsfield spoke words of consolation: "The noble Earl has expressed his regret that my noble friend sitting on my right and myself should be abroad at the same time: he has been pleased to add that he considers that the absence of the noble Marquis and of myself from the Cabinet will diminish the personal importance of those that remain. My Lords, I can conceive no circumstance—ahem!" (business with handkerchief)—"more calculated to add to it." Salisbury was now his right-hand man, and for two excellent reasons: he was both brave and intelligent. "Courage is the rarest of all qualities to be found in public men", said Beaconsfield, adding that Salisbury was "the only man of real courage that it has ever been my lot to work with." But Salisbury was brainy as well as plucky. On hearing one of his acquaintances state that under no circumstances should he think it right to say what was not true, Salisbury remarked "I am glad that I have been warned: I shall be careful never to trust him with a secret." He made the strangest of discoveries for a politician: that insincerity was the concomitant of weakness. And another almost as strange: "No lesson seems to be so deeply inculcated by the experience of life as that you never should trust experts. If you believe the doctors, nothing is wholesome: if you believe the theologians, nothing is innocent: if you believe the soldiers, nothing is safe." With such a man Dizzy was in harmony, though it took some time, as we have seen, for Salisbury to be in harmony with Dizzy. At the time of the Berlin Congress, however, old disagreements had been smoothed away; they were hand-and-glove; and Bismarck under-estimated the younger man when he said: "I think nothing of their Lord Salisbury: he is only a lath painted to look like iron. But that old Jew means business."

The last thing Beaconsfield did before setting off for Berlin was to pen a line to Lady Bradford, begging her to write frequently—"Anything about you and yours will always interest me, even at a Congress"—and closing "With deep affection." Only a few months before this, he had told her that his weakness was his heart, a weakness he should long ago have outlived, and that the only real happiness was that which sprang from the affections. He took four days to reach Berlin, being entertained by the King and Queen of the Belgians on the way. The moment he arrived at the Kaiserhof Hotel in Berlin he received a message from Bismarck asking for a personal meeting. They had not seen one another for sixteen years, an interval that had changed Bismarck from a tall pallid man with a wasplike waist into a monstrous giant with red face and huge belly. He talked in a sweet and gentle voice, with a very refined enunciation, which contrasted curiously with the ogre-like body, the rabelaisian and recklessly frank things he said. He was to be President of the Congress, and he had little respect for any participant except Beaconsfield. Each took the other's measure from the start, and they were soon on agreeable terms. Prince Gortchakoff, the Russian Chancellor, was there, and Beaconsfield found him so courteous and caressing that "it is quite painful to me to occasion him so much annoyance, particularly as he tells me he only came to the Congress to make my acquaintance." On the opening day there was an amusing scene which Beaconsfield described in a letter to Queen Victoria but would not have admitted to a serious biography because it lacks the dignity of history. Gortchakoff, a shrivelled old man, was leaning on the arm of the gigantic Bismarck, who was suddenly seized with an attack of rheumatism, both of them falling to the ground. Bismarck's dog, seeing his master apparently struggling for dear life with an opponent, sprang to his rescue, and it was with some difficulty that the rheumatic Bismarck saved Gortchakoff from being seriously mauled. Yet even dignified history is illuminated by this episode, which shows that a dog is less tenacious than a man, for Bismarck could not save Gortchakoff from Beaconsfield. Another figure of note at the Congress was the Austrian Foreign Minister, Count Andrassy, who had resuscitated the Hapsburg Empire; while France was represented by Georges Waddington, an Anglo-Frenchman described by Beaconsfield as "a doctrinaire—he is convinced by his own reasoning—he is the slave of his own syllogisms." Italy sent Count Corti, and Carathéodory Pasha put the case for Turkey.

At once it became obvious that Beaconsfield was the outstanding personality of the Congress, and the man who would impose his will upon it. "*Der alte Jude, das ist der Mann*" ("The old Jew, that is the man"), was Bismarck's summary of the situation. Everyone except Beaconsfield addressed the Congress in French; he spoke in English. The reason given for this was that the other plenipotentiaries did not wish to hear a master of his own language speak in any other; but the true reason was that his French pronunciation left much to be desired, and the British Ambassador Odo Russell, accustomed to deal with delicate situations, was deputed by Montagu Corry and the other English secretaries to deal with this. Beaconsfield listened gravely while Russell begged him not to deprive the Congress of an intellectual treat to which everyone had been looking forward. The chief took the insinuation as a compliment, and spared the feelings of his entourage.

The Congress opened on June 11th, and Beaconsfield's determination was clear from the outset that Russia should be excluded from the Mediterranean Sea, for access to which she had gone to war with Turkey; and he insisted at once that the boundaries of Bulgaria, which Russia wished to enlarge and convert into a satellite State, should be drawn according to his own plan. Eventually he gained his point by the simple but dangerous method of telling Count Corti in confidence at a banquet that he would break up the Congress if Russia did not accept his proposals, which would mean war between the two nations. He knew that Corti would at once pass this information on to Bismarck, who for his own purposes wanted the Congress to be successful. But Dizzy was leaving nothing to chance, and asked Corry to order a special train to be ready for their return home should Russia refuse to fall in with his wishes. Bismarck heard what he had said to Corti, heard too of the train, and did an unprecedented thing: he called on Beaconsfield. "Am I to understand it is an ultimatum?" he asked. "You are", he was told. "We should talk over this matter. Where do you dine today?" "At the English Embassy." "I wish you could dine with me." Beaconsfield accepted the invitation. After dinner, at which Bismarck ate and drank as much as he talked, they retired to another room, where they smoked, "the last blow to my shattered constitution", reported Dizzy, "but I felt it absolutely necessary." He convinced Bismarck that the ultimatum was not a sham; and before going to bed he heard that the Tsar had capitulated. "What is the use of Power if you don't make people do what they don't like?" he once asked. The following morning, June 22nd, he was able to telegraph the Queen that "Russia surrenders, and accepts the English scheme for the European frontier of the Empire, and its military and political rule by the Sultan. Bismarck says 'There is again a Turkey-in-Europe'." The Queen replied "It is all due to your energy and firmness." But it had not been easy. "I am brought forward as the man of war on all occasions, and have to speak like Mars", he said.

His victory, which had been won by many hours of mental and physical strain, resulted in a violent attack of gout, and Dr Kidd was summoned from London. Though suffering severely, he yet managed to get the only other really important matter settled: Russia's position in Asia Minor, won by her in the recent war. Beaconsfield was emphatic that Batoum on the Black Sea should be a free and commercial port, and that Turkey should have a frontier line in Asia Minor that would put her in a favourable position if attacked and at the same time make it difficult for Russia to expand southwards towards India, Mesopotamia or Egypt. After much haggling, Russia yielded these two points, and Beaconsfield had successfully accomplished the main objects of his mission. His own diplomatic method was direct and concise. "It was easy to transact business with him", said Bismarck; "in a quarter of an hour you knew exactly how you stood with him; the limits to which he was prepared to go were clearly defined, and a rapid summary soon precisionised matters."

The other parts of the Treaty, such as the occupation and administration of Bosnia and Herzegovina by Austria, were of small account compared with those which vanquished the recent victor in the war with Turkey.

Before taking to his bed Beaconsfield had attended several great banquets, had stayed with the Crown Prince and Princess at Potsdam, and had visited the wife of Wilhelm I, the Empress Augusta, who, said Salisbury, was very foolish, "and B's compliments were a thing to hear." The dinners and receptions were a frightful strain on his weakening physical system. "I begin to die at ten o'clock and should like to be buried before midnight", he confessed to Queen Victoria. The amount of food that the Germans and Austrians managed to eat was a source of perpetual surprise. "I watched her with amazement, that so delicate and pretty a mouth could perform such awful feats", he wrote of the Countess Karolyi, and Bismarck's achievements at the table were gargantuan. But he enjoyed the long talks he had with the German Chancellor. At one of them Bismarck asked whether horse-racing was still popular in England. More than ever, replied his guest. "Then there never will be Socialism in England", cried Bismarck. "You are a happy country. You are safe, as long as the people are devoted to racing. Here a gentleman cannot ride down the street without twenty persons saying to themselves, or each other, 'Why has that fellow a horse, and I have not one?' In England the more horses a nobleman has, the more popular he is. So long as the English are devoted to racing, Socialism has no chance with you." In further conversation it became clear to Beaconsfield that the Chancellor's idea of progress was to seize something, for when he heard that England had acquired Cyprus he said "You have done a wise thing. This is progress. It will be popular; a nation likes progress." He looked upon England's withdrawal from the Ionian Isles as the first sign of her decadence. Beaconsfield was fascinated by Bismarck's monologues, rambling, amusing, coarse, candid, egotistical, and let him ramble on. The only drawback was that the listener had to smoke: "If you do not smoke under such circumstances, you look like a spy, taking down his conversation in your mind. Smoking in common puts him at his ease."

The Treaty was signed on July 13th. The Congress had lasted a month. Another month would have killed him, said Dizzy, whose arrival home on the 16th was signalised by popular acclamations. All the way from Charing Cross to Downing Street a dense crowd shouted its approval and sang loyal songs. Salisbury was with him, and both of them responded to the cheers by appearing at the windows of No. 10 Downing Street, Beaconsfield telling the people that "Lord Salisbury and myself have brought you back peace; but a peace, I hope, with honour." The Queen insisted on giving him the Garter and wished him to accept a Marquisate or Dukedom. He declined everything except the Garter, requesting that it should also be bestowed on Salisbury, with which she promptly complied. On August 3rd the two Ministers drove to the Guildhall through wildly enthusiastic multitudes to receive the freedom of the City. Beaconsfield was in pain all the time but managed to fulfil his task. The Treaty was accepted by the Lords without a division, and by a large majority in the Commons. Hartington, the Opposition leader, dared not put forward a hostile resolution, and the innocuous one he moved was described by Dizzy as "a string of congratulatory regrets." Indeed the Prime Minister's achievement was of such a nature that England's prestige on the continent was advanced to a point it had not attained since the days of Wellington after the battle of Waterloo; and in 1878, unlike 1815, her position had been won without bloodshed at the expense of a great Empire which had just concluded a triumphant campaign. Next to leaving Turkey as a power in Europe and guardian of the Straits, Beaconsfield's object had been to break up and prevent the alliance between the autocratic powers of Russia, Germany and Austria; and this too had been contrived by his personal influence with Andrassy and Bismarck. It was in fact a great diplomatic victory for a democratic country, won by a single determined individual, unique in modern history and likely to remain so.

THE BERLIN CONGRESS, 1878 (*facing*)

Portraits, left to right: Baron Haymerle, Count Károlyi, Count de Launay, Prince Gortchakov, W. H. Waddington, Lord Beaconsfield, von Radowitz, Prince Hohenlohe, Count Corti, de Möuy, d'Oubril, Count de St. Vallier, Desprez, Count Andrassy, Lothar Bucher, Prince von Bismarck, von Holstein, Dr. Busch, Herbert von Bismarck, P. A. Shuvalov, Sadullah Bey, Lord Odo Russell, Count von Bülow, Lord Salisbury, Carathéodory Pasha, Mehemed Ali Pasha.

THE BERLIN CONGRESS, 1878

By Anton von Werner

THE EARL OF BEACONSFIELD, 1879

Photograph taken at Osborne

The success of his policy and his personal popularity made Gladstone frantic, and he spat venom. He called the Treaty "an insane covenant", its negotiation "an act of duplicity of which every Englishman should be ashamed", its chief author worse than a despot, and so on and so forth. Beaconsfield replied to this tirade at a Conservative party dinner given to Salisbury and himself in the Riding School at Knightsbridge on July 27th; and in speaking of the term "an insane covenant" he referred to Gladstone in words that will probably be remembered when their subject is forgotten:

> Which do you believe most likely to enter an insane convention, a body of English gentlemen honoured by the favour of their Sovereign and the confidence of their fellow-subjects, managing your affairs for five years, I hope with prudence, and not altogether without success, or a sophistical rhetorician, inebriated with the exuberance of his own verbosity, and gifted with an egotistical imagination that can at all times command an interminable and inconsistent series of arguments to malign an opponent and to glorify himself?

Gladstone did not appreciate this view of himself, and wrote to ask for a list of the epithets with which he was charged as having applied to Dizzy's measures and personality, a request which suggests that he was never quite conscious of what he was saying. Beaconsfield regretted that he was much pressed with affairs, and as the research would cover a period of two and a half years he would ask others to undertake it; but he quoted his rival's recent outburst, and mentioned an occasion when Gladstone had accused him of degrading and debasing the great name of England. As far as we know, the correspondence then ceased.

Chapter XXIV

AFGHANS AND ZULUS

THE aristocrats who had formerly sneered at Dizzy now cheered Beaconsfield, for the author of *Vivian Grey* had become the master of Europe, and the unspeakable outsider had grown into a stately senator. The mask he had once adopted to hide his emotions had in process of time superseded his naturally animated countenance, and without that inscrutable expression, that rare enigmatic smile, that perplexing stare, those drooping eyelids, he would not have been Dizzy. By taking thought he had created his public personality. The slight drawl in his speech, the sepulchral tone, the deliberate and impressive manner, the sententious terminology, the long silences, were as much a part of the creation as, in later years, the dyed black hair, the stays, and the curl on the forehead which was kept in position by the art of the coiffeur. The bent figure was often to be seen in the late seventies, leaning on the arm of Corry, moving down Whitehall with a rather shuffling gait, clothed during the cold weather in a great coat lined with astrakhan, easily recognisable from the tuft on his chin and the deathlike pallor of his face. Though he loved the solitude of the country, he liked to see the crowds in the London streets; and in walking with a friend along Pall Mall, he refused to turn right at the Athenaeum Club and so take a short cut to the Houses of Parliament down the Duke of York's steps, saying: "No, no! Not that way: it's so damned dull!"

So striking was his appearance that it became the ambition of nearly every artist to paint him. Whistler longed for the opportunity and did everything in his power to bring it about, trying to enlist the interest of every notable person of his acquaintance who knew Dizzy, and even begging the American Ambassador to use his influence. But the Premier was not to be inveigled. Then, one day, Whistler saw his ideal model sitting alone in

St James's Park, abstracted, absorbed. Though not subject to the emotion, Whistler felt shy; but his desire gave him courage and he approached the still and somewhat sinister figure, introduced himself nervously, spoke of the people they both knew, referred to his own work, and at last said that the one great object of his life was to paint the most famous statesman of the age. Not a movement, not a sound, not a flicker of an eyelid, from the sitting sphinx. Whistler stopped speaking, and there was a glacial pause; after which, though the eyes remained lifeless, the lips of the inanimate being moved slightly and six words issued from them: "Go away, little man, go away."

Whenever his illness and his duties permitted, he continued to dine out, and perhaps his frequent silences caused his utterances to be remembered by the other guests. At one public dinner the food was served up cold, and when he tasted the champagne he observed "Thank God, I have at last got something warm!" He could not accustom himself to the poor wine at the tables of so many wealthy men. "An Englishman, incapable otherwise of a shabby action, will nevertheless order inferior claret at dinner", he lamented. But he spared their feelings. Once, when the ladies had retired, his host asked him to take more claret. "No, thank you, my dear fellow", he said. "It is admirable wine, true Falernian, but I have already exceeded my prescribed quantity, and the gout holds me in its horrid clutch." Afterwards, when the host mentioned this to his wife, she exclaimed: "Claret! Why, he drank brandy and water all dinner-time." His invariable politeness was shown in the last years of his life whenever he met old acquaintances whose names had slipped his memory. "I get over it this way", he confided to someone. "I always say 'How is the old complaint?', for most people have something; and while they are answering I have time to collect my thoughts and recall the name." He continued to entertain on a lavish scale, and he wished the peers who dined with him would attend the House of Lords in equal numbers; but his failing memory occasionally bothered him: "I want an earl to complete my table. I believe there are a hundred of them, but I'll be hanged if I can remember the name of one."

He was not much attracted to his fellow-authors. He met Browning at someone's table, "a noisy, conceited poet"; and when asked whether he had read a novel that was making a stir, he replied "When I want to read a novel, I write one." Nor did he care for the very few pieces he saw in the theatre. "Monty and I are going to the play tonight to see some nonsense, which everybody is going to see—*Parasol* or *Pinafore*—a burlesque—a sort of thing I hate." This was the first of the great Gilbert and Sullivan successes, which was the rage in '78. But one man's thrill is another man's boredom, and Dizzy said that, except at Wycombe fair in his youth, he had never seen anything so bad. Nevertheless he must have enjoyed Gilbert's caricature of W. H. Smith, whom he had made First Lord of the Admiralty in July '77, because he used to speak of him as "*Pinafore* Smith", an excellent example of his detachment from the humbug of party politics. Two years later he saw Henry Irving for the first time. The play was *The Corsican Brothers*; and though he had never witnessed anything so cleverly staged, he thought Irving "third-rate, and never will improve, but good enough for the part he played." Another form of entertainment made little appeal to him: "A long dreary sermon from the Bishop of London, which made me bitterly repent I had placed the mitre on his head in 1868." But he does not seem to have thought highly of the ecclesiastical pundits. When Lady Bradford approved the promotion of Maclagan (afterwards Archbishop of York) to the see of Lichfield, Dizzy wrote: "It seems a success with all 'schools of Church thought', *alias* Church nonsense."

Had Beaconsfield appealed to the electorate soon after the Berlin Congress, his party would undoubtedly have returned to power for another six or seven years, but he did not wish to take advantage of his success in that way, and he remained in office for nearly two more years, during which certain disappointments at home and disasters abroad, for which he could scarcely be held responsible, swung the political pendulum in favour of his opponents. In England there was a trade depression, resulting in reduced wages, disputes, unemployment and strikes; and a series of bad harvests precipitated the ruin of the nation's agriculture which he had foreseen when the Corn Laws were repealed; so that his downfall, when it came, was partly due to a policy that he had condemned; and the irony of this circumstance was not lost upon him.

At the close of the parliamentary session in '78 he went to Hughenden, whence he wrote to Victoria that he no longer felt "that continuous flow of power, which becomes the servant of an Empress and a Queen." A visit to see her at Osborne made his bronchitis worse than ever, though she insisted on his taking every precaution, and refused to let him visit the Prince of Wales on his yacht in order to meet the King and Queen of Denmark because it would have meant going a short distance in an open boat; so the mountain came to Mahomet, and he lunched with the Prince and his royal guests in lodgings at Cowes. Back at Hughenden, he gave orders that his secretaries were not to approach him except on urgent and critical business; but public affairs kept him at work, and the autumn was one of alarms and incursions. He enjoyed the solitude, and he loved his library: "Books are companions, even if you don't open them." Any social excitement, anything that interfered with the mechanical regularity of his habits, upset him; and as the world would not leave him alone, he was constantly upset.

Apart from the efforts he made to get all the articles in the Treaty of Berlin carried out, his main anxiety in the latter part of '78 was caused by the Viceroy of India, Lord Lytton, and the Amir of Afghanistan, Sher Ali. It had been impressed upon Lytton when he became Viceroy in '76 that the north-west frontier of India should be secured, owing to Russia's growing friendliness with the Amir, to counter which it was proposed that a British mission should visit Kabul, the capital of Afghanistan. But the Amir was shifty, and showed no disposition to receive a mission, while claiming material support from Great Britain in case of aggression. Clearly he was conspiring with Russia, and it became vitally necessary to safeguard India by occupying the main passes on the Afghan frontier. In December '76 Lytton concluded a treaty with the Khan of Kelat, which gave Britain the military control of Baluchistan and the right to garrison Quetta. This protected India on the extreme north-west. But there was still grave danger of a Russian invasion through the Khyber and Michnee passes north of the Punjab, and the Amir was doing his best to stir up the local tribes in a holy war against the British. The situation became acute in July '78, when a Russian mission arrived at Kabul and was received with honour by a ruler who expected Great Britain to guard his independence. Lytton at once determined that a British mission should also be received with honour at Kabul, and despatched one. But he made the mistake of sending it by the Khyber pass, where it was stopped by the Amir's troops. Beaconsfield was annoyed, firstly because Lytton had been told to wait until Russia had replied to the Cabinet's remonstrance, secondly because he had been advised to send the mission, when the proper time came, by Kandahar. He had definitely disregarded his instructions, and, as Dizzy said, "When Viceroys and Commanders-in-Chief disobey orders, they ought to be sure of success in their mutiny." However, the thing was done, and since Britain had been affronted the Cabinet supported, if with reluctance, Lytton's action. An ultimatum was sent to the Amir demanding a written apology for his hostile behaviour and the permanent presence of a British mission in his country. Before his reply could come the Prime Minister had to appear at the Lord Mayor's banquet.

Beaconsfield was not, like Gladstone, a vote-snatcher and a moraliser. He did not rush round the country fomenting righteous indignation, nor did he put a case in such a light that it favoured his personal aims. Instead of protesting at the Guildhall that, while feigning friendship with England and expecting help from her if attacked, the Amir had given an honourable reception to a Russian mission and forcibly prevented a British mission, an action that necessitated the Government's ultimatum, the Premier calmly and clearly stated his intention to rectify the north-west frontier of India, so that the country should be safe from invasion. His colleagues were disturbed by his honesty, his opponents delighted, and the Liberal press and party promptly gave tongue, describing the Government's policy as a wanton and warlike provocation. In case he had not provided them with enough to scribble and gossip about, he also referred in his speech to the newspaper and platform comments on the Berlin Treaty, the terms of which, said the critics, were not being implemented. Having explained that the major conditions had already been fulfilled, and the less important ones would certainly be observed, he remarked: "The government of the world is carried on by Sovereigns and statesmen, and not by anonymous paragraphers, or by the hare-brained chatter of irresponsible frivolity."

His party were not pleased by his outspokenness, but he did not expect them to be, for he had once said: "They are all middle-class men, and I have always observed through life that middle-class men are afraid of responsibility." He remained undaunted, and instructed Lytton to take action on the day the ultimatum expired. He even risked the frown of Majesty a few days after his City speech by accepting an invitation from Prince Hal, as he called the heir-apparent, to stay at Sandringham. The Queen telegraphed that she highly disapproved of his going, as he was taking a great risk by travelling in such cold stormy weather. He thought that she was getting jealous of his friendship with her son; but he went all the same, enjoyed an agreeable visit, and may have caught a cold, because he arrived sneezing at Windsor not long afterwards for a royal audience, "during which, strictly, I believe, you may not even blow your nose."

What the liberals described as an unjust war was at any rate successful, largely owing to the ability of General Sir Frederick (afterwards Field-Marshal Earl) Roberts, who routed the Afghan army and quickly became master of the situation. Sher Ali fled, and his son Yakub Khan became Amir, signing a treaty which stipulated that a British representative should reside at Kabul, that British assistance should be forthcoming in case of attack by other powers, that the Amir should receive a subsidy, and that certain districts should remain under British control with the object of settling a frontier defence for India. This was in May '79, and the man who negotiated the treaty, Sir Louis Cavagnari, an able administrator who had spent twenty years in both military and political branches of the Indian service, was appointed Resident at Kabul. He went there in July with a staff and escort which, at his own request, were as small as possible. On September 2nd he telegraphed to the Viceroy that all was well. The next day the Residency was stormed by Afghan troops, possibly with the connivance of the Amir, and all the defenders were massacred. Beaconsfield was momentarily stunned by the news. "This is a shaker", he wrote to Salisbury. But having reflected "It is fortunate that Parliament is not sitting: there is nothing to paralyse us", he acted with his usual promptitude and energy. Lytton had just reported that nearly all the people who had received honours or votes of thanks from parliament for their services in the recent affair were utterly worthless. "And these are the men whom, only a few months or weeks ago, he recommended for all these distinctions!" exclaimed Beaconsfield. Fortunately there was one notable exception, Roberts, who repeated his former triumphs and was in Kabul a month after commencing operations. While there he discovered that the "unjust war" was at least an expedient one, for the seizure of letters between Sher Ali and Russian agents brought to light "a very serious conspiracy against the peace and security of our Indian Empire." The hostile tribes continued to give trouble, and Roberts made a famous march from Kabul to relieve a British force at Kandahar; but as a result of the second Afghan War India established a defensible frontier and Russian expansion was arrested in that quarter.

Having been hustled into one war against his wish, the Prime Minister was hurled into another against his will. He was at Hughenden for Christmas '78, fighting his various ailments. Yet he did not complain of life: "I have had a good innings and cannot at all agree with the great King that all is Vanity." On January 1st, 1879, he wrote to Lady Bradford: "My present physicians are Dr Solitude, Dr Silence, Dr Warmth; and two general practitioners, Regular Hours and Regular Meals . . . I don't want any companion, unless it were you." A fortnight later he announced that, after ten weeks of suffering, his asthma, bronchitis, and all the grisly crew, had been driven away by the thaw or the gout, and he felt he could grapple with anything when well and in reasonably good spirits; but the grisly crew soon returned. Every week in April '79 baskets of primroses, made up into little bouquets, arrived from Osborne, and the head gardener had orders to send them when the Queen was elsewhere. But Victoria was having serious disagreements with her chief Minister, who experienced the truth of his saying: "There is nothing so exhausting as the management of men . . . except perhaps the management of women."

For some time there had been trouble in South Africa. The Transvaal Republic was in a condition of bankruptcy and anarchy, and the Boer inhabitants were constantly fighting the natives on their borders, while treating those inside their country with inhuman harshness. The most famous and bellicose of these native tribes, the Zulus, occupied the country between British Natal and the Boer Republic. Their king, Cetywayo, was on good terms with the British but hated the Boers, and would have attacked the latter in force if he had not been restrained by the former. Among the English administrators of South Africa there was a growing fear of a general Kaffir war; and to ease the situation the British authorities decided to annex the Transvaal as a preliminary to forming a federation of the various states, giving each a free Constitution. The annexation took place in April '77; and though some of the leading Boers objected to it, no general dissatisfaction was exhibited at the time. But the Zulu king was not pleased. It seemed to him that he was being encompassed by white people; no longer could he fight the Boers, who were now protected by the British; and with the Zulus fighting was as necessary as breathing.

The atmosphere became tense; and the High Commissioner of South Africa, Sir Bartle Frere, having studied the situation on the spot, came to the conclusion that there could be no tranquillity or safety in the country until Cetywayo's power was destroyed. This was not the view of Beaconsfield, who believed that if the Zulu chief were treated fairly and reasonably, especially concerning his claim to certain lands that had been the subject of bitter contention between himself and the Boers, he would remain friendly with the British. Frere, however, wished to force the issue, and allowed the Boers to remain on the disputed land, though a Commission had decided in favour of the Zulus. He also asked the Home Government for reinforcements in case of hostilities. The English Cabinet sent them, but instructed Frere that they must only be used for defence. The danger of a general native revolt against the white men, headed by the Zulus, was now imminent, and Frere, who had been encouraged by the Colonial Secretary to believe that the Cabinet agreed with his forward policy and would support him in asserting the sovereignty of Great Britain throughout South Africa, ignored his instructions. Without consulting the Home Government, he sent an ultimatum to Cetywayo ordering him to make reparation for the outrages committed by his people, to disband his celibate army, and to accept a permanent British Resident in his country. Frere knew quite well that Cetywayo would reject the ultimatum, and when no answer arrived a British force, commanded by Lord Chelmsford, entered Zululand. On January 22nd, 1879, the enemy surprised one column of this force at Isandhlwana, eight hundred white soldiers and nearly five hundred natives being wiped out to a man. The news came as a shock to the English people, who were scarcely aware that a war had broken out, and as a knock-out blow to Beaconsfield, whose illness returned in full force, prostrating him. He did not leave his house for about a month, and performed his duties between visits from his doctor. The disaster was followed by a feat of heroism at Rorke's Drift, where a handful of men, protected by an improvised barricade of rice bags and biscuit tins, held out all through one night against waves of Zulu warriors.

But no feats of heroism could soothe the British public after the deplorable affair at Isandhlwana, and there was a loud outcry against Frere for disobedience and Chelmsford for incompetence. Beaconsfield was not the man to yield to popular clamour; he never sacrificed a good servant of the State even when his orders had been disregarded, and never made a scapegoat to save his own face, being loyal and chivalrous to his subordinates and to those who were doing a job on the spot. He had great difficulty with his Cabinet, the members of which were easily stampeded by mob orators and press philippics, and several of whom required "considerable private handling", he told the Queen. But he persuaded them to keep their heads; and it was agreed that Chelmsford must be given a chance to repair his error, while Frere, who had a fine record as an Anglo-Indian administrator, must be rebuked but retained. Unfortunately Frere attempted to vindicate his conduct, which further antagonised the Cabinet, and as the weeks drifted by the news from the Cape made Beaconsfield think that Chelmsford was incapable of retrieving his early disasters. Towards the end of May the Cabinet were sitting almost daily, and the Prime Minister was dealing with Afghans as well as Zulus. Though his eyes were misty with work, and gout or asthma held him in its grip, he made all the decisions and obtained the backing of his colleagues.

It was at length determined that Sir Garnet Wolseley should be sent out as High Commissioner and Commander-in-Chief for Natal, the Transvaal, Zululand, and adjacent territories, an appointment that would leave Frere as Governor and High Commissioner of Cape Colony, and Chelmsford as second-in-command on the scene of action. Beaconsfield knew there would be storms from his royal Mistress, and in the hope of disarming her sent a letter of congratulation on her birthday, wherein he touched upon the vastness of her Empire, "the hallowed influences of her hearth", and the bright intelligence and condescending sympathy which charmed and inspired his labours. But she refused to be cajoled; and after giving strong reasons against the Cabinet's decision, the main one being that it would amount to a lack of confidence in Frere at a moment of great difficulty, she concluded that she "would sanction the proposal submitted if her warnings are disregarded, but she would *not approve it*." A correspondence then ensued which showed that, if the Queen could be firm, her Prime Minister could be firmer, and she had to give way. Then he encountered obstruction from the military authorities, who had their own pet generals, and looked on Wolseley with disfavour. The headquarters staff at the Horse Guards raged furiously; from the Duke of Cambridge, Commander-in-Chief, downwards, they were all jealous of Wolseley, calling him an egotist and a braggart. But so was Nelson, wrote Dizzy to the Queen: "Men of action, when eminently successful in early life, are generally boastful and full of themselves"; and he admitted that he too would have been the same if he had not had the immense advantage of being vilified and abused for forty years, which had taught him self-control, patience, and circumspection. "The Horse Guards will ruin this country", he declared, "unless there is a Prime Minister who will have his way." Wolseley went; but his duties were mainly of a civil nature, because, after having exhibited much vacillation and incompetence, Chelmsford practically finished the war by smashing the main Zulu forces at Ulundi within a week of his substitute's arrival. Wolseley eventually became a Viscount, a Field-Marshal, and Commander-in-Chief of the British Army in succession to the Queen's cousin, the Duke of Cambridge, who had held the post for forty years.

A disturbing feature of the campaign had been the loss, in a small outpost affair, of the ex-Prince Imperial of France, who had persuaded his mother, the ex-Empress Eugénie, who in turn had persuaded Victoria, to let him go to the front. Beaconsfield did everything he could to prevent it, "but what can you do when you have to deal with two obstinate women?" Since he was not permitted to join the British forces, the young man went as a mere traveller; but when he reached Natal, probably with private letters from the Queen and Empress, Chelmsford gave him a staff job. As the British Government were on friendly terms with France, Beaconsfield was made uneasy by the public sympathy the Queen wished to display over the death of a pretender to the French throne. Somehow he managed to prevent her from expressing her feelings in too marked a form; but he was relieved when the Prince's burial at Chislehurst was safely over. The Queen telegraphed that she was highly pleased at the funeral arrangements and the public manifestations of sorrow. "I hope the French Government will be as joyful", drily commented Dizzy. "In my mind nothing could be more injudicious than the whole affair." However, it did not provoke a *casus belli*.

War has to be paid for, and the Chancellor of the Exchequer, Sir Stafford Northcote, proposed to increase the duties on tea. This would have raised a howl from the tea-drinking liberals, and the Prime Minister suggested that the necessary amount should be borrowed by the issue of Exchequer Bonds. The Chancellor was worried; but after his chief had conveyed to him how greatly he was esteemed and regarded by his colleagues, he assented.

It had been a wearying session for Beaconsfield, and its close did not bring him peace. First he dutifully faced the usual City feast, where, after three or four hours of futile conversation, the glare of gas, and nothing to eat, he had to rise in a condition of mental confusion and bodily exhaustion and make a speech that would be criticised in detail for more than a month. Next he had to deal with the irritation of his Sovereign, who expected him to receive Lord Chelmsford at Hughenden. He refused to do so, saying that he would only give the returning General, who had bungled the war, an official interview at Downing Street. The Queen was grieved and astonished at his attitude. He was grieved and distressed at her displeasure; but he stuck to his guns; and though she received the General at Balmoral, he would only ask to Hughenden two subordinate officers who had distinguished themselves, Sir Evelyn Wood and Colonel Redvers Buller. He felt himself to be in disgrace, and, intending no doubt that his letter should be shown to the person chiefly concerned, he wrote to Victoria's close friend, Lady Ely: "I love the Queen —perhaps the only person in this world left to me that I do love; and therefore you can understand how much it worries and disquiets me, when there is a cloud between us."

Victoria was much too fond of him to let such disagreements

affect her feelings or her judgment, and reflection probably convinced her that he was almost invariably right. She even remained calm when the Prince of Wales stayed for a night at Hughenden in January, 1880. Dizzy was anxious that Prince Hal should not be bored, and so made up the party with the nearest Victorian equivalents to Falstaff and Poins, their names being Bernal Osborne and Lord Rosslyn, friends of the Prince in his frolicsome hours and described by their present host as "two clowns, and both capital ones." In the evening Dizzy hoped they would play nap, which would have left him free, but the Prince insisted on whist, partnering with Osborne against Beaconsfield and Salisbury. "He beat us, which does not displease him." In fact he thoroughly enjoyed himself, and much to Dizzy's relief the Queen wrote that she highly approved of the visit. "I thought, on the contrary, we should have had our ears boxed", he said.

In March, 1880, the Cabinet decided to advise the Queen to dissolve parliament, and the electoral campaign that followed was made notable by a second pilgrimage of passion in Midlothian by Gladstone, who denounced the devil and all his works, as personified by Dizzy and symbolised by his policy, and announced himself as the champion of freedom, justice and humanity. Beaconsfield himself spent the electoral period quietly at Hatfield, which had been lent him by Salisbury, who was in the south of France with most of his family. Other members of the family came and went, and all seemed to do as they liked in a very free and easy household. "I drink Grand Château Margaux of 1870—by special orders", he wrote to Lady Bradford; "but, as it is not given to anyone else, I feel awkward, but forget my embarrassment in the exquisite flavour." Trade depression, a number of bad harvests, two wars, and Gladstone's apostolic fury, had their effect; though when someone asked Dizzy for a party cry, he put his finger on the true cause of the Conservative defeat: "You need not trouble yourself about that. The only cry that ever interests the people is 'that damned Government'." He took his loss of power with his usual stoicism, saying that he had always longed to pass the spring and summer among the woods of Hughenden, which he had never been able to do. Lord Barrington lunched with him at the Carlton Club, found him well, and noted the charming temper with which he bore this stroke of ill-fortune in the sunset of his career. Many friends, especially women, sent to enquire how he was. "As well as can be expected", was the answer, as if he had been confined. He blamed no one for what had happened, did not think it necessary to explain the defeat or invent excuses for it, and even sympathised with the chief official of the Conservative party organisation, W. B. Skene, the casual mention of whose name shortly after the catastrophe educed from Dizzy in his deepest tones: "What! has that unhappy man not fled the country?"

The Queen could not find the words to express her feelings, though she found a good many. She was astonished, distressed, shocked, annoyed and ashamed at what had happened. She was unable adequately to convey her sorrow at "having to part with the kindest and most devoted as well as one of the wisest Ministers" she had ever had; and she suddenly began to address him in the first person, hoping that they would constantly correspond with one another, that she would still benefit from his advice, that the Conservatives would soon return to office stronger than ever, and that he would allow her to bestow a barony on his nephew in remembrance of his great services. Beaconsfield described his separation from the Queen as almost overwhelming: "His relations with your Majesty were his chief, he might almost say his only, happiness and interest in this world." He declined the barony for his nephew, but requested that honour for his secretary, Montagu Corry, who had just inherited Rowton Castle and seven thousand acres in Shropshire, with an income exceeding £10,000 a year. Corry became Lord Rowton, and is remembered today for his doss-houses, the first of which was founded in 1892.

The leader of the party now returned to power was Lord Hartington, and Beaconsfield told the Queen that her right and constitutional course was to ask him to form a Government. But Hartington explained that no Liberal Government could exist without Gladstone, who would serve under no one. With extreme reluctance she then sent for Gladstone, who accepted the chief office. Beaconsfield left Downing Street on April 25th, 1880, and two days later took leave of his Sovereign, who presented him with her statuette in bronze and shook his hands when he kissed hers. But their close friendship persisted. She constantly sought his advice, wrote him affectionate letters, and told him how often he was in her thoughts and how his picture on the wall rejoiced and comforted her. "Oh!" she once exclaimed, "if only I had you, my kind friend and wise councillor and strong arm to help and lean on! I have *no one*." And for the five years of Gladstone's Administration she watched with anguish and an aching heart the decline of England's European prestige which her dear Lord Beaconsfield had raised so high.

He was to stay with her three more times after he had ceased to be her Minister; and on the first of these occasions, while sitting next to him at dinner, she gave vent to her joy in his company and her grief at losing him: "I feel so happy that I think what has occurred is only a horrid dream!"

Chapter XXV

BENDYMION

AND so, for the first time in his life, Dizzy was able to enjoy the woods, gardens and park lands of Hughenden during the months of May, June and July. He arrived there on May 1st, 1880, in what he called a state of coma, and there he remained for the rest of the year, apart from a few short visits to London on party business, when he stayed at the Seamore Place residence of Alfred de Rothschild, who had placed a suite of rooms at his disposal, leaving him to do what he liked. The quietude of the country restored him, and springtime was a fresh revelation. "I cannot live without cuckoos and nightingales and pink may", he decided. His peacocks pleased him too, but he preferred to see them basking on the lawn, silent and motionless; their struttings and screamings jarred upon him; and thunderstorms in their neighbourhood were unnerving: "At every crack all the peacocks scream. I hardly know which sound is the most infernal. The mixture quite a day of judgment."

His greatest pleasure was in his books and his beeches. Favoured visitors were introduced to both. He loved to chat about literature in his library, where his chief treasures were some Aldine editions of Latin and Italian authors, locked up in a black wooden cabinet, the exterior of which was decorated with modern Dresden china plaques. He adored some of the Greek and Latin poets, but did not think highly of the moderns. Tennyson, though not in the front rank, was the only one who might last, he said. Everyone who stayed with him had to see his trout stream, with its little lake and diminutive island, and the views from his "German forest". He was much concerned over the trees in his park, and issued peremptory instructions that horses must not be allowed to injure them; but he allowed anyone to walk about the park, and thought it disgraceful that so many rich landed proprietors kept working people out of theirs: "I for one cannot and will not do anything so absurd." He was also careful to see that the cottagers on his estate lived in as much comfort as he could procure for them, and he ordered his agent to attend to smoky chimneys, which destroyed all the pleasure of home life, and to see that their gardens were well supplied with flowers and trees. He stopped and talked to all the country-folk who saluted him on his walks, asking them about the crops, the state of the market, their private affairs. He lived on genial and easy terms with his poorer neighbours. A Wycombe man met his coach one day, and thinking it was empty called out to the driver "How is the old cock today?" Beaconsfield put his head out of the window and pleasantly replied: "The old cock is much better, thank you."

When alone his habits were governed by the clock. He was called at 7.30 in the morning, when he had something to eat, and another light meal about three hours later. At dinner, a simple repast, ten minutes elapsed between each course while he read a favourite book, Latin or Italian Renaissance or eighteenth-century English. He never felt dull, for he "peopled the air with imaginary personages." At 11 he went to bed. His visitors of course lived more luxuriously, and the usual process of a large breakfast, a considerable lunch, a solid tea, and a lengthy dinner, displaced his spartan meals and early hours. He was an amiable host, and did his best to make everyone feel at ease. Sometimes he was asked to do things he did not like, but under pressure he nearly always yielded. A lady wished him to read W. H. Mallock's *The New Republic*, which everyone was talking about. He begged to be excused. She persisted, saying that a civil word from him would secure Mallock's adhesion to the Tory party for ever; so he took a sheet of paper and wrote: "Dear Mrs ——, I am sorry that I cannot dine with you next week, but I shall be at Hughenden. Would that my solitude could be peopled with the bright creations of Mr Mallock's fancy!" Once a friend who wished his son to adopt a political career requested Beaconsfield to give the lad a word of advice. The ex-Premier obliged: "My dear young friend, never ask who wrote the Letters of Junius, or on which side of Whitehall Charles I was beheaded; for if you do, you will be considered a bore—and that is something too dreadful for you at your tender age to understand."

With the disappearance of the cuckoos, the nightingales and the pink may, and the coming of summer, Beaconsfield's asthma left him for a while, and he was heard to observe: "My idea of a happy future state is one of those long midsummer days when one dines at nine o'clock." It was a great relief, but it did not make him wish to engage in social life. Asked by the Princess of Wales to a garden-party at Marlborough House, when the Queen would be present, he made some excuse, remarking to a friend: "Fallen Ministers are not company for Princesses and Princes, who, very wisely, favour popularity and power." There was however a more urgent reason for avoiding such functions. All that spring and summer he was busy writing a new novel, which he called *Endymion*, a strange production for an ex-Premier in his seventy-sixth year. Like some other men of action, Cromwell, Clive, Wellington, Lincoln and Henry Lawrence, he had the poetic temperament without the poetic talent, and his novels are so many attempts to reveal his feelings. Their failure is due to the fact that he could not create living characters. It has been said that his social scenes, wherein peers and politicians rub shoulders at great receptions, are the best in the language. If so, it is merely because no great writer has bothered to depict peers and politicians rubbing shoulders. A man cannot give life to a scene without giving life to the people who take part in it; and Dizzy's characters lack the vitality of their creator, though they can be as pithy in *Endymion* as in the other novels:

"Knowledge is the foundation of eloquence."

"Nobody should ever look anxious except those who have no anxiety."

"Time is the great physician."

"One cannot ask any person to meet another in one's own house, without going through a sum of moral arithmetic."

"Inquirers who are always inquiring never learn anything."

"It was a grand idea of our kings making themselves Sovereigns of the sea. The greater portion of this planet is water; so we at once became a first-rate power."

"Sensible men are all of the same religion." "And pray what is that?" "Sensible men never tell."

As we should expect, Endymion resembles Benjamin in many ways. Both are indebted to women for their rise in life, beginning with a devoted sister. Each falls in love with a married woman, whose husband conveniently dies, leaving her rich enough to bestow her hand and her dividends on himself. Each becomes Prime Minister. High life is painted, as usual, in high lights: the palaces are as glorious as ever, the gardens as beautiful, the chief characters as wonderful, and the whole effect like nothing on earth. Great literature is never literary, and this author is so much interested in style that his sense of reality forsakes him when he writes fiction. *Endymion* is the last view of Dizzy's dreamland, though he would have continued to dream in fairy-tales had he lived, for he began a new story immediately he finished this one. The queer thing is that even his satire of individuals lacks the semblance of reality. We have already noticed that, while polite to aristocrats, he could be very unpleasant to artists; and there is a vignette of Thackeray as 'St Barbe' which caricatures the original as grossly as his pictures of dukes and duchesses idealise their prototypes. We can recognise Thackeray in St Barbe's remark after dining with a wealthy family: "I declare when I was eating that truffle, I felt a glow about my heart that, if it were not indigestion, I think must have been gratitude." But the general picture of a vain and envious being is so far off the mark that it merely proves how hurt Disraeli must have been by the parody of *Coningsby* which Thackeray did for *Punch*. Dizzy himself was not jealous of other people's achievements, and he considered envy a most objectionable vice. "I have a thousand faults, but not that detestable one", he said at the end of his life. It is probable that he attributed Thackeray's parody to envy, which would have added to the annoyance he felt over the ridicule of his work. Most authors are highly susceptible to adverse criticism, and often mistake the honesty or levity or stupidity of their critics for envy or jealousy or hostility. The man who could stand any amount of personal derision and political abuse with equanimity, could not endure the laughter of those who thought his dreams absurd.

Mystery surrounded the progress of *Endymion*. No one knew it was being written. This was another record of his secret life, and he kept it secret, not only from Mr Baum, his valet, but even from Lady Bradford. Though he seems to have been unaware of it, the writing of the novel gave him some relief from the heartache which the exercise of power had failed to give. When completed, he placed the arrangements for publication in the hands of his secretary, Lord Rowton, who displayed a business sense that staggered the author: "I know no magic of the Middle

Ages equal to it", said he. "And you are the Magician, best and dearest of friends." The gentleman, anxious to prove himself a man of business, is often mean. The business man, anxious to prove himself a gentleman, is sometimes generous. Rowton actually persuaded Longman to part with £10,000, the largest sum ever paid for a literary work up to that time. Later, Beaconsfield offered to cancel the contract, as the three-volume edition which appeared in November '80 did not pay for the advance; but Longman refused, and the issue of the popular edition early the following year quickly squared the account, the general public's passion for living in high society resulting in a large sale.

But the mystery was kept up to the last moment, and when Norton Longman went down to Hughenden for the manuscript he wondered whether he was there to complete a business deal or to assist in some occult rite. Beaconsfield was rather nervous and asked whether he ought to have his study lighted, but on reflection thought it might excite his valet's suspicion and said they had better light the candles themselves, which made Longman feel that they were about to commit sacrilege. Arriving in the study, Beaconsfield said: "We must light all the candles, Mr Longman; I can't get on without plenty of light . . . We must have your room lighted also. But Mr Baum can do that." The valet was duly instructed, and having shut the door with the air of a conspirator Beaconsfield produced three red despatch boxes. "Are you ready?" he asked. Longman signified that he was ready, but he did not know for what. "Can you carry two?" "Yes." Three volumes of manuscript, each tied up with red tape, were then produced from the three despatch boxes, and the conspirators solemnly tip-toed down the passage with their precious loads to the guest's bedroom, where his host closed the door with the utmost circumspection. The volumes were placed on the table, and Longman was asked what he was going to do with them. He had an inspiration: "My Glad——" he began, but thought better of it and added: "My bag." But his Gladstone bag had disappeared. They searched under the bed, in the wardrobes, everywhere, but could not find it. Had Mr Baum designedly hidden it? Impossible to ring for him, as that would give the game away. At last it was found in the dressing-room; and having reverently deposited *Endymion* within it, the ceremony was concluded.

Beaconsfield's health was again bad in the autumn of '80, and he rarely visited London. But one day Colonel Bridges, who was reputed to be the best-looking man in the army, saw him in Hyde Park, leaning heavily on the arm of Monty, whom Bridges knew and saluted as they passed. Hearing his name called, the Colonel turned back. "Lord Beaconsfield would like to be introduced to you", said Monty. After shaking hands, Dizzy, one of whose eyes was closed, forced it open with his finger and thumb, looked at Bridges, said "You're a bloody lot handsomer than Monty", and, letting the eyelid drop, moved on. He still received occasional visitors at Hughenden. Lytton, who resigned the Viceroyalty of India the moment Beaconsfield left Downing Street, came with his wife, who, noted their host, "rules her husband, but that I suppose is always the case where marriages are what is called happy." Lord Ronald Gower stayed there in September and wrote an interesting account of his sojourn.

"I am the unluckiest of mortals", said Beaconsfield; "six bad harvests in succession, one worse than the former, this has been the cause of my overthrow; like Napoleon, I have been beaten by the elements! Bismarck and I were perfectly *d'accord* . . . He is one of the few men that at my age I have been able to feel real attachment for; but all that is now over, and were he to come to England I should not ask to see him; there is no such thing as sympathy or sentiment between statesmen. I have failed, and he would not care now to see me; nor I him." Beaconsfield declared that he wanted to resign the leadership of the party, but they would not let him. "All becomes chaos when I am away", he said, pacing the room and waving his arms. He assured Gower that he did not know what it was to feel bored for a moment.

One evening in his library, by a blazing fire, he talked of the past, of the three lovely Sheridan sisters, of the delightful dinners in the rooms of one of them, Mrs Norton, over a public house near Storey's Gate. "Dreams! dreams! dreams!" he murmured, gazing into the fire. He constantly spoke of "my dear wife", as if she had been his good angel. He thought he would live for another two years, the Queen for another twenty; and he was right about the Queen. But every minute spent in thinking of death is a minute given to death, which already has an eternity in store for everybody, and Beaconsfield did not waste his life with thoughts of an after-life.

Apart from his dreams and his books, his mind was chiefly occupied with "the Arch-villain" Gladstone, whose policy by the end of 1880 had successfully produced a revolution in Ireland, a revolt in the Transvaal, and a slump in England's continental prestige. "I think the A.V. so wicked a man, that he would not hesitate to plunge us into a great war to soothe and save his maniacal vanity", wrote Dizzy, whose view was justified by the publication in *The Times* of a letter from the Prime Minister thanking the public for their sympathy during his recent illness. "Did you ever hear anything like that!" exclaimed his rival to Gower. "It reminds one of the Pope blessing all the world from the balcony of St Peter's." But Beaconsfield was scrupulously polite to the family of the Arch-villain, one of whose daughters asked him at a reception about a certain foreign diplomatist who was present. "That", said he, "is the most dangerous statesman in Europe—except, as your father would say, myself, or, as I should prefer to put it, your father." The reflection that he must continue the fight against the man who was undoing everything that he had done discouraged him: "It is no easy thing to step out of the profound solitude in which I live—often not speaking to a human being the whole day—and walk into the House of Lords and make a speech on a falling Empire." He may have been thinking of Gladstone when someone enquired "Which passion gives pleasure the latest? The conventional idea is, of course, Avarice." His answer was surprising: "No! Revenge. A man will enjoy that when even Avarice has ceased to please." Yet no one practised the wisdom of forgiveness or overlooked injuries so systematically as he. His revenge in this case was taking the form of portraying Gladstone in the novel he had just begun, under the name of Joseph Toplady Falconet, the first name recalling Joseph Surface, the second the author of 'Rock of Ages', the third a field-gun; the combination signifying an explosive and religious humbug. The completed portrait would no doubt have been the best in the Disraelian gallery, as we may guess from the artist's final sketch of his subject in a private letter: "It was easy to settle affairs with Palmerston, because he was a man of the world, and was, therefore, governed by the principle of honor: but when you have to deal with an earnest man, severely religious, and enthusiastic, every attempted arrangement ends in unintelligible correspondence and violated confidence."

During the autumn of '80 Beaconsfield saw less and less of Rowton, who was amusing himself as a young man should; indeed it would have distressed the gout-and-asthma-ridden statesman if Monty had spent much time at Hughenden, for it would have meant that he was being deprived of his pleasures. But there were so many letters to be written, and so many people to be seen, that an active and constantly attendant secretary was a necessity; and when, towards the end of the year, Monty had to accompany an invalid sister to Algiers, Lord Barrington took his place. With the sum he had made on his recent novel Beaconsfield acquired the lease of a house in Curzon Street, Mayfair, and after spending the first days of 1881 in Rothschild's mansion at 1 Seamore Place, he moved into his new residence on January 10th.[1] "I always intended to die in London", he said; "it gives one six months more of life, and the doctor can come to see one twice a day, which he cannot in the country."

It was an exceptionally severe winter, and he was seldom free from one or another of his maladies; yet he went to many dinner-parties, attended debates in the House of Lords, and actually sat for a portrait by John Millais, which was left unfinished. At one of the dinners, being offered a cigar, he observed: "You English once had a great man who discovered tobacco, on which you English now live; and potatoes on which your Irish live; and you cut off his head." Early in March there was a big debate in the Upper House, and Beaconsfield made his last important speech against the Government's intention to abandon Kandahar, one passage of which found its way into school-books:

> But, my lords, the key of India is not Herat or Kandahar. The key of India is London. The majesty and sovereignty, the spirit and vigour of your Parliament, the inexhaustible resources, the ingenuity and determination of your people—these are the keys of India.

The speech was a great strain on his enfeebled constitution, and he depended on drugs to help him through it.

[1] Bricks and mortar have done their best to keep his memory from fading. All the houses with which he was closely associated, in Theobalds Road, Bloomsbury Square, Grosvenor Gate, Curzon Street, as well as those at Bradenham and Hughenden, have so far escaped the ravages of Goths, Huns and Vandals. (1950.)

A curious personality called to see him at about this time, a Marxian socialist who was to found and lead a group of reformers: Henry Mayers Hyndman. The Curzon Street furniture, noted this visitor, was old-fashioned and upholstered in red damask. The curtains and wallpaper were also red; much gilding was everywhere apparent; and the whole was a gorgeous symphony in scarlet and gold. Beaconsfield entered the room, dressed in a long red gabardine, moving slowly and painfully, his head bowed, one eye completely closed, the other partially so. With his deeply-lined, sallow, sphinx-like face, the curl on his forehead, the lower lip protruding forcefully, he looked like an Egyptian mummy; and the newcomer felt as if he were about to converse with a statue. As Hyndman unfolded his plan for the betterment of the world, Beaconsfield bowed his head between the paragraphs. "Utopia made to order", he said during a momentary lull, and his voice seemed to come from the bowels of the earth: "A pleasing dream; not, I fear, easily realised in fact. And how would you begin?" Hyndman knew how to begin, how to go on, but never when to stop, though he paused at one moment to say "You admit that?" "I admit nothing, Mr Hyndman; I am listening to you." Another instalment from Hyndman, following which the motionless figure asked: "Suppose all you say is true, what then?" Hyndman said what then at some length; but when he referred to the democratic movement, Beaconsfield took him up: "Why not say Socialist movement? That is what you mean." Hyndman's explanation of what he meant continued for about half-an-hour, and when he paused for breath Beaconsfield remarked that private property and vested interests would thwart his designs: "I do not say it to discourage you, but you have taken upon yourself a very—heavy—work—indeed, and—" he smiled—"even now you are not a very young man to have so much zeal and enthusiasm. It is a very difficult country to move, Mr Hyndman, a very—difficult—country—indeed, and one in which there is more disappointment to be looked for than success. But you do intend to go on?" Hyndman certainly did. "Then I shall have the pleasure of seeing you again", said Beaconsfield. But they did not meet again in this world.

Though he had been laid up with gout for two days, Beaconsfield gave a dinner-party on March 10th, receiving his guests with the aid of a stick, and on the 15th he made his last appearance in the Lords. "I only live for climate and I never get it", he said despairingly, as the bitter winds of March began to blow. He dined at Marlborough House with the Prince of Wales on the 19th; but on the 23rd he took to his bed with a chill and a return of his worst enemy, asthma. Lady Bradford visited him, and a few of his colleagues came to talk about the defeat of the British at Majuba Hill in Natal. He told them what to say about the Government's unpatriotic policy, and they said it. His friends felt that he should have the advice of the best available chest authority, Richard Quain, and his own doctor, Kidd, raised no objection. But Kidd was a homoeopathist, and ordinary practitioners were not allowed by their trade union rules to consult with such. However, after receiving the assurance that Kidd would act entirely under his advice, that the patient had so far been treated allopathically, and that it would be disloyal to the Queen if he refused, Quain appeared at Curzon Street. To relieve Kidd, another physician also attended during the nights.

Death should be met boldly, said the dying man, and the doctors and nurses were impressed not only with his fortitude under affliction but by his gentleness and kindness. Violent spasms shook him at intervals and left him gasping for breath. He fought death, but knew it was coming, and spoke of it without fear. The doctors did their best to hearten him with talk of progress, but they did not convince him. "His words are hopeful, but his countenance is that of a disappointed man", he said after one of them had spoken cheerfully. "I feel I am dying. Whatever the doctors may tell you, I do not believe I shall get well", he warned a friend. On reading a bulletin which stated that his health was maintained, he said "I presume the physicians are conscious of that. It is more than I am"; and he objected to the word 'well' in another bulletin which reported that he had "taken nourishment well." When an air-cushion was brought for his greater comfort, he refused it with the words: "Take away that emblem of mortality." On March 31st he corrected the proof of his final speech in parliament, saying "I will not go down to posterity talking bad grammar"; but public affairs had ceased to interest him.

Lord Rowton returned from Algiers; but the sufferer was too weak to stand the shock of seeing him; and it was some days before Monty joined George Barrington and Philip Rose

(Beaconsfield's old friend and executor) as a bedside ministrant and companion. The Queen was deeply distressed. Her letters and telegrams arrived daily, and the sick-room in Curzon Street was regularly supplied with spring flowers from Osborne or Windsor. She longed to visit him, but thought it better that he should be "quite quiet". She begged him to be "very good and obey the doctors and commit no imprudence." But if he would like to see her, she would be delighted to come. On April 5th she sent a letter from Windsor Castle by special messenger, with the request that it should be read to him, if he could not himself read it, as there was nothing agitating in it. He took it in his hand, but feeling unequal to a personal perusal said "This letter ought to be read to me by Lord Barrington, a Privy Councillor." It was the simple and ingenuously affectionate expression of a woman who instinctively knew that her "dearest Lord Beaconsfield" would soon be taken from her, and that she was about to feel, as she later confessed, that terrible void which makes the heart sick. She sent him primroses, "your favourite spring flowers", and said "You are very constantly in my thoughts, and I wish I could do anything to cheer you and be of the slightest use or comfort."

Just before Easter Day he seemed to rally, and the Queen telegraphed "Thank God for this good news, which overjoys us." His friends thought he might like to receive the Sacrament on that day, as he was accustomed to do at Hughenden; but Quain would not let them suggest it to him, as it would make him feel that they had given up hope. During the short period of apparent well-being which so often precedes a final relapse, he said "I had rather live, but I am not afraid to die", and made his last joke: "I have suffered much. Had I been a Nihilist, I should have confessed all." Early in the morning of Easter Tuesday, April 19th, 1881, his friends knew that the end was at hand. A few minutes before his heart ceased to beat, he partly raised himself from the bed, drawing his shoulders up and stretching his body out, as he used to do when rising from his seat in the House to make a speech. His lips moved; but no words came. Then he sank back, the fight over, the spirit gone, the face tranquil.

BIBLIOGRAPHICAL NOTE

The main biographical source for any work on Disraeli is the six-volume *Life*, begun by William Flavelle Monypenny, the first of whose volumes appeared in 1910, and finished by George Earle Buckle, the last of whose volumes appeared in 1920. Apart from that, there are Disraeli's Home Letters (1885), his letters to Lady Londonderry (1938), and his letters to Lady Bradford and Lady Chesterfield, edited by the Marquis of Zetland, 2 vols. (1929).

The Bradenham Edition of the novels and tales has been used, with introductions by Philip Guedalla, 12 vols. (1926–7).

In addition to the above, over a hundred books dealing with the man and his period have been consulted, to enumerate which were "wasteful and ridiculous excess", since the majority are mentioned in the Monypenny-Buckle *Life*.

INDEX